D1536313

THE CISTERCIANS

Texts written with the collaboration of:
Julie Roux
Historical and religious advisors:
the monks of the abbey of Acey,
Nicolas D'Andoque
Translated by Barbara Jachowicz-Davoust

S U M

Saint Anthony

1

HISTORY

FROM THE DESERT TO CLUNY

HISTORY OF THE CISTERCIAN ORDER

2

ABBEYS

CLAIRVAUX AND ITS LINEAGE

M A R Y

Arcades of Fontenay cloister

Cloister capital in Santes Creus

1

History

1

FROM THE DESERT TO CLUNY

It has been just over two thousand years since the death of the Son of Man at Golgotha and his Word began to be spread around the Mediterranean Basin by men and women whose lives often ended with their martyrdom. In Egypt, Paul, then Anthony, retired to the solitude of the desert in order to live the evangelical ideal, thus providing the roots of monasticism. Influenced by the Desert Fathers, marked by the exceptional personalities of Pachomius, Basil, Jerome, Martin, Augustine, Honoratus, John Cassian, Benedict of Nursia, Columba and Benedict of Aniane, monasticism developed over time, from the East to the West, and became an essential element of the history of Christianity in the first millenium.

St Anthony visits St Paul the hermit, Issenheim Reredos

The Origins of Monasticism

Starting in the East during the second half of the 3rd century, the desire to strictly observe evangelical precepts led some Christians to withdraw from the world in order to live a life of renunciation and prayer in the desert, making a complete offering of the self to God. Paul settled in Thebaid around 250, and in about 270 Anthony entered deep into the desert of Pispir, before ending his days on Mount Qolzum in 356. Other "Desert Fathers" called hermits or anchorites retired to the desert of Nitria in Egypt, like Saint Amun in about 315, or to the desert of Scete like Saint Macarius of Egypt in 330. During the 4th century, eremitic communities were also founded in Palestine and in the Sinai. Several Desert Fathers were the authors of the *Apophtegmata* – phrases and anecdotes that became the texts of reference for the monastic tradition. In about 320, in Tabennisi in Thebaid, Pachomius founded the first monastery, called a *laura*. The monks obeyed the abbot and followed his written Rule which organized communal life but also allowed them to practice individual asceticism. Starting in 357 in Cappadocia, Basil pursued the monastic experience inaugurated by Pachomius to its limits. His disciples solemnly pronounced the vows of obedience, which placed them under the abbot's authority, and of stability, which forbade them leaving the monastery. Basil wrote the *Long* and *Short Rule*, allotting the monks' time between manual labour and prayer, defining their renunciations and organizing material life: group labour, common refectories and dormitories. Several monasteries were thus created at the end of the 4th century in Syria and Palestine where, at the same time, anchoritic life took on various and original forms. The *grazers* wandered the land, eating grasses and roots; *dendrites* lived in hollow trees; *stylites* like Simeon, spent their lives on top of columns. In the West, monasticism began to take hold under the influence of Athanasius, the bishop of Alexandria and author of

Reference Dates

Paul settles in Thebaid	250
Birth of Anthony	251
Anthony retires to the desert of Pispir	270
Pachomius founds the first monastery	320
Macarius of Egypt settles in the desert of Scete	330
Death of Saint Anthony	356
Basil in Cappadocia	357
Martin founds the community of Ligugé	360
Athanasius writes the life of Saint Anthony	372
Jerome goes into the Chalcis desert	374
Honoratus founds the monastery of Lérins	410
John Cassian founds Saint Victor's monastery in Marseilles	415
Romain and Lupicin create a hermitage in Condat	425
Evangelization of Ireland by Patrick	450

Saint Simeon's Basilica in Syria

Cappadocia landscape

ANTHONY, THE STAR OF THE DESERT

Abbot Pambo questioned Saint Anthony: "What should I do?" The old man replied, "Do not trust justice, do not regret anything past and be master of your tongue and your stomach."
Apophtegmata of the Desert Fathers.

Anthony was born in about 251, at Qeman in Upper Egypt, into a wealthy Christian family. His parents died when he was eighteen years old and he devoted himself to the upbringing of his younger sister.
In the chapel of his village, he heard the call of the Lord to the rich young man, "If you wish to be perfect, sell all you have and follow me." Renouncing the world, he sold his house and all his lands, distributed the profit to the poor and went to live in the cabin of an old ascetic on the outskirts of the village. But the Devil's haunting voice disturbed his thoughts, reminding him of "the goods he left behind, the care he took of his sister, the desire for glory...". In order to resist more easily, Anthony left the old hermit and went into the desert where he locked himself into the darkness and disturbing isolation of an empty tomb. Through fasting, sleepless nights and prayer, Anthony fought Evil and its accompanying cortege of fierce, phantasmagorical animals that did not stop violently attacking him, wounding his body until he lost consciousness. After several months, Anthony went deeper into the desert of Pispir and settled in an abandoned Roman fortress. During his journey, the Devil placed a basin of silver and gold bullion in his path. But in vain. For twenty years, locked in the fortress, Anthony continued his struggle against the powers of evil, refusing all contact with men, only allowing them to hear his screams of terror echoing behind the walls. Around 305, some disciples settled nearby, in individual cabins. But soon Anthony retired to Mount Qolzum, forty kilometres from the Red Sea, where he lived a life of beatitude as a reward for his victory over Evil. Before dying at the age of over a hundred, he asked his disciples to bury him in a secret location to prevent anyone from idolizing him. Athanasius, the bishop of Alexandria, faced with the rise of Arianism which denied the divine nature of Jesus Christ, found, in Anthony's victorious struggle against Evil, the proof that "God became man so that man would become God" and hence the proof of the Son of Man's divinity. Immediately after Anthony's death, Athanasius wrote the story of Anthony's life in Greek and, translated into Latin in 372, it spread throughout the West.

Temptation of St Anthony, Issenheim Reredos

The Life of Saint Anthony, exiled in Trier from 335 to 338, then in Rome until 346. On his return to Rome in 382, Jerome, a Dalmatian who had gone to live as a hermit in the Chalcis desert in 374, brought the fruit of his experience and solid knowledge about the Desert Fathers, whose lives he described in his *Lives*, before finishing his days in Bethlehem. In Gaul, Martin, a Roman who had become a monk after being a soldier, founded two hermitages: at Ligugé in 360, then in 372 in Marmoutier, near Tours, where he was elected bishop in 371. On the Mediterranean coast of Italy and Provence, areas in contact with the East, hermitages and monasteries multiplied. Near Carthage, after his conversion in 386, Augustine founded monastic communities in Tagaste in 386, as well as in Hippo in 388. In 410, Honoratus founded the monastery of Lérins on an island in the gulf of Cannes, before taking over the bishop's seat in Arles, where others from Lérins, Hilarius and then Cesarius, succeeded him. Around 415, John Cassian, after being a monk for twenty years in a monastery in Bethlehem, founded Saint Victor Monastery in Marseilles and wrote the *Coenobitic Institutions*. In 429, Germain of Auxerre christianized Brittany – Great Britain – and in 430, Palladius did the same in Ireland where Patrick took over from him in 450. In 435, in the Jura, Romain and his brother Lupicin created a hermitage, the future abbey of Condat. And in about 490, Nursia in the Umbrian Appenines saw the birth of Benedict, whose Rule was to become the charter of Western monasticism.

Martin shares his coat, tapestry in Montpezat de Quercy church

Etymologies

Abbot

From the Aramaic *abba*, meaning father, chief, master of a monastic community.

Monk

From the Greek *monachos*, solitary. A monk lives away from the world, either alone or in a community, after pronouncing vows to follow the rules of an order.

Anchorite

From the Greek *anachoresis*, meaning departure, a fleeing from the daily world.
A contemplative monk who retires to the outskirts of society, in solitude.

Hermit

From the Greek *eremos*, desert.
A monk who lives in solitude, retired to an isolated place.
(Synonym: anchorite)

Dendrite

From the Greek, *dendron*, tree.
An anchorite who lives alone in trees.

Stylite

From *stylus*, column in Greek.
A person alone living on a platform at the top of a column.

Coenobitic

From the Greek, *koinos bios*, community life. As opposed to the hermit or anchorite, the coenobite lives on the margins of society but within a community.

Benedict agrees to be abbot, fresco in cloister of Monte Oliveto Maggiore (detail)

Benedict of Nursia

Very few sources exist about the life of Benedict of Nursia other than the second book of dialogues of Gregory the Great. Benedict was born around 490 in Nursia in Central Italy's Umbrian mountains. His parents were wealthy landowners and expected him to take up an administrative career. They thus sent him to Rome at an early age in order to study law and rhetoric. But Benedict decided to understand "learned ignorance" and chose to go and live as a hermit, first of all near the village of Afile, then at Subiaco, where, for three years, living in a cave, he subjected himself to a life of extreme asceticism. His reputation grew and nearby he founded twelve small monasteries which drew numerous candidates for eremitic life, including those who were to become his disciples, Maurus and Placid. In 529, he settled further south at the summit of Monte Cassino, where he established a monastery. Starting in 534, and probably until his death in 537, Benedict elaborated a Rule, the consequence of his long experience, that defined a totally monastic way of life. The number of his disciples increased and Benedict founded another monastery in the neighbouring town of Terracina while his sister Scholastica ran a community of nuns near the mother abbey. In 581, Lombards destroyed the abbey at Monte Cassino where Benedict was buried. In 673, a Frankish monk discovered his remains among the ruins and transferred the precious relics to the abbey at Fleury sur Loire.

Reference Dates

Birth of Benedict of Nursia	**490**
Benedict lives in Subiaco as a hermit	**500**
Benedict founds the monastery of Monte Cassino	**529**
Benedict begins to write his Rule	**534**
Death of Benedict	**547**

Monte Cassino monastery is destroyed by Lombards	**581**

Saint Benedict's Monastery, Subiaco

The Rule of Saint Benedict

"Listen, O my son, to the precepts of thy master and incline the ear of thy heart; and cheerfully and faithfully execute the admonitions of thy loving Father "
Prologue to the Rule of Saint Benedict

The Rule of Saint Benedict was characterized by its clarity and balance. Its application was as much the spiritual guidance of the monks as the organisation of their material life and the correct functioning of the monastery which contained an autonomous religious community. The cenobitic monks who compose it "live together, do battle in the service of God, guided by the Rule and an abbot". The monastery is a "school in the service of God" where the brothers live in humility and silence, poverty and piety, mutual love and obedience. The Anchorites corresponded to a higher level, reserved for those who had already been tried in the monastery, "who are no longer in the first fervour of their religious life".

Destruction of Monte Cassino

The newcomer who desired to enter the monastery was rather harshly welcomed. Indeed, he had to wait four or five days before the door was opened for him. The postulant was then placed under the direction of an elder who observed him to test his faith and his vocation. After one year of noviciate, during which the novice learned about the Rule and meditated upon it, after agreeing to respect it, the novice was accepted into the heart of the community. He solemnly pronounced three vows: obedience, steadfastness and con verting moral standards. From then on he was forbidden to leave the monaster he had to obey the superior in every matter, and promised to live in chastity to renounce the world and, especially, live in humility, poverty and piety. After the ceremony of the vows, his clothes were taken from him and he pu on the monk's habit. If he was rich, all his goods were distributed to the poor The abbot was himself a monk elected to head the monastery, chosen becaus of "his merit" and the "wisdom of his teaching". In the monastery he held "th place of Christ", his task was to lead hi brothers towards God, to make sure that they respected the Rule. It was his responsibility to make important decisions after consulting with the other monks. He governed his brothers with

Benedict feeds the monks

Benedict breaks a poisoned glass

ʒour but also love, compassion and oderation. He must not forget that he mself was a "servant rather than a aster". If a monk committed an fence, the superior punished him by tting him apart from the community -, depending on the seriousness of the fence, by corporal punishment, with clusion from the monastery being the

Monks disobeying the Rule

ost serious disciplinary action. Eight riods of prayer set the rhythm of a onk's life: Vigils took place between o and three in the morning; Lauds, t daybreak; Prime, at the beginning the day; Terce, during the morning; xt, in the middle of the day; Nones, the afternoon; Vespers, at the end the day; and finally, Compline, before tiring for the night. Outside the Hours prayer, the monks' time was harmo- ously balanced between *lectio divina*, e reading of sacred texts, and manual oour, necessary for a life of autarchy d proof of humility. During meals, ken in common and in silence in the fectory, the weekly reader read a cred text to his brothers. The food as frugal but sufficient, composed of o cooked dishes accompanied by a tle bread and wine. Mealtimes were riable according to the seasons and riods of fasting. In general, the monks e two meals a day, at noon and after spers. During periods of fasting, the

Benedict takes the hermit's habit

unique meal took place around three o'clock in the afternoon. In the dormitory, where a lamp "burns all through the night", each monk had a bed where he slept fully clothed in order to be always ready to get up and go to prayers. The monks' habit consisted of a tunic and a cowl, more or less thick depending on the season and the local climate. Nobody owned anything within the monastery where everything was held in common. It turns out today that Benedict was greatly inspired by a previous Rule, known by the name of Rule of the Master, which had in turn undergone Cassian's influence. Benedict simplified it and adapted it to his own time, defining it himself as "a little rule for beginners". The Rule of Saint Benedict did not establish itself immediately. More realistic and concrete than the rules defining Celtic monasticism, it was first of all adopted in English monasteries before its adoption in Germany, particularly by Saint Boniface in the abbey he founded at Fulda at the beginning of the 8th century. The reconstruction of Monte Cassino Abbey by Abbot Petronax in 718, and the support of the Frankish kings gave the rule new influence. Charlemagne had a copy of the Benedictine rule made and kept it in his palace. Saint Gall Abbey still contains a copy of this manuscript, made under Charles the Bald. And the synods that took place in 816, 817, 818 and 819 in Aachen, within the framework of the reform started by Benedict of Aniane, finally imposed the "Holy Rule" as the unique rule.

Benedict frees a tied-up peasant

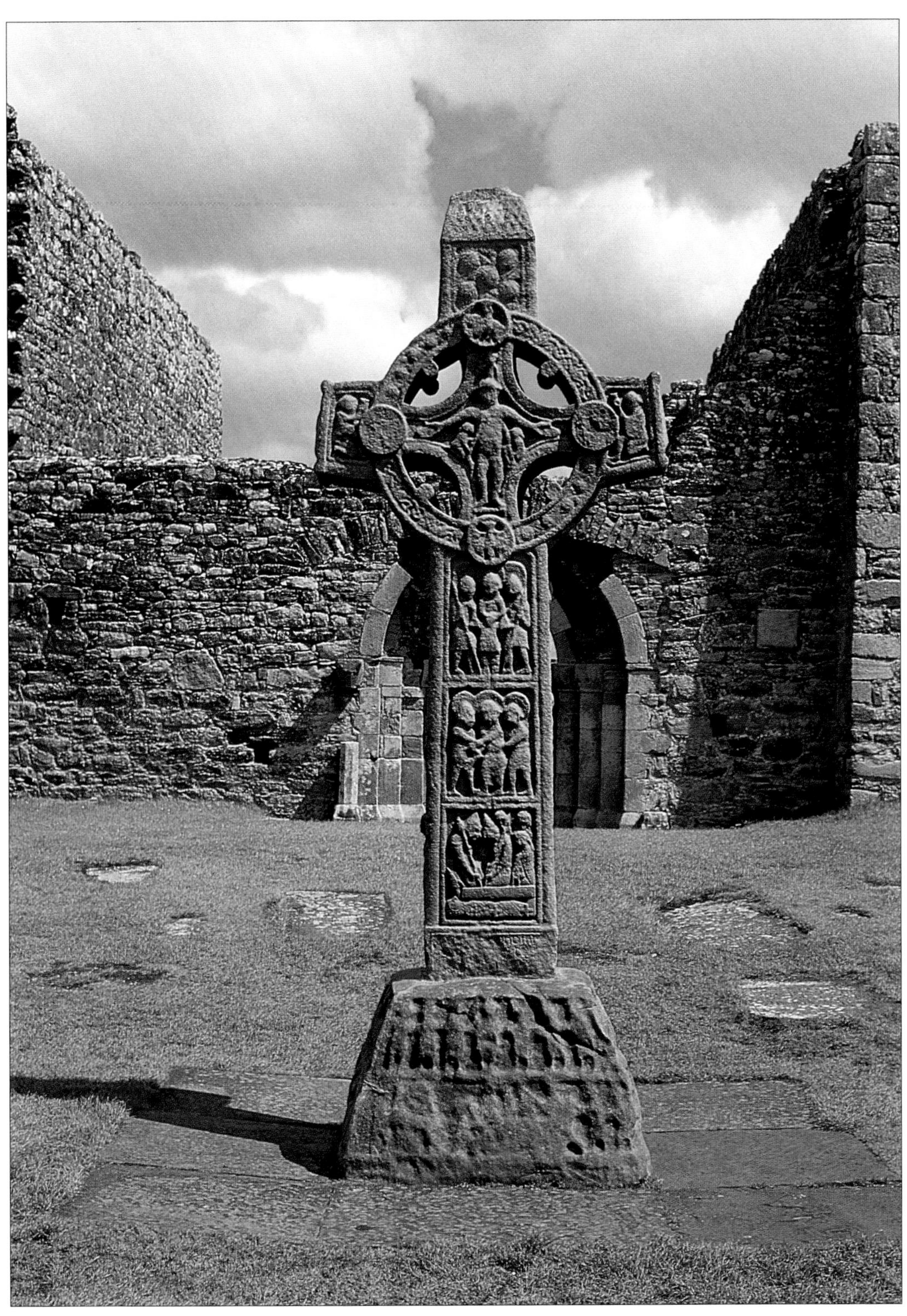

Clonmacnois with the Cross of the Scriptures in the foreground

Progress of the Benedictine Rule

Ireland was christianized during the 5th century and many monasteries were founded in the middle of the following century: Clonmacnois by Kieran, Glendalough by Kevin, Derry by Columba, and Bangor by Comgall. A monk from Bangor, Columban, went to Gaul in about 590 and founded the monastery of Luxeuil in the Vosges mountains. After some conflict with Merovingian power, particularly with Brunehaut, in 614 Columban settled in Bubbio, near Milan in Italy. This was after the creation of what was to become the abbey of Saint Gall near Lake Constance by his disciple Gall in 612. At Columban's death in 615, Columban foundations were numerous in eastern Gaul but also in the region around Paris, in Normandy, Picardy, Vendée and Flanders, as well as in Bavaria and northern Italy. However, the Columban Rule, extremely strict like the other Celtic rules, did not manage to establish itself. Meanwhile, Pope Gregory the Great (590-604), the biographer of Saint Benedict, worked to spread the Benedictine Rule not only in Italy but also in England, in the Kingdom of Northumbria where he sent missionaries to replace Celtic monks. Throughout the 7th and 8th centuries, Benedictine monasticism progressed in Western Europe. The Rule of Saint Benedict appeared in Gaul during the 620's, at Alta Ripa Monastery near Albi. However, the monasteries were usually

Reference Dates

Birth of Columban	540
Foundation of Glendalough by Kevin	541
Foundation of Clonmacnois by Kieran	541
Foundation of Luxeuil by Columban	575
Foundation of Bobbio by Columban	614
A monk from Fleury brings the relics of St Benedict back to his abbey from Monte Cassino	673
Birth of Witiza, the future Benedict of Aniane	750
Foundation of a *cella* at Aniane by Benedict	782
First synod in Aachen	816
Partition of Verdun	843

St Kevin's Church in Glendalough

Tympanum detail in Saint Génis

open to the world, contrary to the original principles. In Germany, monks participated in evangelizing the population, and in the Frankish kingdom, especially under Charlemagne, abbeys became the instruments of political power. The most powerful ones, whose abbots exercised far-reaching powers, collected taxes and revenues, dispensed justice and enjoyed immunity from the authority of the counts, the representatives of imperial or royal power. A complete centre of agricultural, commercial and economic activity, the monastery was a far cry from Benedictine ideals. Charlemagne did not hesitate to name abbots himself, sometimes naming laymen, nor to dispose of a monastery's goods. Furthermore, he allowed them to carry out pastoral activities that were normally allotted to the secular clergy. In an attempt to promote arts and literature, he created renowned schools within the abbeys and set up copyists' workshops. These activities were contrary to enclosure, an expression of renunciation of the world and the essential foundation of monasticism, and hence provoked a certain slackening of discipline. A return to more authentic monasticism appeared necessary. This restoration was accomplished thanks to Benedict of Aniane, to whom King Louis the Pious, Charlemagne's son, entrusted the task of carrying out a reform. The Chapter of 817, due to Benedict of Aniane, imposed the Benedictine Rule in all monasteries and called for the respect of all its fundamental principles. In 818, a second chapter re-established free abbey elections. However, the reform was not wel-

IN TUSCANY

Sant'Antimo *(below)* was allegedly founded at the end of the 8th century by the future Charlemagne. The "Carolingian" chapel, whose chevet abuts in the south that of the Romanesque church, was the original abbey church.

Abbey of Sant'Antimo

CELTIC MONASTICISM

The evangelizing missions of Germain of Auxerre and Patrick, sent in the 5th century from Gaul to Brittany – today's Great Britain – and Ireland, preached a Christianity strongly influenced by monastic ideas. The new converts considered renunciation as an essential element of their religious life. The most fervent of them, on whom the missionaries conferred the priesthood, gathered communities of men, women and children, who imposed monastic life upon themselves. Starting in the 6th century, Celtic monasticism was organized and developed rapidly with the foundation of monasteries destined for a brilliant future, not only in Ireland but also in Scotland, on Iona, and in Britain, at Sherbourne and Canterbury. In Brittany, in Armorica, Gildas founded Rhuis, Guénolé and Landévennec. The monks obeyed their abbot, the all-powerful chief, who established a Rule for them. Celtic monasticism advocated renunciation of the world and exalted poverty, chastity and humility. Its asceticism, with its frequent and difficult fasting and corporal punishment, was generally very rough and the manual labour was exhausting. The monasteries adopted a coenobitic way of life, but each monk had his own cell. For Celtic monks, coenobitism was understood as preparation for eremitism, the ultimate expression of renouncing the world. And it is true that the most ardent, after testing life in the monastery, left to accomplish their "flight into the desert" alone, usually in the form of a long sea journey. Upon their return to land, in a preferably arid and isolated location, they founded a new monastery. The choice of a retreat from the world did not exclude acting within society. On the contrary, by maintaining their piety and virtues, the retreat prepared the Celtic monk to better transmit his faith. Therefore, many monks became priests and said holy offices for the faithful, as well as evangelizing pagan peoples. One example is Saint Columba who, in 563, left Ireland to found a new monastery in Scotland, on the island of Iona. He evangelized the Scottish Picts, crowned the king of the Scots in 574, then pursued his action in Northumbria, the kingdom of the Angles, which extended from the south of Scotland as far as Wales. In 590, another monk, Columban, left Ireland for Gaul. Celtic monasteries rapidly became active centres of intellectual and artistic life. They became renowned seats of learning, where pupils learned the Latin language, which was foreign to Celtic culture but necessary for reading the Bible, and liturgy. They also studied astronomy, in order to determine the cycle of the liturgical year. Celtic monks daily recited the hundred and fifty psalms that Saint Benedict had spread over a week, as well as the *loricae*, incantatory litanies that concluded with a spontaneous poetic phase, inherited from Druidic and bardic traditions. At the request of monks, local artists placed themselves at the service of religion, beginning the art of illumination, among others.

Canterbury cloister

Saint Patrick's tombstone

Columban's tomb, Bobbio

BENEDICT OF ANIANE

Born about 750, Benedict, whose real name was Witiza, son of Agulfe, Wisigothic Count of Maguelonne, was raised at the court of Pepin the Short. He took part in the battle of Pavia where, with his brother, he narrowly escaped drowning. To thank God, in 774 he entered Saint Seine Abbey in Burgundy. Fascinated by monastic ideals, he subjected himself to strict asceticism, studied the great rules that he gathered in one collection, the *Concordia regularum*, and adopted that of Saint Benedict, whose name he chose at conversion. He left Burgundy and, on property belonging to his family at Aniane, founded a monastery following the Benedictine Rule. The quality of its monastic life encouraged many vocations and made Aniane the most prestigious monastery in the Carolingian empire. Benedict of Aniane participated in the struggle against the Adoptianist heresy – for the Adoptianists, Christ was a man adopted by God – which flourished in Aquitaine and was professed by Bishop Felix of Urgel. In 804, William the Great, Duke of Toulouse and Marquis of Septimania, retired to Aniane. He had become a legendary personality in the *Geste of William of Orange* and two years later, with the help of Benedict, founded nearby a monastic *cella* that was to become Saint Guilhem le Désert. Thanks to the help of Charlemagne's son, Louis the Pious, then governor of Aquitaine, Benedict visited several houses in Poitou, Languedoc, the Rhône valley and in Burgundy. When he became emperor in 814, Louis the Pious placed Benedict at the head of the monastery of Cornelimünster, near Aachen, and entrusted him with diffusing monastic reform throughout the empire. Benedict of Aniane gave increasing importance to the liturgy in the monks' daily activity, to the detriment of manual labour, to the extent that the holy offices took up most of the Cluniac *horarium* in the 11th century. The synods held in Aachen in 816, 817, 818 and 819 finished the work of imposing Benedict of Aniane's reform. He died in Germany in 821.

Saint Guilhem le Désert

MOORS AND NORSEMEN

Charlemagne, having conquered the Moors on Montmajour Hill, allegedly founded the monastery there (*above*). The Carolingians were also at the origin of Saint Mary's Abbey at Bains d'Arles, destroyed in 858 by Norsemen and rebuilt in 881 in Arles sur Tech (*opposite*).

Montmajour Abbey

Tympanum detail, Arles sur Tech

comed with universal enthusiasm and, by the middle of the 9th century, traditional monasticism was in danger once again. During the reign of Louis the Pious, then again during the dislocation of the empire and the partition of Verdun in 843, royal power was weakened to the advantage of local lords. To increase their power and wealth, these lords interfered in the management of monasteries and seized their possessions. Furthermore, at this time, Europe was the object of new invasions by Saracens, Huns, and especially, Norsemen, whose raids did not spare the monasteries. Each one looked to its local lord for protection and thus came under his obligation, laying the foundations of the feudal system. And many monks, condemned to exile, wandered the countryside carrying the relics of their saints with them.

Abbey basilica of Saint Benoît sur Loire

Cluny

At the beginning of the tenth century, while the Church was under the influence of laymen, new attempts at reform of the regular clergy appeared, particularly in Burgundy and Lorraine, where the work of Benedict of Aniane had evoked the most interest. This was the context within which, in 909, William, Duke of Aquitaine and Count of Mâcon, later called "the Pious", ceded to Bernon, the abbot of the monastery of Baume les Messieurs, a property near Mâcon on which he was to found the Benedictine monastery of Cluny. Placed under the patronage of apostles Peter and Paul and under the protection of the Holy See, it was free of any civil supervision, in particular for the election of the abbot which was the duty only of the community. Bernon was succeeded by Odon in 926. In 931, by a privilege accorded by Pope John XI, the abbot of Cluny could take the head of any monastery that any lay abbot was willing to entrust to him, as was the case of Fleury sur Loire, and he could welcome to Cluny any monk belonging to an unreformed community. Maïeul became the abbot in 954, and it was under his abbacy that the second church of Cluny was consecrated in 981, receiving on this occasion the relics of Saints Peter and Paul. In 994, Odilon took charge of the abbey of Cluny, to which the privilege of exemption was accorded in 998 by Pope Gregory V. This was confirmed and extended to all the Cluniac establishments by John XIX in 1024. This network of priories and abbeys attached to Cluny, the *Ecclesia cluniacensis*, was ruled by a certain number of customs concerning its liturgical, practical and even political aspects, because the Cluniacs had truly become lords exercising a certain number of royal powers, such as dispensing justice. Under the abbacy of Hugues de Semur (1049-1109), Cluny underwent its greatest period of expansion, to the extent that in the 12th century it included nearly twelve hundred houses spread throughout France, England, Northern Italy and Spain. This same abbacy also

Reference Dates

Foundation of Cluny	909
Abbacy of Bernon	909
Abbacy of Odon	926
Abbacy of Aynard	942
Pilgrimage to Compostela by Godescalc, Bishop of Le Puy	951
Abbacy of Maïeul	954
Cluny acquires the relics of Peter and Paul	981
Council of Charroux	989
Abbacy of Odilon	994
Councils of Bourges	1038
Abbacy of Hugues de Semur	1049
Start of construction of Cluny III	1088
Former Cluniac Urban II preaches the First Crusade. Consecration of Cluny, Saint Gilles, Our Lady of Le Puy and Saint Sernin	1095
Abbacy of Pons de Melgueil	1109
Abbacy of Peter the Venerable	1122
Convocation of the First General Chapter	1132

Remains of Cluny narthex

Fresco in St. Germain of Auxerre

Judas' kiss, Saint Gilles

Pray for us in Compostela

The discovery of the tomb of the apostle James the Greater in Galicia in 820 gave rise to a pilgrimage. In the 10th century, pilgrims gathered from all over Europe, following roads described by the Cluniac monk Aymeric Picaud in his *Liber peregrinationis*, written about 1130. *Via Tolosana, via Podensis, via Lemovicensis* and *via Turonensis* "all become one" at Puente la Reina to form the *Camino francés.* In Chapter VIII, Aymeric indicates the "holy bodies that rest along the route to Santiago and that pilgrims should visit", such as the relics of Saint Foy (*below*) in Conques, in a basilica where "for the glory of God, the Rule of Saint Benedict is observed with the greatest care".

saw the beginning of the construction of Cluny III, which was finished only fifty years later. This church, totally destroyed during the 19th century, whose nave was a hundred and eighty-seven metres long and eighty metres wide at the transept, was the greatest church of Christianity before Saint Peter's in Rome and a masterpiece of Romanesque art, then at its peak. For the Cluniacs were great builders whose shrines were distinguished by their grandiose proportions and the wealth of their decoration. Inspired by the ideas of Benedict of Aniane, they exalted the praise of God and, bit by bit, extended the length of holy offices, to the detriment of manual work, thus breaking with the organisation wanted by Saint Benedict. They took part in all the great undertakings of their time. Following the Councils of Charroux in 989, and Bourges in 1038, the so-called "black monks" worked alongside bishops to establish the Peace and the Truce of God within a feudal society torn by internal wars between rival lords. The papacy depended on them to put into practice the Gregorian reform and, in particular, to restore ecclesiastical discipline that had notably slackened. Pope Urban II, who preached the First Crusade in 1095 at Clermont, was a Cluniac. They participated in developing the pilgrimage to Santiago de Compostela, with their abbeys and priories used as stages along the routes to Santiago. Under the abbacy of Pons de Melgueil (1109-1122) the Cluniac church went through a critical period following repeated criticism of its luxurious tastes while new orders preached and practised a return to the values of Benedictine ideals. Peter the Venerable (1122-1156) attempted to solve these problems by establishing a system of direct exploitation of Cluniac properties, making them independent of donations. In 1132, he convoked the first General Chapter. The institution of an annual General Chapter was ratified by the statutes of Hugues V (1199-1207) who thus made Cluny into a true monastic order. Cluny's influence on religious life continued until the French Revolution, although it was never able to regain the prestige and influence of the first centuries.

Statue of St Foy in Conques

Fantastic animals, mosaic in north transept, Ganagobie Priory

Jeremy, Saint Pierre Abbey pier, Moissac

Vézelay tympanum

Romanesque Art

From the year 1000 to the end of the 12th century, a new form of art developed at the same time as Latin or Roman languages were developing, hence providing its name of Romanesque. Born in Tuscany, Burgundy, Provence and Catalonia, it spread throughout all of Western Europe and was expressed in architecture, but also in sculpture and painting. Churches, sometimes built above crypts, consisted of a nave, which was sometimes flanked by side aisles, ending with a semidome apse. In pilgrimage churches, these apses contained ambulatories with radiating chapels. One of the most important structural Romanesque developments was the vault. The earliest were barrel-vaults, later reinforced by transverse ribs. In some places, Lombardy stripes decorated chevets and steeples. In the beginning, the material used was small stones joined by mortar and hewn stone was used only to frame openings or in bases before it came into general use. During the 11th century, sculpture was limited to a block of marble worked on a single plane or on capitals before appearing on tympana or cloisters in the 12th century. In these “stone books”, artists showed Jesus Christ, the Virgin Mary, biblical or evangelical themes in which vices and virtues, angels and devils, monsters and grotesque characters confronted each other.

Narthex frieze detail, Cluny

Chevet of St Foy Abbey Church, Conques, built in the mid-11th century

THE 11TH CENTURY TURNING-POINT

After the year one thousand and despite the schism in the East in 1054, the Roman Catholic church was greatly expanding. Its area of influence extended to eastern Europe and the Scandinavian countries. The number of shrines multiplied. Raoul the Clean-shaven, a Cluniac monk born about 985, wrote, "It looked as though the entire world, in mutual agreement, had thrown off its old rags to cover itself in a white robe of churches." In the Iberian peninsula, the re-conquest progressed. In 1085, the king of Castile, Alfonso VI, recaptured Toledo and in 1118, the king of Aragon, Alfonso I the Warrior, managed to re-conquer Zaragoza. In 1096, the great barons Godefroi de Bouillon, Raymond IV of Toulouse, Bohemond de Tarento and Robert Courteheuse, preceded by Peter the Hermit and his pitiful groups of followers, set off to deliver the tomb of Jesus Christ in Jerusalem, which they captured in 1099. However, starting in 1076, the most prominent dignitaries of Catholic Christianity, the pope and the Holy Roman emperor, whose power extended over the kingdoms of Germany, Italy and Burgundy, violently opposed each other. At stake was the place of the Church within feudal society. The lords and kings, who granted lands and gave donations to the bishoprics, parishes and abbeys, rapidly wished to be in charge of naming bishops, priests and abbots themselves. In Rome, even the election of the pope was not free from pressure by the emperor and the Italian lords. Each of these positions corresponded to ecclesiastical advantages and their holders were not primarily concerned with their pastoral missions. Indeed, many were busier dealing with simony, trafficking in church objects and properties, and nicolaism or the non-respect of clerical celibacy. An attempt at the moral restoration of clerical life was undertaken at the Council of Reims in 1049. Work on the spiritual restoration of the lay Church, called the "Gregorian reform" after Pope Gregory VII (1073-1085) began in 1059, when Pope

Reference Dates

Romuald founds the Order of the Camaldoli	1012
John Gualbert settles in Vallombrosa in Tuscany	1039
Robert of Turlande founds La Chaise Dieu	1043
Council of Reims	1049
Schism in the East	1054
Decree by Pope Nicholas II on papal elections	1059
Stephen retires to Grandmont	1074
Gregory VII's decree on investitures	1075
Henry IV in Canossa	1077
Bruno founds the Carthusian Order	1084
Call of Urban II for the First Crusade	1095
Foundation of Citeaux	1098
Foundation of the Order of the Templars	1119
Foundation of the Order of the Hospitallers of Jerusalem	1120
Norbert founds the Order of the Premonstrants	1120
Concordat of Worms	1122

Crusader, fresco in temple at Cressac

Holy Sepulchre Church, Jerusalem

Nicholas II decreed that, from then on, the pope would be elected by cardinals, in other words the priests of the Roman parishes, and the bishops of neighbouring dioceses. In 1075, Pope Gregory VII published a decree on investitures, forbidding all laymen from investing a cleric with ecclesiastical functions. The princes and, above all, the emperor, for whom the bishops were powerful vassals, refused to submit. The quarrel finally ended only on September 23, 1122 with the signature of the Concordat of Worms between Pope Calixtus II and Emperor Henry V. The emperor was to be allowed to choose the holders of ecclesiastical advantages, but only the pope had the right to spiritually invest a bishop.
The world of monasticism was also affected by this renewal and the return to the great principles of the Desert Fathers and to the source of the Benedictine Rule began. It took on multiple forms. A new form of monasticism started, first of all in Italy. In the 10th century, Nil created eremitic communities at Rossano in Calabria near Monte Cassino, and at Gaeta. After joining Saint Michel de Cuxa in 974 along with Orseolo, the Doge of Venice, in 1012 Romuald retired to the isolation of the Appenines, at Camaldoli. After 1043, Peter Damian, Romuald's biographer, imposed in the abbey of Fonte Avellana a regime that was even stricter than the one prescribed by his model. Already in 1039, John Gualbert had created an establishment inspired by Camaldoli at Vallombrosa in Tuscany. Eremitic initiatives multiplied also in Germany and France. Géraud de Sales settled in Perigord, in a place close to the future abbey of Cadouin;

An emperor in Canossa

The decree about investitures promulgated by Pope Gregory VII in 1075 weakened the authority of the lords, kings and emperors by depriving them of powerful vassals. Emperor Henry IV (1056-1106) sharply opposed the pope and, ignoring the decree, continued naming the bishops he wanted. The pope excommunicated him in 1076. Seizing the opportunity to weaken imperial power, the German lords soon aligned themselves with the pontiff. Left alone, Henry IV chose this moment to cross the Alps into Italy and went to the castle of Canossa, the property of Countess Matilda of Tuscany, where Gregory VII was staying. For three days, barefoot and wearing only a shirt, kneeling in the snow, the emperor begged forgiveness and submitted to papal authority on January 28, 1077. Humbled, Henry IV seemed to have accepted pontifical authority. But in 1085, the emperor, who had found supporters in Italy, entered Rome and named an anti-Pope, Clement III. Chased out of the Eternal City, Gregory VII, vanquished, died in exile in southern Italy in 1085.

Canossa Castle

Capital, Saint Michel de Cuxa

Saint Michel de Cuxa

A church dedicated to Saint Germain l'Auxerrois was located in Cuxa, at the foot of Canigou Mountain in the Pyrenees. Benedictine monks settled there in 878. A new church was consecrated in 975 and dedicated to Saint Michael, under the abbacy of Garin, a Cluniac. Garin brought numerous relics from his travels in Italy and the Holy Land, and attracted to Saint Michel de Cuxa (*above* and *opposite*) Pietro Orseolo, the Doge of Venice, and Romuald. During the 11th century, Oliba had the chancel encircled by an ambulatory, and the cloister was built in the 12th century. Commendam in the 16th century provoked a deterioration in monastic life. On January 27, 1793, revolutionaries expelled the last monk from Cuxa and vandalized the monastery, which was then sold as state property. In the 19th century, the abbey was in ruin. At the beginning of the 20th, entire sections of the cloister were sent to the United States. They are visible today at the Cloisters Museum in New York City. Cistercians settled in Cuxa from 1919 to 1965, followed by monks from Montserrat.

Saint Michel de Cuxa

Serrabone Priory

Garin in the Alps; Stephen, in Muret near Grandmont, in 1074; Gérard at the Sauve Majeur in 1079. Bruno was born in Cologne in 1030. After refusing the bishop's seat of Reims, in 1082 he stayed at Molesme where he met the abbot Robert, who was to be one of the founders of Citeaux, then settled with two disciples at Sèche Fontaine in Burgundy. He was disappointed with this experience and it was in the frozen desert of the Chartreuse that he created the first Carthusian monastery in 1084. Called to Rome by Urban II, he did not return to the Chartreuse, but he did found another house in Calabria in 1091. Guiges, the fifth prior of the Chartreuse wrote the Carthusian Rule for this contemplative order, which united monasticism and steadfastness. Communities of canons, such as those at Saint Ruf near Avignon, or Serrabone in Catalonia, also multiplied. They adopted their rule from the precepts of Saint Augustine, but remained in contact with society, carrying out pastoral duties, or, like the Premonstrants founded by Norbert in 1120, preaching. Within the context of the crusades and the *Reconquista*, the beginning of the 12th century saw the birth of religious and military orders such as the Templars in 1119, and the Knights Hospitaller of Jerusalem in 1120. Finally, new orders or monasteries adopted the Benedictine Rule: in 1043, Robert of Turlande created La Chaise Dieu in the Livadrois region of France, after a visit to Monte Cassino in 1040; in 1100, Robert of Arbrissel settled his disciples at Fontevrault. Two years earlier, on March 21, 1098, Robert, Alberic and Stephen had arrived in a place called *Cistels*...

CASA DEI

At his death in 1067 at La Chaise Dieu (*below*), Robert of Turlande had founded fifty priories. In 1084, one of his successors, Seguin, donated land to Bruno in the Chartreuse in order to install his community.

Cloister, La Chaise Dieu

THE UNWRITTEN RULE OF SAINT AUGUSTINE

Augustine was born in Tagaste, in what is now Algeria, in 354. After studying in Carthage, he became a professor of rhetoric and taught in the capital of Roman Africa, then in Rome and Milan. A Manichean auditor, he was eventually won over by the preaching of Ambrose, the bishop of Milan, and converted to Christianity at the same time as his son, Adeodat, in 387. Returning to Tagaste, he founded a first community that he installed on his father's property and which adopted a monastic rule brought from Bethlehem by Alypius, one of his disciples. In 391, Augustine was ordained for the priesthood in Hippo and organized a new lay community for which he wrote his *Praeceptum*. As the bishop of Hippo in 396, he had to deal with a conflict in a nun's monastery of which his sister was the abbess, and on that occasion Augustine wrote a letter providing further information about his understanding of monastic life. Augustine preached in different towns, struggled with various heresies such as Donatism and Pelagianism, while simultaneously producing a large number of writings. At his death, which occurred during the siege of Hippo by Vandals in 430, he left behind him a considerable amount of literary, theological and philosophical work that was to make him into one of the four great Latin fathers of the church. Besides his *Confessions*, relating his spiritual itinerary, or the *De Trinitate* and *The City of God*, there remained his remarkable correspondence as well as hundreds of sermons. In fact, Augustine did not really write a rule, but rather defined a framework. Cesarius, the bishop of Arles from 470 to 542, was the first to refer to it for a community of nuns in difficulty. Starting in the 11th century, regular canons in charge of implementing the Gregorian reform adopted an Augustinian rule. These clerics, often called canons of Saint Augustine, took for themselves monastic values with their respect for their vows and the practice of meditation and prayer, just like the Benedictines. In particular, they renounced all personal possessions, an element that Augustine especially emphasised. But unlike the Benedictines, they had pastoral duties and evangelized the faithful in a priory that took the place of a parish church. In 1121, under the influence of Norbert, the canons of Prémontré, in Picardy, imitated them although their principal vocation was preaching – later they were to become teachers – outside their enclosure, just like the preaching friars of Saint Dominic, who adopted the Rule of Saint Augustine in 1215.

St Augustine teaching the hermits

2

History of the Cistercian Order

It was in a place called *Cistels* that Robert of Molesme, Alberic and Stephen Harding founded their *Novum Monasterium* on March 21, 1098. Their main motivation was a wish to return to the principles of Saint Benedict's Rule. After some difficult years, Stephen provided the Order of Citeaux with its impetus and its institutions. Bernard of Clairvaux left the imprint of his charisma. The abbeys founded by the Order or which were incorporated into it multiplied. The Cistercians played an important role in the life of the Church and society; some were elected popes or named bishops. Starting in the 13th century, the Order had to struggle to remain faithful to itself. Trials were overcome and the founders' spirit lives on still today in the members of the Cistercian family.

Vault in refectory, Molesme

Robert and twelve monks clearing land at the Novum Monasterium

Statue of Stephen Harding, Citeaux

In a place called Cistels

This sentence appears at the foot of the statue of Stephen Harding (*above*): "In this place stood the first church of Citeaux, consecrated on November 16, 1106 by the Bishop of Châlons, where its founding fathers Alberic and Stephen as well as Saint Bernard devoted themselves to prayer." On March 21, 1998, seven hundred Cistercian nuns and monks from all over the world joined together in Citeaux to commemorate the nine hundredth anniversary of the arrival of Robert, Alberic and Stephen on March 21, 1098.

Robert, Alberic and Stephen

Crosier of Robert of Molesme

Born in 1030 near Troyes, in his youth Robert was a monk at Moutier la Celle, a Cluniac monastery of which he became prior in 1050. In 1069, he was called by the monks of Saint Michel de Tonnerre, who named him their abbot. In 1071, he directed a group of hermits settled in the forest of Colan. In 1075, Robert gathered together his disciples in a monastery that he founded in the woods of Molesme, near Tonnerre, and for which he had chosen the Benedictine Rule. Molesme attracted vocations, created priories and received donations. The success and wealth of the abbey distanced it from the ideals that had given rise to its foundation. In 1090, the prior Alberic and a monk, Stephen, left Molesme for a new solitude at Oigny when others, with Robert, guided by the same purpose, retired to Aulps in the Chablais, where Alberic and Stephen joined them. Robert and his companions returned to Molesme in 1093 and attempted to impose the strict respect of the Benedictine Rule. But conflict arose so Robert, Alberic, Stephen and four monks requested permission to leave Molesme. It was granted by Hugues, Archbishop of Lyons and the papal legate. On March 21, 1098, Robert, Alberic, Stephen and twenty-one other monks created their *Novum Monasterium* on an allodium ceded to them by the Viscount of Beaune, south of Dijon, in a wooded, marshy place called *Cistels* – reeds in Old French, "uninhabited, except for wild animals". Eudes, the Duke of Burgundy, supported the undertaking and enlarged the property by several arpents, including, among other things, the vineyard of Meursault. However, in Molesme, the monks requested Robert's return and called on Pope Urban II. The pope asked his legate, Hugues, to settle the problem. The synod of Port d'Anselle in June 1099 decided that Robert should return to Molesme, while it legitimized the foundation of the New Monastery of which Alberic, one of the most fervent supporters of the break with Molesme, became the abbot. On October 19, 1100, Pope Paschal II granted his protection to the isolated little monastery in the Cistels forest, whose future remained uncertain.

Under the authority of Alberic, the community tried to return to the sources of Benedictine monasticism. Rapidly, Alberic abandoned the original location for another several hundred metres away where, in November 1106, the bishop of Chalôns came to consecrate the abbey church. In 1109, at the death of Alberic, the New Monastery was completely destitute, in agreement with its founders' ideals. However, life was so difficult in this New Monastery, which could barely supply its own food, that new voca-

Reference Dates

Foundation of Molesme	1075
Foundation of Citeaux	1098
Paschal II grants his protection to Citeaux	1100
Consecration of the Citeaux abbey church by the bishop of Chalôns	1106
Death of Alberic, beginning of the abbacy of Stephen Harding	1109
Arrival in Citeaux of Bernard of Fontaine	1112
Foundation of La Ferté	1113
Foundation of a priory for nuns in Jully. The first prioress, Elizabeth, is the wife of Bernard's older brother, Guy, who himself entered Citeaux. She is succeeded in 1128 by Hombeline, Bernard's sister	1113
Drawing up of the Original Charter	1114
Foundation of Pontigny	1114
Foundation of Clairvaux and Morimond	1115

Foundation of Preuilly	1118
Calixtus II approves the Original Charter and the writing of the Original Exordium	1119
Foundation of Bonnevaux	1119
Foundation of l'Aumône	1121
Foundation of the first Cistercian abbey for nuns in Tart	1125
Stephen Harding gives up his position	1133
Death of Stephen Harding	1134

St Bernard, Fontaine lès Dijon

tions were discouraged and the new recruits needed to ensure the monastery's survival were not forthcoming. It was Stephen who succeeded Alberic. Stephen Harding was an Englishman, who had stayed at Vallombrosa in Tuscany, and a faithful disciple of Robert and Alberic. The new abbot enlarged the property with donations from the chatelaine of Vergy. To improve it, he employed laymen to help the monks, ageing and obliged to attend holy offices, to work the land. Starting in 1111, material improvements brought new recruits attracted by the monks' reputation for fervour and holiness. Among the new arrivals in 1112 was the son of the lord of Fontaine, Bernard, followed by thirty companions. The number of monks at the New Monastery, which had taken the name of Citeaux in 1119, allowed it to diffuse. In 1113, its first daughter abbey, La Ferté, was founded. It was followed in 1114 by Pontigny, then Clairvaux in 1115, of which Bernard was the abbot, and Morimond. After a four-year pause, foundations began again with Preuilly in 1118, La Cour Dieu and Bonnevaux in 1119, L'Aumône and Loroux in 1121. Until 1131, the year in which three were founded: La Bussière, Le Miroir, and Saint Andrea de Sestri in Italy, Citeaux did not create any other daughters although the Cistercian area increased greatly because its daughters in turn, especially the first four – La Ferté, Pontigny, Clairvaux and Morimond – had also begun to diffuse. This development, over space and time, of what was already the Cistercian Order threatened its cohesion and altered its fundamental principles.

The Fifth Daughter of Citeaux

Preuilly (*below*) was founded on the lands of the Count of Champagne in 1118. It created Vauluisant in 1129, La Colombe in 1146 and Seine Port in 1148. The latter was the future abbey of Barbeaux who adopted Rancé's reform at the end of the 17th century.

Preuilly Abbey

Diffusion, Substitution and Incorporation

The creation of a new Cistercian community can be carried out by diffusion, by substitution or by incorporation. In the first case, the mother abbey sends a group of monks onto land it received as a donation and founds a new abbey, her daughter,

Chevet, Fontenay Abbey Church

Arches of the nave at Buildwas, daughter of Savigny

who can diffuse in her turn. Morimond thus founded the German abbey of Camp in 1123, which by 1236 included thirty-two monasteries affiliated to it throughout Germany and central Europe. In the second case, the monks of the mother abbey repopulate a non-Cistercian abbey, replacing a former community. Hence, the abbey of Orval in Belgium, founded in 1070 by Benedictines from Calabria and then occupied by canons from Trier Cathedral, was repopulated in 1132 by Cistercians from Trois Fontaines.

Finally, in the third case, some non-Cistercian communities that agreed to respect the Charter of Charity and other customs were incorporated into the Order under the supervision of one of the abbeys. This was the case of the abbey of Savigny in 1147. It brought with it the twenty-four houses it controlled when it became a daughter of Clairvaux.

Cloister at Furness, daughter of Savigny

Tympanum at Sturzelbronn, granddaughter of La Ferté

The Charter of Charity

The *Charter of Charity*, conceived by Stephen Harding starting in 1144, laid out the institutions and structures of the Cistercian Order. Pope Calixtus II approved the Charter by the bull *Ad hoc in apostolici* of December 23, 1119. Essentially, the Charter organized affiliations and started the General Chapter. The founding abbot of a new abbey, called the father-abbot, had to visit his daughter abbey once a year. He advised it, presided the election of its abbot and controlled its monastic constancy. The authority exercised by the father-abbot was spiritual rather than judicial. Indeed, although all the Cistercians chose to live the same way, according to strict respect of the Rule of Saint Benedict, although they adopted the same chants, the same prayers, each abbey retained its autonomy and, in no case could the father-abbot interfere in an abbey's management. In order to maintain unanimity and cohesion, as well as the respect for the initial ideals, the Charter called for an annual meeting of all the abbots at Citeaux, under the direction of the abbot of the mother abbey. This meeting, called the General Chapter, made important decisions about the Order and punished breaches of the Rule. During deliberations, each abbot could intervene with equal rights. Furthermore, the Charter established that abbeys, although autonomous, were also jointly interdependent and that they had to support each other spiritually and materially. Finally, the abbots of the first four daughters of Citeaux – La Ferté, Pontigny, Clairvaux and Morimond – were in charge of supervising observance of the Rule in the mother abbey. If the abbot of Citeaux appeared to be moving away from it, they were to call him back to order and, in extreme cases, could meet to consider his dismissal. At the death of the abbot of Citeaux, they were to organize the election of the new abbot, that they were to preside and to which they were to summon the abbots of their choice. In 1120, the General Chapter settled complementary measures to the articles of the Charter of Charity, *capitula*, that joined the statutes, or *instituta*, established in 1134. The entire structure was the legacy of Stephen Harding.

Fontenay chapter house

Therefore, as soon as Pontigny was created in 1114, Stephen provided the Order with a structure. He established the *Original Charter* that, progressively completed until 1119, formed the final version of the *Charter of Charity* to which other measures were added before the statutes of 1134. It was also in 1119 that Stephen had the history of the New Monastery written up under the title of *Original Exordium.*

The life of a Cistercian monk was based on the search for isolation and poverty in order to attain, through prayer, communion with God. A Cistercian abbey was placed under the patronage of Our Lady, "Queen of Heaven and Earth". It was founded with the agreement of the bishop and built far from any inhabited place, near running water that would allow fishing, irrigation and to turn the paddles of a mill. The monastic community worked its own land, lived in self-sufficiency on the margins of its time and refused ecclesiastical advantages. Within the monastery, novices, professed monks and lay brothers lived all together. The novice lived his apprenticeship of monastic life under the supervision of an elder. After his noviciate, in front of the abbot and the community, he pronounced solemn vows of steadfastness, obedience, and conversion of moral standards, by which he became a professed monk. Clothed in an unbleached tunic, the monk conformed to St Benedict's Rule and lived in silence. His day was punctuated by Hours for prayer, with the rest of his time devoted to reading holy texts, *lectio divina,* and manual work. A characteristic of the Cistercian rule was that every day, after the singing of Prime, the monks met in the chapter house for the monastic chapter. After the reading and commentary of a chapter of the Rule, each confessed his sins or faults. The professed monks slept fully dressed in the dormitory and took their meals together in the refectory, listening to sacred texts read from the pulpit. Originally, the lay brothers were laymen recruited by Stephen to help the monks with the heavy work. They nonetheless participated in morning and

Hours of Prayer

Vigils (Night Office)

June 2-3 a.m.
December 1:30-2:50 a.m.

Lauds (at dawn)

June 3:10 a.m.; December 7:15 a.m.

Prime (at sunrise)

June 4 a.m.; December 8 a.m.

Terce

June 7:45; December 9:20 a.m.

Sext (noon)

June 10:40; December 11:20 a.m.

Nones

June 2 p.m.; December 1:20 p.m.

Vespers

June 6- 6:45 p.m.
December 2:50-3:30 p.m.

Compline

June 7:50 p.m. December 3:55 p.m.

Dormitory in Val Abbey, daughter of La Cour Dieu, founded in 1125

Huerta, pulpit

Rules of Life

Books that an abbey should possess

Missal, The Gospels, Epistles, collection of prayers, gradual, antiphonary, hymn book, psalter, lectionary, Rule, calendar.

Monk's clothing

Simple and ordinary, without a cloak, nor shirt. The outside of the cowl should be plain, daily shoes should be of cow's leather.

Food

A pound of rough bread and a hemine of wine per day. Dishes without meat or fat, except for the ill.

Enclosure

The monk may not live outside the enclosure, but can go to the granges. Women are not allowed in the monasteries or the granges.

Lay brothers, detail of Stephen's tomb, first abbot of Obazine

evening offices. A first rule concerning them was written in 1133, then in 1145 it was completed and annexed to the statutes of 1134. In any case, by 1150 they were friars. After their noviciate, having learned about the Benedictine regime, they renounced all their personal belongings and submitted to the abbot's authority. The lay brothers wore beards, were dressed in brown robes and lived in granges or in a building reserved for them at the monastery. In the abbey church, their chancel was separated from that of the professed monks by the rood screen. They could never become monks.

In 1133, when he retired a year before his death, Stephen had accomplished a considerable amount of work. The Order included about seventy abbeys throughout Champagne, Burgundy, Franche Comté, but also in Italy, Germany and England. Between 1120 and 1125, Stephen had even founded in Tart, near Citeaux, a first establishment for nuns.

Fontfroide, lay brothers' walk

Le Relecq, granddaughter of Aumône, founded in 1132

Stephen Harding and Saint Vaast offering the model of their abbey to the Virgin

Granges

"To exploit, maintain and preserve all this properly, we can have, nearby or far from the monastery, granges that will be guarded and administered by lay brothers."

Working the land was a basic given of the Cistercian Rule. A first originality of the Cistercians was that the monks themselves worked the fields around their abbeys, unlike the indirect exploitation common in the Middle Ages. The abbey's location, far from inhabited places, was carefully chosen. At the edge of a forest, on flat ground or in the heart of a valley, it was generally set near a river or stream. Starting with this first, often modest, settlement, the properties exploited by the abbey increased over the years thanks to donations, at first on the site itself, but further away afterwards. Hence, a Cistercian abbey could own property of five to eight thousand hectares, or even twenty-eight thousand in Clairvaux. These included lands growing cereal grains, pastures and vineyards. In order to organize the exploitation of these lands, particularly those the most distant from the monastery, the Cistercians built granges, guarded and administered by teams of lay brothers, under the supervision of the abbey's cellarer. They were usually spread over a radius of five to twenty kilometres around the cloister, from which they were not supposed to be more than a day's walk away. The number of granges owned by an abbey varied according to the amount of property it possessed: Citeaux had nineteen, Clairvaux about twenty, Fontenay about ten, Fountains had twenty-six, Alcobaça, fifteen, Eberbach sixteen. Two granges owned by neighbouring abbeys had to be at least two leagues apart. Each grange managed the exploitation of a property large enough to consist of several dozen hectares of cultivated land, one or several hundred pastures, woods and ponds. In the vineyards, the grange was organized around a smaller property, called a cellar. Some of these vineyards have remained famous – those of Chablis belonged to Pontigny, Le Clos de Vougeot to Citeaux. However, the Cistercians' economic activities were not limited to agriculture. Some abbeys, like Balerne in the Jura, owned deposits of salt, others like Fontenay ran forges, or like Chaalis, manufactured tiles and ceramic objects. In the second half of the 12th century, lay brothers appeared at markets selling their abbey's products that visitors

Framework in Beaumont Grange

Vaulerent Grange

Woodcutting monks

could buy at the abbey itself. The granges where the teams of lay brothers lived consisted of outbuildings, which contained tools and sheltered cattle. Some even owned a small oratory, abolished in 1204 by a decision of the General Chapter, which feared the granges would be accepted as authentic monasteries. To help the lay brothers, unpaid and religious labour that was not always sufficient, the Order planned the hiring of salaried workers, *mercenarii*, hired during harvests or to work on the abbey's construction. At the head of each grange, and on a suggestion by the cellarer, the abbot named a master of the grange from among the lay brothers. He directed the other lay brothers and the *mercenarii*.
The cellarer made sure that the lay brothers respected their monastic obligations, with the help of the grange master. He sent them to the various granges and allocated the work.
During the first half of the 13th century, it became ever more difficult to recruit and direct exploitation was progressively abandoned, so the granges with their original organization disappeared. With their granges, the Cistercians had provided themselves with an extremely efficient organization and had far-reaching knowledge in agronomy, forestry, animal breeding, fisheries and hydraulics. Thanks to their network of granges, their sense of organization and the development of their knowledge, the Cistercians made an important contribution to clearing and improving land in Europe during the 12th and 13th centuries.

Cougnaguet Mill

Fontenay Forge

Saint Bernard, detail from St Bernard's Reredos, Majorca Museum

Bernard of Clairvaux

Bernard's arrival in Citeaux

In 1134, at the death of Stephen Harding, the Order had acquired solid structures and a certain authority, the foundations for a tremendous development that took place from 1133 to 1153 and to which Bernard of Clairvaux made a great contribution. Born in 1090 in Fontaine lès Dijon, Bernard was the son of the lord of Fontaine, Tescelin, and of Aleth de Montbard, mid-level nobles but related to powerful and influential lords. Tescelin and Aleth had seven children, six boys and a girl, and although his brothers were destined to become knights, Bernard was the only one, perhaps because of his fragile health, to be entrusted to the canons at Saint Vorles's collegiate church in Châtillon sur Seine. There he discovered the Bible, the Fathers of the Church, theology, and studied the Latin language and its authors. Bernard was gifted with exceptional intelligence and sensitivity, which flourished during his studies. On his return to the family castle at Fontaine at the age of eighteen to lead the life of a young aristocrat, he slowly felt the stirrings of a vocation for monasticism. In 1112, aged twenty-two, with thirty companions, including four of his brothers and two maternal uncles, he entered as a novice at the New Monastery in the nearby forest of Cistels. In June 1115, Stephen Harding placed Bernard at the head of the abbey of Clairvaux in the district of Bar sur Aube. Thanks to the dynamic influence of its abbot, Clairvaux soon began to diffuse in its turn. Trois Fontaines Abbey was founded in 1118, that of Fontenay in

Reference Dates

Birth of Bernard	1090
Bernard enters Citeaux as a novice	1112
Foundation of Clairvaux	1115
Foundation of Clairvaux's first daughter, Trois Fontaines	1118
Foundation of Fontenay	1119
Drafting of *Apology to William of Saint Thierry*	1123
Synod of Troyes	1128
Bernard supports Innocent II	1130
Council of Pisa	1133
Debate in Sens between Bernard and Abelard	1141
Bernard leaves to preach in Languedoc	1145
Bernard calls for a second crusade in Vézelay	1146
Foundation of Fontfroide	1146
Foundation of Alcobaça	1148
Foundation of Poblet	1151
Death of Bernard	1153

St Bernard's Pond in Fontenay

Clairvaux storeroom

Narthex detail, Moissac

1119, another at Foigny in 1121. Starting in 1124, Bernard became the foremost representative of the Order, following an affair that involved him personally and opposed Cluny and Citeaux. His nephew, Robert of Châtillon, who had been offered as an oblate to Cluny, but who had professed in Clairvaux, secretly left his monastery, at the request of the Cluniac prior Matthew, to enter Cluny, despite his vow of steadfastness. Bernard was deeply affected and demanded Robert's return. The Cluniacs, supported by the Holy See, refused. Bernard responded by writing his nephew a fiery letter about the Cluniacs, which he made public and whose terms went beyond the initial stake. He reproached the black monks with gluttony, their lack of spirituality at holy offices, their contempt for manual labour. A short time later, he published his *Apology*, dedicated to his friend William of Saint Thierry, in which he opposed Cistercian austerity, poverty and simplicity with the Cluniac lifestyle. He denounced their greediness, their interest in their appearance, as well as the grandeur and luxury of their churches and cloisters with their costly and mannered decoration. "In the cloisters", he wrote, "what is the point of those ridiculous monsters, those horrible beauties and those beautiful horrors? What is the point of those foul monkeys, those ferocious lions, those monstrous centaurs? And those half-human beings?" Written in 1125, when the Cistercian Order was flourishing and becoming the new monastic model, although one that inspired jealousy and was sometimes criticized for its excesses and self-importance, under

REPROACHING A NEPHEW

In the letter to his nephew Robert, Bernard wrote: "But what? Is salvation rather in the refinement of clothing and the opulence of dishes than in austere food and modest clothing?"

Cloister of La Prée, daughter of Clairvaux, founded in 1141

A PROLIFIC BRANCH

Under the abbacy of Bernard, Clairvaux's affiliation developed considerably, since the number of abbeys belonging to the lineage of Clairvaux was over a hundred and seventy by 1153. Among the foundations or incorporations during this period of expansion were abbeys such as Noirlac, Mellifont, Poblet and Eberbach, but also other lesser known ones like La Bussière, Vaucelles, La Bénisson Dieu, La Prée, Fontmorigny...

La Bénisson Dieu Abbey church

La Bussière pigeon house

Fishpond and bakery, Fontmorigny

Vaucelles watchtower

The Krak des Chevaliers

THE KRAK DES CHEVALIERS

This castle belonging to the emir of Homs was captured in 1099 by Raymond IV of Saint Gilles, then by Tancred in 1110. The Knights Hospitallers occupied it from 1142 to 1271. The fortress *(above)*, an eagle's nest overlooking Homs plain, suffered from several earthquakes but was rebuilt at the beginning of the 13th century. This "bone placed across the Muslims' throat" repelled numerous attacks, including Saladin's, but fell in 1271 into the hands of the Mameluks. Its conqueror, Baibars, erased all the Latin inscriptions in the chapel, which he transformed into a mosque, except one: "May be you accorded abundance, wisdom, beauty, but fear, above all, pride which destroys everything."

Bernard's brilliant and caustic quill the *Apology* took on its defence and destroyed its adversaries' arguments. Soon, Bernard became one of the most important personalities of Western Christendom. In 1128, he was present at the synod of Troyes, gathered to define the mission and structures of the Order of the Knights Templar, founded in 1119 to defend the Frankish states of Syria and Palestine after the First Crusade. In his *In Praise of a New Knighthood*, that he wrote for the new military orders, the Templars or the Knights Hospitallers of Jerusalem, while exalting holy war Bernard enjoined their members to lead a life close to the monastic ideal, to be chaste, to renounce glory and the futile values of the world and to undertake a quest for spirituality. During the schism of 1130, the abbot of Clairvaux took the side of Innocent II against Anacletus and subsequently, on numerous occasions, conscious of the quality of Cistercian candidates, Bernard intervened in episcopal and pontifical elections to support the candidatures of monks from his own order. In 1138, the prior of Clairvaux, Godefroy de la Roche Vanneau, won the episcopal seat of Langres against a Cluniac; in 1145, a Cistercian, Bernard Paganelli, Abbot of Saint Anasthasius near Rome and a former monk in Clairvaux, became pope under the name Eugene III. This exceptional openness to the world, required for the good of the Church, reinforced the Order's prestige and authority and, after 1134, was tolerated by the General Chapter. In 1139, alerted by William of Saint Thierry, Bernard denounced, in front of Abelard's students in Paris, the

The Schism of Anacletus

In 1130, the Roman church suffered from a schism following a double pontifical election opposing Innocent II and Anacletus II, whose faction held the majority in Rome. Furthermore, Anacletus had the support of Roger II of Sicily, a descendant of knights from Normandy, who controlled the territories south of the Papal States. On Italian lands, he turned out to be an adversary too powerful for Innocent II. Thus, the latter left Rome for France, where he asked for help from other political powers. Emperor Lothair III was slow in responding but the king of France, Louis VI, called a special council in Etampes in the spring of 1130. Bernard, who was present, ardently supported Innocent II and convinced the king to recognize his legitimacy. Pursuing his action within Innocent's faction, of which he became the head, the abbot of Clairvaux met the king of England, Henry I, whom he convinced to join the cause. In 1133, Bernard was in Italy with Innocent who tried, with the Emperor's military support, to establish himself in the north. In April, Innocent II entered Rome at the side of Bernard and Lothair. The conflict appeared to be resolved in his favour. However, once the emperor returned to Germany, he was once again forced to flee. In Pisa in 1135, he asked for a second military intervention by Lothair and united his supporters, including Bernard, in a council. The case of Milan, a bastion of Anacletus, retained attention. Innocent, who had forced the dismissal of the archbishop Anselm, who supported his adversary, decided to send a delegation of two cardinals, accompanied by Bernard, to conquer and persuade the Milanese population. The arrival of the abbot of Clairvaux provoked general enthusiasm and stirred up crowds who hurried to see and touch him and even acclaimed him as the archbishop. However, after his departure, although the Milanese nobility had decided to promote the foundation of a Cistercian abbey, a daughter of Clairvaux, which took the name of Chiaravalle – an Italianized name of the mother abbey – the supporters of Anacletus regained influence and Bernard was forced to intervene a second time to rally the city to his cause. In 1137, the schism had not yet ended. Despite attacks by Lothair, Roger II still controlled the Mezzogiorno, while Anacletus was living in Rome. In the springtime, Bernard vainly attempted to win the Sicilian's favour. The death of Anacletus in 1138 hastened the end of the conflict, when his successor submitted to the authority of Innocent II in May, 1138.

Chiaravalle

ONE HERESY CAN HIDE ANOTHER

"What evils does the heretic Henry cause to the Church of God: the basilicas contain no faithful, the faithful have no priests; the priests no honour, and to say it in one word, there remain only Christians without Christ."
Saint Bernard

Funerary garden in Sarlat

It was at the beginning of 1116 that a former monk, Henry of Lausanne, began to preach in Le Mans. Later, he became the disciple of another heretic, Pierre de Bruys, whom he joined in the lower Rhône River valley. The two men did not recognize the authority of the church, rejected baptism for children, claimed that Adam's original sin was not transmitted to his descendants and denounced episcopal luxury. In 1134, the archbishop of Arles had Henry arrested and made him appear at the Council of Pisa in 1135. Henry retracted and met Bernard who suggested he enter Clairvaux. Henry once again began his heretical statements, especially in the area of Toulouse. The abbot of Cluny, Peter the Venerable, denounced him in 1138 in his treatise *Contra Petrobrusianos* where he noted that the inhabitants of Saint Gilles had burned Pierre de Bruys alive. Bernard contradicted Henry's heretical theses in the two longest sermons of his *Song of Songs*. In one, he claimed that heretics should be brought back to the path of righteousness "not by arms but by arguments destroying their errors". Bernard's interest in this question led him to write to Alphonse Jourdain, Count of Toulouse, to ask him to intervene. And in May and June of 1145, accompanied by the bishop of Chartres and the legate Alberic, the bishop-cardinal of Ostia, he undertook a journey that took him from Bordeaux to Albi, passing through Poitiers, Périgueux, Sarlat, Tulle, Cahors and Toulouse. The progression of this missionary journey is perfectly well-known thanks to the detailed report made of it by Geoffroy of Auxerre. Plague was raging in Sarlat and the inhabitants proclaimed its eradication as a miracle by the abbot of Clairvaux. The lantern of the dead remains as testimony. In Toulouse, Bernard was received by the canons of Saint Sernin's, the population gave him a warm welcome. A public controversy was organized – Henry was invited along with other heretics to whom Geoffroy of Auxerre gives the name of Aryans, and who a few years later would be called Albigensians or Cathars. But none of them came. In Verfeil, the Christian dualism called Catharism was already strongly established, particularly in the local seigniory. Geoffroy of Auxerre immediately called it the *castrum* de *Sedes Satanae*. Bernard was unable to address the inhabitants who hid in their houses and made noise to drown out his speech. Allegedly Bernard left the *castrum* damning it "Verfeil, may God dry you up!", a play on words since *verfeil* meant *verte feuille* (green leaf) in local dialect. In 1148, Henry was condemned to prison in perpetuity by the Council of Pisa. But the Albigensian heresy was ever more present in the regions of the Languedoc where, fifty years later, the Cistercians were called upon to play an important role in solving this *negocium pacis et fidei* that was the Cathar crisis.

Baptistry, cathedral and tower in Pisa

theses of their master and in June, 1140, he confronted Abelard before an assembly of bishops, who condemned the theologian's positions. Called on by ecclesiastical authorities, the abbot of Clairvaux continued his action in the service of Christianity. From May to July 1145, he undertook a journey through south-western France to preach against the heretical teachings of Henry of Lausanne. When Eugene III organized a second crusade, he naturally called on his former abbot. Despite these affairs that took him far from his monastery, Bernard remained an exemplary monk and abbot. A talented and prolific writer, he wrote superb sermons on the *Song of Songs* and his influence in the fields of spirituality and liturgy, architecture and art was considerable.

As the intellectual guide of the Order, Bernard actively participated in its development and expansion although he never became abbot of Citeaux. In 1133, Guy, Abbot of Trois Fontaines Abbey, the first of Clairvaux's daughters, was named as the head of the Order, and after one month he was replaced by Raynard, a monk from Citeaux, who was to remain in position until his death around 1150. Over a period of twenty years, from 1133 to 1153, under Bernard's influence, diffusion continued and many communities of monks and canons were incorporated into the Order, bringing the houses they were linked to with them. At Bernard's death in 1153, the Order included three hundred and fifty establishments, or two hundred and eighty more than in 1133. Citeaux's contribution to this development was minimal, even though it incorporated

Saint Sernin's Basilica, Toulouse

About Abelard

In Epistle 189, Bernard wrote, "I did not find it was appropriate to compromise with weak human reasoning, divine faith whose certainty rests on truth itself."

St Bernard teaching monks, *Les Heures d'Étienne Chevalier*, Condé Museum

THE SECOND CRUSADE

"Since you command it, even more, through your intermediary, it is God who commands it."
Letter from Bernard to Eugene III

In 1144, the Franks had lost Edesse in Syria and in 1145 a Cistercian, Eugene III, succeeded Lucius II on the throne of St Peter. Raymond of Poitiers asked Manuel Comnenius, the Basileus, for help but was refused. Therefore, on December 1st, he addressed the West. The king of France had taken a vow of making a pilgrimage to the Holy Land, but the pope's calls to French and Italian nobles to engage in a second crusade found little response. On March 1, 1146, Eugene III asked Bernard to revive the flame. And on March 31, 1146, in Vézelay, the second crusade was officially launched in the presence of the king. Was Bernard present and did he really make that fiery speech? Nothing is less certain, but a short time later he addressed a letter to the nobles of France, Italy and Germany to ask them for their help in the operation. In the same letter, he also asked the German princes to put an end to the pogroms of the Jews in the Rhineland. Since Emperor Conrad III was still not showing much enthusiasm, Bernard went to Flanders and Germany during the summer of 1146. During this voyage, his preaching had the desired effect and on December 27, 1146, in the cathedral of Spier he convinced the emperor and the German knights. He also responded to the letter sent to him by Hildegarde von Bingen telling him of the questions that her visions were posing for her. When he returned to Clairvaux on February 2, 1147, he was accompanied by about sixty young candidates for monastic life. On February 16 and 17, Bernard took part in a meeting held in Etampes, preparation for the departure for the crusade, where he named Abbot Suger of Saint Denis as one of the men in charge of administering the kingdom in the absence of Louis VII. On March 13, Bernard joined a Diet that organized preventive armed action against the Slavs who, at the eastern border of the Empire, had decided to take advantage of the Crusaders' absence to cross the frontier. In May, Conrad III and his army set out and, in June, Louis VII followed. The failure of the siege of Damascus in July, 1148 put an end to this crusade. A new expedition was envisaged at the beginning of 1150 and Bernard was considered to be put in charge of it, but the project eventually came to nothing. Subsequently, the Cistercians were asked to contribute to the organization of the third and fourth crusades. Thus, Gerard, Archbishop of Ravenna, a former Cistercian, was named papal legate to preach the third crusade in Italy. He died in 1191, under the walls of Saint John of Acre. In 1198, Luke, Abbot of Sambucina, intervened in the organization of the fourth crusade. In 1202, Guy, Abbot of Les Vaux de Cernay, protested in the name of the pope to the heads of the crusader's army on the eve of the assault against the Christian town of Zara in Dalmatia. Peter, Abbot of Locèdio, accompanied the Crusaders to Constantinople and participated, after the capture of the city on April 13, 1204, in the election of Baudouin of Flanders as the first Latin Emperor. The Cistercian foundations in the Byzantine Empire and the Near East date from the time of the crusades. Morimond created Belmont in 1157, south-east of Tripoli; Belmont diffused to Cyprus with Beaulieu, where the entire community of Belmont took refuge in 1289, after the fall of Tripoli. As for Daphni, a Greek monastery near Athens, it was incorporated into Citeaux in 1217, in the affiliation with Bellevaux.

St Bernard preaching the Second Crusade in Vézelay

Cloister in Furness Abbey, daughter of Savigny

Obazine. For Clairvaux, which benefited from its abbot's influence, this expansion was impressive. Clairvaux's lineage included Eberbach and Himmerod in Germany; Fountains in England; Cherlieu, Hautecombe, Noirlac, Acey, Grandselve, Fontfroide and Savigny in France; Fossanova, Chiaravalle, Casamari and Tre Fontane in Italy; Mellifont in Ireland; Villers in Belgium; Alcobaça in Portugal; Poblet and Santes Creus in Spain. As for Morimond, it was reinforced by Aiguebelle and L'Escale Dieu that in turn founded Fitero, Veruela and La Oliva in Spain, and Flaran in Gascony. Its German branch filled out with Maulbronn, and then spread to Camp, its granddaughter. The two other first daughters of Citeaux, Pontigny and La Ferté, developed more modestly. Another direct daughter of Citeaux, Bonnevaux, in the Dauphiné region, directly founded Léoncel and its daughter Mazan, Le Thoronet, Sylvanès and Sénanque. At the death of Bernard, abbeys descended from Clairvaux represented over half the total number of Cistercian abbeys.

In 1147, William of Saint Thierry began to write the biography of his master and friend, but he died the following year. The work was continued by a monk from Bonnevaux, then by Geoffroy of Auxerre, Bernard's secretary. This biography had to be included in the demand for canonization that was addressed to Alexander III in 1163. But Bernard was canonized in 1174 on the basis of another biography, written by Alan of Lille. He was proclaimed a doctor of the Church in 1830.

The Monks' Functions

The abbot

This was the father, *Abba*, of the community. He was elected by the monks. Saint Benedict's Rule gave him the place of Jesus Christ in the heart of the community.

The prior

He was named by the abbot, whom he seconds. He is the premier (*prior*) of the monks. A sub-prior is seconded to him.

The treasurer

He managed the community's finances.

The cellarer

Responsible for administration, he was the "spokesman" of the abbey. He controlled the granges.

The sacristan

He was the organizer of ecclesiastical activities.
He made the hosts and rang the hours of holy offices.

The cantor

Master of the choir during holy offices. He organized the friars' processions. When there was no librarian, he was curator of the books.

The hospitaller

Attached to the cellarer, he welcomed guests.

The porter

He guarded the entrance of the abbey.

The infirmarer

Took care of the sick. He gathered medicinal plants in the garden and prepared medicines from them.

The novice master

Was responsible for training the novices.

Mary, Mother of the Monks

"Some, her presence makes them conquerors by making them triumph over vices; for others, her maternal intercession ensures the possession of the highest virtues; to some, she opens the secret of interior contemplation; to others, at the end of their lives, she provides a safe road, so that no enemy force may frighten those being guided towards Christ by the mother of God's unique son."
Amadeus of Lausanne,
Homilies in Praise of Blessed Mary

The Virgin, protectress of the Cistercians by Jean Bellegambe

Following the example of the monks of Molesme, the founders of Citeaux placed their order under the patronage of the Virgin Mary, whose cult developed rapidly starting in the 11th century. A mediating figure between Heaven and Earth, the human and the divine, the faithful and God become man, Mary, the Mother of God, occupied a special place in Cistercian spirituality. In the image of her virginal purity, the Cistercians adopted a white-coloured habit, and chose to follow in her footsteps. In the way that she reconciled work and contemplation in her care for her new-born son, the Mother of the Lord seemed to provide the proportions for monastic life as it was understood by the monks of Citeaux. "When [the Virgin] nourished, dressed her child [...], all that was part of corporal activity; but when she considered his divinity, contemplated his power and tasted his sweetness, then it was the part of Mary", wrote Abbot Aelred of Rievaulx (†1167) in his *Sermon for the Nativity of Mary*. According to the analysis by the historian Sylvie Barnay, accomplishing a synthesis of action and contemplation in her acts of which Christ is the unique object, the Virgin provided all her strength and her authority to the Cistercian reform, founded on work and prayer, in conformity with the original Rule of Saint Benedict. Overcoming the paradox evoked in the Gospels through the figures of Martha, always in action, and her sister Mary, the contemplative, the Mother of the Lord reconciled action and contemplation, showing the way to the Cistercians for whom she was the model. This is illustrated in the text of the apparition of the Virgi to the harvesting monks, written down for the first time in around 1174; the prior Cesarius (†1240), former novice master at Heisterbach, provides one version of it in his *Dialogus miraculorum*. "It is said that, at a certain moment of the harvest, when the community [of Citeaux] was taking in the harvest in the valley, the blessed Virgin Mary, Mother of God, Saint Anne her mother and Saint Mary Magdalene came from a hill [...]. They descended into the eart of this valley in strong light, wiped ne sweat from the monks and made breeze by fanning their sleeves." hus, Mary allowed the monks to parake in the spiritual rest in God, even vhile they were working. Through er, monastic life was united with rayer. A source of unity, Mary was at ne same time a model to be imitated nd a spiritual mother full of concern, omforting and calming the monks vhile accompanying them in their ausere existence. In his *Sermon for the Nativity of Mary*, Aelred of Rievaulx learly expressed the Virgin's spiritual naternity of the Cistercian Order. 's she not our mother? Through her, ve are born, through her we are nourshed, through her we grow in virtue." Comparing childhood to the first stage of the soul's ascension towards God, Cistercian thinking in the 12th century aw in the monks the "foster brothers" of the Child Jesus, the spiritual neworns of Mary. She nourished them ymbolically with her milk, a celestial everage representing divine grace, eading to spiritual growth. "Let us join vith Jesus while he sucks at the niple...", wrote Adam of Perseigne †1221) in one of his *Letters*. "Mary's reasts are filled with Heaven, they omfort with unutterable sweetness." During the first decades of the 13th cenury, this theme of lactation was very opular in exemplary literature and religious painting. Described by the monk Peter of Celles (†1183) as the "very amiliar nursling of Our Lady", Saint Bernard, the poet of Mary, was often hown physically drinking her milk, he source of the Word of God. The act of conceding indulgences to he faithful of Saint Vorles's Church n Châtillon sur Seine thus reports a lescription of lactation dated 1340. n this church, "a certain image [...] of the blessed Virgin Mary, miraculously presented her Son [to Saint Bernard] and among other things taught him about the Catholic faith... The image lifted her hand to her breast and miraculously produced three drops of milk [...] into the open mouth of her devoted saint. Hence, having received these drops from the breast of the aforementioned image [...], he composed several devoted praises [...] and devotedly wrote the *Salve Regina*". Here the attribution of the *Salve Regina* to Saint Bernard passes through Mary's milk, elaborating a word coming from Heaven.

St Bernard and the miracle of lactation

Transept of Bonnefontaine Abbey, granddaughter of Clairvaux, founded in 1154

Necessary Adaptations

By the time of Bernard of Clairvaux's death, the Order had developed considerably. Until 1250, although expansion had slowed, it was nonetheless noteworthy. In 1153, the Order included three hundred and fifty houses, becoming about six hundred and fifty in 1250. However, this development evolved differently. First of all geographically: of the three hundred new abbeys, sixty-two were located in an area corresponding to present-day France, whereas in 1150, it was the case for nearly one out of two. The Order strengthened its presence in the Anglo-Saxon and Germanic countries, in Italy and the Iberian peninsula, established itself in Eastern Europe, Greece and the Near East. Subsequently, the dynamism of Clairvaux weakened while Morimond became more active through its granddaughter, Camp. Citeaux did not create new abbeys until the first half of the 13th century – Royaumont in 1228, and L'Epau in 1229. Furthermore, this new generation of abbeys was often the action of the second or third generation, which incorporated existing communities as well as creating new ones. Finally, starting in 1200, the number of houses of Cistercian nuns, thanks to the diffusion of Tart and Las Huelgas, founded in Spain in 1187 with the support of Alfonso VIII and Alienor Plantagenet, progressed rapidly. There were four hundred of them by the end of the 13th century.

Reference Dates

Foundation of the Order of Calatrava	1158
Alexander III accords the privilege of exemption to the Cistercians	1169
Raymond V of Toulouse writes to the abbot of Citeaux to denounce the progress of the Albigensian heresy	1177
Third Lateran Council	1179
Legation in Languedoc of Pierre de Castelnau and Raoul, monks from Fontfroide, joined in 1206 by Arnaud Amaury from Citeaux	1203
Battle of Las Navas de Tolosa	1212
Fourth Lateran Council	1215
Foundation of Royaumont by Saint Louis	1228
Foundation of Saint Bernard's College in Paris	1245

Latrine buildings in Royaumont, daughter of Citeaux founded in 1228

Valcroissant, founded in 1188

FREDERICK BARBAROSSA

Frederick Barbarossa (1152-1192) dreamed of reconstituting the Roman Empire. He was faced with Lombard resistance in Italy. In 1159, he opposed Alexander III with an anti-Pope. But beaten in Legnano, the emperor begged for the pope's pardon in Venice in 1177.

These hundred years from 1150 to 1250, even while tracing a slowdown in the Cistercian Order's development, covered a century of profound changes. First of all, factors of instability appeared. The multiplication of the number of abbeys, their distribution and distance, the incorporation of establishments possessing their own customs, all threatened the Order's cohesion and unanimity. Several events outside the Order also created conflict within it, such as the double pontifical election of 1159. Alexander III had been elected by the cardinals when Victor IV received the support of Frederick Barbarossa. Most of the abbeys located in the Germanic zone supported the latter, as did the abbot of Citeaux, Lambert, who, as the former abbot of Morimond, had retained narrow ties with Morimond's German daughters. The abbots of Clairvaux and Pontigny forced him to resign in 1161. The length of abbacies was considerably reduced. Abbots were often chosen among the elders of the abbey, when they were not called to other functions within the Church. Thus, at the head of Clairvaux, which had had only one abbot, Bernard, from 1115 to 1153, nine different abbots succeeded each other between 1153 and the end of the 12th century. Secondly, the Cistercians became integrated into the Church and society. They took on pastoral duties, providing precious help to the secular clergy. Nominations for bishops and cardinals from within their ranks multiplied, a favourable comment on the quality of their clerics. They also supplied numerous papal legates who took on

CISTERCIAN SEMANTICS

In the solitude surrounding his abbey, the Cistercian monk enjoys the joy and beauty of a superior order, reflected in the name given to the monastery. Attached to this place that he has chosen never to leave, he is sensitive to its charm, evoked in names like Beaubec (beautiful stream), Beauvoir (view), Beaupré (field) or Bellevaux (beautiful valley); its silence and sweetness – Bonnevaux, *Bonnae valles*, Cherlieu, *Carus locus*, Chambons, *Campi boni*, or Vaux la Douce. A place of light and celestial clarity, Cistercian abbeys were called Clairvaux, *Clara vallis*, Vauluisant, *Vallis lucens*, Lum Dieu, *Lumen Dei*, Clairmarais, *Clarus mariscus*, or Clairmont, *Clarus mons*. Sometimes the abbey kept the original place name which took on another, spiritual, dimension when it was latinized. Bouras was *Bonus radius*, Candeil translated by *Candelium*, evoking the light of candles, Lucelle by *Lucis cella*, the house of light. The abbey symbolized the whiteness of virginity and purity when it was called Aubepierre, *Albae petrae*, white stones, or Auberive, *Alba ripa*, white shore. Water surrounding the monasteries sprang forth in the names Clairefontaine, Fontenay, *Fontenaium*, Sept Fons, Fontfroide, or again, Aiguebelle, *Aqua bella*, and Sénanque, *Sana aqua*. A place of renunciation, where the monk found completeness in the love of God, the monastery was called Morimond, *Mori mundo*, die to the world, Loc Dieu, *Locus Dei*, place of the Lord, L'Amour Dieu or La Merci Dieu. Where humility led to the celestial kingdom, L'Escale Dieu, *Scala Dei*, the Lord's ladder. Refuge and peace provided Bonport, *Bonus portus*, Bonrepos, Port du Salut or La Valette, *Vallis laeta*, happy valley.

Fontfroide cloister

Window in San Galgono

Cloister arcades in Maulbronn

OPUS FRANCIGENUM

Gothic art was born towards the middle of the 12th century. While re-doing the chancel and transept of Saint Denis, begun in 1140, its abbot Suger was one of its first promoters. This art used architectural elements like intersecting ribs, which lightened vaults and distributed thrust, and, starting in 1200, buttresses to reinforce walls which, cut away and with large openings, let light stream in through ever more important stained glass windows. Furthermore, this art systematically preferred pointed (Gothic) arches to round or Romanesque ones. From Île de France it spread throughout Europe where it was able to adopt, according to location, various styles of expression and was interpreted by architects towards ever greater heights. This audacity led to the great cathedrals of the 13th century. Coexisting with Romanesque art during the 12th and 13th centuries, Rayonnant in the 14th, Flamboyant in the 15th, it was the Renaissance that called it Gothic in the 16th century, as a pejorative comment on Barbarian peoples. The churches and cloisters of many Cistercian abbeys, like Rievaulx, Maulbronn, Eberbach, Fossanova, San Galgano, Cadouin, sometimes in ruins, are the testimony of this art characteristic of the last third of the Middle Ages, also expressed in enamel work, illumination and, of course, sculpture.

Chevet rose window at Santes Creus

Men of Faith and Men of Letters

The initial project of Citeaux did not plan a school within the Order's abbeys and emphasized the importance of manual work. However, many Cistercians were literate and books, always necessary for carrying out the Offices and for the monks' private reading, have always been present in abbeys. The first Cistercians worked to give their Order an authentic liturgy. Stephen Harding undertook an enormous task of exegesis by revising the text of the Vulgate and took advice from the master of the rabbinical school in Troyes about the interpretation of certain Hebrew terms. In 1109, the two illuminated volumes of the *Bible of Saint Stephen* were completed. The Cistercians of the second generation profoundly influenced the spirituality of the Middle Ages. The fervour, enthusiasm and talent of Bernard of Clairvaux inspired some of his brothers. First-rate scholars, knowledgeable about Greek and Latin authors, mystics adoring the Word, nourished by biblical manna, they were theologians, poets and historians. Their names were William of Saint Thierry, Guerric of Igny, Hélinand of Froidmont, Aelred of Rievaulx, Gilbert of Hoyland, Isaac of L'Etoile or Adam of Perseigne, to mention only the most famous. They had "renounced everything, except the art of writing well", according to Etienne Gilson. Bernard began his career as a writer before 1125, with the *Apologia*, a real satire of the Cluniac way of life. He did not stop writing until his death, leaving a considerable body of work behind him. He composed admirable sermons on the *Song of Songs*, and, in his treaty *On the Love of God*, Dom Le Bail wrote, "For Saint Bernard, the question of love is a drama, the drama of a being who feels inevitably destined to love, thus it is not a paradox to claim that St Bernard wrote only a single treatise on spirituality and that he elucidated one single aspect of the soul's relation with God: Love." Besides his abundant correspondence, he left two great works from his late years, the *Life of Saint Malachy* and *De Consideratione*, written for one of his former monks who became pope as Eugene III. The writings and mystical works of his friend and biographer William of Saint Thierry, especially the famous *Golden Letter or Letter to the Friars of Mont Dieu*, which was to serve as a guide for numerous generations of monks, were for a long time attributed to Saint Bernard. Born in Liège before 1075, William met the abbot of Clairvaux in 1118. Having become abbot of the Benedictine abbey of Saint Thierry, he tried to reform the monasteries of the archbishopric of Reims. In 1135, Bernard authorized him to join the Cistercian Order and William professed at Signy Abbey, where he remained until his death in 1148. A contemporary of Bernard and William, and of Anglo-Saxon origin like Aelred of Rievaulx, Isaac of L'Etoile was born about 1110. He studied in France, at the schools of Laon. In 1143, he entered Pontigny and, four years later, was elected abbey of L'Etoile. Then, in his quest for solitude and poverty, he retired to the Island of Ré where, between 1167 and 1169, he founded the monastery of Notre Dame des Châteliers with several companions. He died there about 1178, leaving fifty-five sermons. Cardinal Lubac included him among "the most profound metaphysicians of his century". History was a popular subject among Cistercians, the authors of chronicles and hagiographic essays. Hélinand of Froidmont, born in 1160, dead after 1229, distinguished himself by his immense *Chronicum amplum ab exordio mundi*, in forty-nine volumes that retraced the history of the world since its creation. A troubadour at the court of Philip Augustus before renouncing the world in 1182 and retiring to the Cistercian abbey of Froidmont in the Beauvais area, Hélinand was also the author of a superb poem in French, the *Verses of Death*, written between 1194 and 1197. Cistercian mysticism seems to have had a great influence on the literature of the Middle Ages. The history of the *Quest for the Holy Grail* by Christian of Troyes and his successors appeared as a mystical work saturated with the supernatural and the divine. The perfect knight, valiant, noble and chaste, Galahad was the only one who managed to contemplate the Holy Grail. This victory seemed possible only through conversion, through a spiritual death in this world and a re-birth in the humility and the love of Jesus Christ.

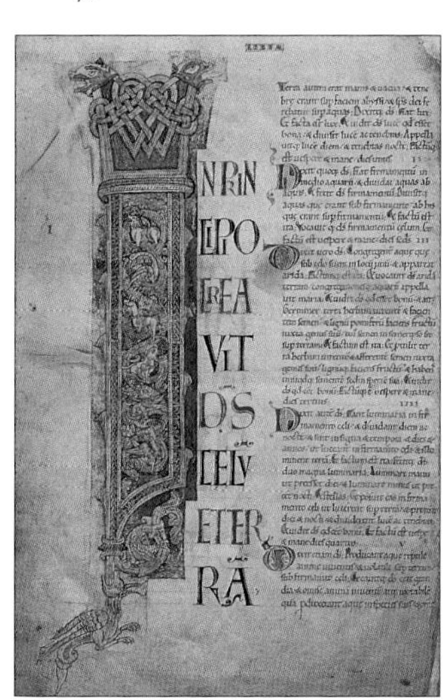

Letter, Stephen Harding's bible

Innocent III, St Benedict's Monastery, Subiaco

specific missions, such as those entrusted to them by Pope Innocent III in the struggle against the Albigensian heresy. Cistercians also turned towards studies. In 1237, some of them attended courses at the University of Paris and, in 1245, Saint Bernard's College was founded in the same city. Their contact with temporal powers multiplied, while recruitment of professed monks came more and more from the aristocracy. Thirdly, breaches of the Rule appeared in some monasteries. Silence was not always respected; monasteries that exploited ever larger territories bought land and sold their products; some joined parishes with their revenues; others abandoned direct working of the land. Voices began to be raised within the ranks of the Order itself. In 1186, Joachim de Flore, the former abbot of Santa Maria de Corazzo, daughter of Fossanova in Italy, in his *De vita sancti Bernardi* made a regular attack on Cluny but also opposed the Citeaux of early days, set up as a model, with the Order of the end of the 12th century. Hélinand of Froidmont, at the beginning of the 13th century, recalled the original demands. Although the "new Order" seemed to distance itself from the founders' ideals, it retained its prestige among religious and feudal powers, but also within the monastic world. The proof is that in 1185, monks from Grandmont, fearing the questioning of the ascetic ideal in their monastery, joined Cistercian abbeys. Above all, the chief abbots and the Order's General Chapter, conscious of the possibility of decline, acted on the institutions. In 1151, the

DIALOGUE BETWEEN TWO MONKS

The debate between Cluniacs and Cistercians, brilliantly engaged by Peter the Venerable and Bernard of Clairvaux, was the subject of a Latin text, *Dialogus duorum monachorum*, written in 1155 by Idung, a former monk of the Benedictine abbey of Prüfening, which had entered the Cistercian order. This dialogue was in fact an animated discussion between a black monk and a white monk, the former reproaching the latter the Cluniacs' instability and praising the foundation of the *Novum Monasterium* by Robert, Alberic and Stephen, who had left Molesme which the author compared to a Cluniac community.

Temporal Conflicts

When Emperor Henry VI died in 1197, Pope Innocent III (1198-1216) who wanted to force political powers to submit to his authority, removed his son Frederick II from the imperial throne, which he ceded to Otto IV. However, Otto did not respect the clauses of his agreement with the pope and was excommunicated and deposed in 1212, after occupying Tuscany. Frederick II succeeded him by promising the pope that he would become a crusader. Since he was in no hurry to fulfil his promise, Honorius III (1216-1227) excommunicated him in 1227. Under threat, the emperor decided to join the crusades, finally to his advantage as he managed to obtain the concession of the Kingdom of Jerusalem from the sultan of Egypt. But despite his engagements to Rome, the emperor continued to covet the Papal States. He was excommunicated a second time by Gregory IX in 1240. Frederick II responded by invading the Church's states and, ignoring the armistice the pontiff offered him, after capturing Ravenna, he marched on Bologna. Gregory IX then decided to call a council in Rome, at Easter 1241, in order to judge the emperor. By letter, he asked the General Chapter of Citeaux to delegate four of the Order's abbots and ordered the bishops not to let themselves be intimidated by the emperor, who had warned the kings of England and France that he would treat anyone who answered the papal call as an enemy. Furthermore, by a secret treaty with his Genoese allies, Gregory IX chartered the fleet needed to carry English and French prelates to Rome. But the emperor, in his resolve to prevent the holding of such a council, knowing that its outcome would be harmful to him, on May 3, 1241 had the Pisan fleet attack the Genoese vessels on their way to the Eternal City. The attack took place not far from the island of Elba. Twenty-two ships were seized, three sunk, and over a hundred prelates were taken prisoner, among them numerous Cistercians: James of Pecoraria, Cardinal-Bishop of Preneste, a former Clairvaux monk before his election as abbot of Trois Fontaines; the abbot of Citeaux, William of Montaigu; the abbot of Clairvaux, William of Dondelberg, who was to die in captivity; and finally, John, Abbot of L'Épau. The Cistercian Peter of Albalat, Archbishop of Tarragona, was one of the few who managed to escape. Saint Louis, the king of France, after a first unsuccessful attempt, finally obtained the captives' freedom by addressing a threatening letter to the emperor. It ended by saying, "Carefully consider and weigh what we are conveying to you and do not retain the prelates in your power; for the kingdom of France is not yet weakened to the point that it will allow itself to be led at your spurs." But Gregory IX died in the meantime, while the imperial army captured Rome, and the council did not take place. His successor, Innocent IV, took refuge in Lyons where, taking up Gregory IX's idea, he called a council for the summer of 1245. At the end of this council, under pressure from two Cistercians, Bishop Peter of Carinola and the Archbishop of Tarragona, Peter of Albalat, the emperor was excommunicated and deposed. Frederick II died in 1250, abandoned by his supporters, but the struggle between his successors and those of Innocent IV continued until 1268, at the death of the last Hohenstaufen. The long-lasting quarrel of papacy and empire finally ended.

Castel del Monte, Frederick II's castle

General Chapter asked Eugene III to approve the Rule once again. In 1152, the Papal Bull *Sacro Sancta* ratified the *Carta posterior*, the updated Charter of Charity, the statutes having been re-compiled. In 1169, Alexander III, de facto, granted the Order the privilege of exemption. Statutes like *De non aedificando* of 1188 limited constructions that were too large, or *De non acquirendo* of 1190 limited investments that would incur too much debt. At the end of the 12th century, Conrad, a former monk in Clairvaux, entered Eberbach, wrote the *Great Exordium* which completed the *Small Exordium* of 1119, and reaffirmed the Order's identity. In 1202, Arnaud Amaury, the abbot of Citeaux, before his legation to Cathar country, proceeded to overhaul the statutes, that were to be only slightly modified by the *Collection of Definitions* in 1250. The statutes of the nuns were written up in 1256.

But all these arrangements of the rules did not prevent the Order from suffering from tension and dissension, starting in 1215, although these were to be expected in an organization that had grown exponentially. They affected the entire structure but the most important were related to the abbot of Citeaux, whose authority was sometimes contested as when in 1238 abbeys refused to receive him. Even the papacy had to intervene and entrusted the problem to a cardinal. In 1262, disagreement between Citeaux and its four great daughters was such that their abbots did not participate in the election of James II as abbot of Citeaux. Order was re-established by the publication of the bull *Parvus fons*, known as the Clementine, published by Clement IV in 1265. The election of the abbot of Citeaux was reserved only for the monks at the abbey itself, but his actions were to be controlled by its four first abbots. What must be retained from these events is that the Cistercian Order was not able to provide the solutions for its own problems and it thus allowed the ecclesiastical hierarchy to affirm its supervisory power over it.

Pope Alexander III

The Privilege of Exemption

According to the Charter of Charity, "when one wishes to found an abbey, one should start by making an agreement with the bishop of the diocese who will receive the new abbey". In 1169, by forbidding bishops to depose an abbot, Alexander III, *ipso facto*, accorded the Cistercians the privilege of exemption, thus removing them from episcopal jurisdiction. This privilege was officially granted in 1184 by a bull of Pope Lucius III.

Pontigny abbey church

Cistercian Art

"O vanity of vanities, but even
more senseless than vain;
the church glitters on its walls
yet lacks everything in its poor."
Saint Bernard,
Apologia to William

Cistercian art appeared to be the translation of the soul and the spirituality of Citeaux. The Cistercians demanded a return to the sources of monasticism, in the tradition of the Desert Fathers, and tried to rid the Benedictine Rule of all the excesses that had been imposed on it over the course of the centuries, in order to revive it in its authenticity. Similarly, they rid their churches and their monasteries of any elements considered superfluous, useless for their religion and for their lifestyle. Renouncing the world to live in poverty and the love of Christ, to whom everything was dedicated from then on, the Cistercian monk banished luxury and splendour from his church. He refused any ostentatious signs of power, even including a steeple. Gold and precious stones which, for Abbot Suger, shone with light similar to divine light, which participated in the splendour and magnificence of celebrating holy offices, had no place in a Cistercian shrine. There was no need for mediating images to reach the sacred; Bernard of Clairvaux reserved them for the ignorant. For the monk who left his body at the monastery's door, where "only souls can enter", images, attached as they are to the world of sensation, might, on the contrary, distract his spirit from its business of meditating the divine word, might release his imagination. The Cistercians stripped their abbeys of the sculptures and paintings that decorated Romanesque churches, to leave only stone, naked, smooth, the colour of the desert. They preferred straight lines, flat chevets rather than the curved lines of an apse. In order that from the simplicity of their buildings, from the purity of the lines, deliberately stripped of any decoration, clarity would spring forth out of the strictness of this architecture built to last. The monk's life was also a quest for the comprehension and intelligence of the sacred text. The Cistercians liked to call their churches oratories. Only des-

Nave in Alcobaça

ned for the use of the community, ey had no second floor or gallery, nd originally, their proportions were uch more modest than those of the luniac churches even though, starting the middle of the 12th century, istercian churches became consider-

Stained-glass window, Obazine

ply larger as their communities creased in size. And the small sanctu-y with a flat chevet was replaced by a rger one, with an ambulatory and diating chapels. The nave, at first cov-red with a barrel vault, generally ghtly pointed, rose starting in 1160, anks to intersecting ribs. The olumns holding up the vaults rested n bases several metres above the ound, to permit the installation of alls for the monks. The capitals on e columns were smooth, or deco-ted with leaves, but never with figura-ve decoration. The facade and the evet were often opened with triple indows and oculi, later with rose win-ows. Stained glass windows, also in sponse to the search for simplicity nd poverty had to be, according to

Capital in Bellaigue

the General Chapter, "white and without images". The first Cistercian master glass-makers thus worked with colourless glass that they cut according to geometric patterns, such as arabesques and knots, or floral patters, before setting the cut glass into lead and assembling it. Subsequently, they covered the glass with a layer of grisaille. The first Cistercian pavements were made of

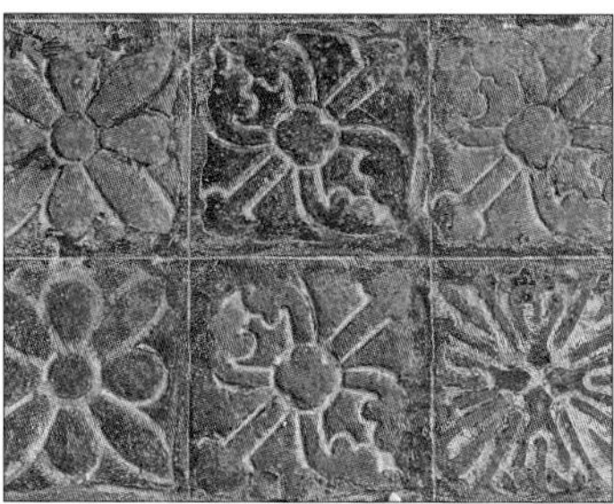

Fontenay, ceramic tiles

red, black or white terracotta tiles, put together to form various geometric figures. Starting in the 13th century, monks made varnished tiles decorated with motifs similar to those on the windows, most often in white on a red background. From the beginning, there had been intense activity in Cistercian *scriptoria*. The first manuscripts made in Citeaux were illuminated according to the monastic tradition, with figures borrowed from Romanesque iconography. The ornamental letters made during Stephen Harding's abbacy were also decorated with figures borrowed from the fantastic Romanesque bestiary, but some of them were worked in a more realistic manner, representing scenes taken from monks' daily life or biblical scenes with characters dressed in 12th century fashions. Under the influence of Bernard, who imposed great simplicity in manuscript decoration at Clairvaux, the General Chapter decreed in 1152 that from then on initials had to be of a single colour, and undecorated. But this prescription was never strictly

Monochrome letter, Bibla Sacra

respected. Hence, Cistercian art was characterized by the sobriety and purity indissoluble from its spirituality and ethics. By raising visual lines with the technique of intersecting ribs, privileging verticality, by replacing the sculptures on Romanesque capitals with floral motifs, Cistercian architecture seemed to mark the end of an era, that of Romanesque art, and announced the coming of the Gothic age.

Buckland, daughter of Quarr, granddaughter of Clairvaux, founded in 1278

Palace of the Popes, Avignon

The Struggle for Survival

Starting in the second half of the 13th century, foundations became less frequent. The Order saw the number of its abbeys increase by only about forty between 1250 and 1300, mainly in the Germanic countries. Recruitment became more difficult since the new mendicant orders attracted ever more vocations. Certain abbeys were also suffering from financial difficulties and went into debt; donations had become rare and direct exploitation of the land was slowly abandoned, often because of a lack of labour. This was the moment chosen by Philip the Fair to make Cistercian abbeys pay tithes. He ended up exempting them from this obligation in 1312 because of their financial situtation, one which was not improved by the poor harvests on French territories during the period 1315-1320. However, the Order maintained its prestige, its contribution to pastoral action remained important and its libraries continued to increase their stocks. Paradoxically, it was the papacy's new policies that revealed its weakness. John XXII (1316-1334), a pope in Avignon, brought in pontifical fiscality to compensate for the loss of revenues from the papal states. Each ecclesiastical dignitary was supposed to receive a revenue, a part of which had to be paid to the pontiff. An abbot had no other choice than to have his monastery bear this burden, directly or indirectly. In 1265, Clement IV had decreed that the popes

Philip the Fair against Boniface VIII

The ever latent dispute between the pope and the king of France worsened in February 1296, when Boniface VIII, supported by the Cistercians, with his bull *Laicis clericos* forbade the clergy to pay the tithe that Philip the Fair wanted to impose without his agreement. The quarrel became nastier when, in 1301, Philip the Fair had Bernard Saisset, the bishop of Pamiers, judged for treason. The pontiff demanded the release of his prelate and convoked a council to be held in November, 1302, in Rome, to "reform the kingdom and correct the king". Philip the Fair made the first move and, in April 1302, called the representatives of all three States of the kingdom to Notre Dame in Paris. With a few exceptions, including Jean de Pontoise, Abbot of Citeaux, the members of the assembly supported him. The pope wanted to excommunicate the king. The latter sent William of Nogaret to present the pope with a subpoena to appear before the council, which would stop the excommunication proceedings. Nogaret arrived in Anagni, where the pope was staying, on September 6, 1303, with men from the Colonna faction who forced their way into the pope's residence at night and threatened him. Humiliated, Boniface VIII died on October 11, 1303. Even though Nogaret's responsibility in the Anagni incident has not been proved, the affair influenced the relationship between Philip the Fair and the new pope, Benedict XI. The king threatened to call a *post-mortem* trial of Boniface, the pope threatened to excommunicate Nogaret.

Reference Dates

Clement IV's bull *Parvus fons*	1265
Jacques Fournier, former abbot of Fontfroide, becomes pope in Avignon under the name of Benedict XII	1334
Clement VI institutes commendam	1342
The Great Schism	1378
Council of Constance	1414
Foundation of the Regular Observance of Saint Bernard in Spain	1438
Foundation of the Italian Congregation of Saint Bernard	1495
Luther posts his 95 theses on the door of the chapel in Wittenberg	1517
Henry VIII breaks with Rome	1534
Beginning of the Council of Trent	1545
Portuguese abbeys form an autonomous congregation	1567
Jérôme de La Souchière writes a reform programme for the Cistercians	1570
Foundation of the Feuillants	1587
Richelieu is elected abbot of Citeaux	1636
Armand Jean Le Bouthillier de Rancé becomes abbot of La Trappe	1664

Avignon, tomb of John XXII

DOMINIC AND FRANCIS

At the beginning of the 13th century, the wealth of the episcopate and prosperity of orders, such as Cluny and Citeaux, contradicted evangelical poverty. Thanks to the aura of their founders, Dominic and Francis, the new mendicant orders underwent considerable expansion and contributed to restoring the Church's image, which was threatened by the development of heresies. Dominic de Guzmán was born in Castile in 1170 into a family of gentry. After finishing his studies, in 1197 he became a canon in the cathedral chapter of Osma and, in 1203, Diègo Acébès, the Chapter's former prior and then a bishop, took Dominic on a long pastoral journey that took them as far as Scandinavia. Upon their return, Innocent III asked them to support the Cistercians in the struggle against the Cathar heresy in the Languedoc. Thus began the great venture of preaching, directed by Dominic after Diego's death in 1207. In 1215, Dominic gathered seven of his companions and, in Toulouse, founded the Order of the Preaching Friars, subject to observing the rule of Saint Augustine. Honorius III approved the Dominican Rule in 1216. In 1217, Dominic scattered his companions, sending them to study in Paris and Bologna then, in 1218, founded two convents in Madrid and Segovia. In the same year, the Preaching Friars settled in Lyons and Rome. By 1221, at the death of Dominic, his Order was also present in Germany and in England. The Dominican way of life mixed action and preaching with monastic life and contemplation.

A novice studied theology while living a cloistered life. Then he pronounced the three vows of chastity, poverty and obedience, before being sent to a convent where he continued his studies and became a priest.

A Dominican preached in his town or his region, attended courses at the university and, in parallel, led a monastic life consisting of fasting, mortification of the flesh, reciting holy offices, meditation and prayer. Above all, he was not supposed to possess anything, nor produce anything with his hands. He lived from alms and donations, which provided him with his daily food and clothing.

Born in Assisi, Italy, in 1181, into a wealthy merchant family, Francis received a middle-class education and, at the age of twenty, dreamed of being a knight. However, after experiencing war, captivity and then illness, the young man considered his life and, little by little, his vocation appeared. Refusing wordly life, in 1206 he undertook the restoration of the church of San Damiano near Assisi. On February 24, 1209, he publicly decided to follow the advice of Jesus Christ to his apostles and to lead an errant life, in poverty and humility, preaching everywhere.

The *Poverello* attracted several companions imbued with the same ideals. They settled beside the church of Saint Mary of the Angels, in a cabin called the Portionculus. Francis and his Minor Friars took care of lepers, dedicated themselves to prayer and, especially, to spreading the word of the gospels. They begged for their food and dressed in rags. In 1223, at the request of Honorius III, Francis wrote up a new rule for his friars who, despite him, constituted an ever more powerful and influential new order, very different from the original little community. Francis then retired to the solitude of Mount Alverno where, in 1224, two years before his death, his body received the five stigmata of Christ. His biographer Tommaso da Celano described him thus: "His entire body was thin, his habit rough, his sleep brief." Francis was canonized in 1228 and Dominic in 1234. Starting in 1233, the mendicant orders were charged with running the tribunals of the Inquisition.

St Dominic, Florence

St Francis, Assisi

were in charge of nomination to ecclesiastical offices, with any other method of nomination, such a free elections for an abbacy, remaining exceptional. In 1311-1312, the Council of Vienne called into question the principle of exemption enjoyed by the Cistercians. John XXII, basing himself on the *Clementine* clauses, named abbots himself. Benedict XII (1334-1342), who had been a monk at Boulbonne and abbot of Fontfroide, tried to restore discipline in his former order with the papal bull, *Fulgens sicut stella matutina* in 1335. Although he did not refer to the *Charter of Charity*, although he did not recommend manual labour but rather emphasized studies, he re-established free elections for the abbots, an annual meeting of the General Chapter and the visits of priors to their daughter abbeys, imposed common dormitories, the non-eating of meat and respect of enclosure, excluded taking any money away from the abbeys and called for prudent management. These prescriptions were only half-heartedly defended by his successors. Clement VI (1342-1352) even instituted the commendam system, through which the pope named abbots no longer from among monks but from the secular clergy, who were often more concerned with their personal interest than that of the monastery in their charge. External events also weighed heavily on the Cistercians: the years 1335-1340 were a time of serious economic depression in Western Europe, already suffering from the Black Death plague epidemic in 1348-1349. The Hundred Years' War arrived leaving its trail of desolation. From 1355 to

Pavement in Benedict XII's *studium*

THE POPES IN AVIGNON

Starting in 1309, Clement V stayed in Avignon. John XXII, the city's former bishop, established the Holy See there. The Palace of the Popes was built under Benedict XII and Clement VI. In 1376, Gregory XI returned to Rome to occupy the seat of Saint Peter.

Fontfroide

Bourges cathedral

ABBOTS NAMED BY THE KING

As the Great Schism drew to an end, the question of the pre-eminence of the conciliar assemblies over pontifical decisions was posed. The problem was the subject of lengthy debates at the Council of Basle from 1431 to 1449, which finally reaffirmed the pope's superiority. But the conciliary system had provided food for thought for the kings, tempted to establish national churches. In France, Charles VII called the clergy together in Bourges in 1438 and promulgated the edict of Pragmatic Sanction. Taking up some of the Basle decrees about the superiority of councils over the pope, in particular the king took for himself the right to intervene in nominating incumbents for major benefices – abbeys or bishoprics – and minor ones – priories, cures – by his "benevolent prayers".
The official birth certificate of Gallicanism, the Pragmatic Sanction was replaced in 1472 by the Concordat of Amboise and then abrogated by the Concordat of Bologna, concluded in 1516 between Francis 1st and Pope Leon X. The monarch acquired the right to name commendatory bishops, abbots and priors, while the pope provided the canonical institution. Although the king's choices remained subject to certain conditions, like the age or knowledge of the candidate, these conditions were not considered for "sublime" persons, exempted from these constraints by their noble birth.

1360, abbeys suffered from attacks by the *Grandes Companies*, then, in 1360, they were beleaguered by *routiers* demobilized by the Peace of Calais. The latter devastated Citeaux, whose monks were forced to take refuge in Dijon.
In 1378, the Great Schism divided Christianity. In question was the designation of a successor to Pope Gregory XI, back in Rome. Clement VII's authority was recognized in France, Scotland, in the Kingdom of Naples, Savoy and in the Iberian peninsula, but Urban VI had the support of the emperor, England, Bohemia, Poland and a large part of Italy. It was not until the Council of Constance in 1414 that support unified around Martin V, elected in 1417. These events could only divide the Cistercian family; the French abbeys chose the camp of Clement VII, except for Pontigny which, given its important German affiliation, took the side of Urban VI. No General Chapter, an essential aspect of the Cistercian institution, was convened until 1422. On that occasion, the supreme Cistercian body could only describe the situation. "Our Order", it declared, "in the different parts of the world where it has spread, appears deformed and fallen in regard to regular discipline and monastic life." It agreed upon the necessity of reform and proceeded with abbey visitations in order to restore discipline. The General Chapter of 1433 organized the Order according to a geographic plan rather than by affiliation, while reaffirming its authority and reinforcing the visitors' powers. The 1439 meeting promulagated new statutes, *Defining Rubrics*, that were intended to enforce a maximum of discipline. Along with these actions, reforming initiatives were taken locally or regionally. In 1425, the monks of Sibculo in the Netherlands restored discipline in their house, and their example was followed in 1430 in Le Jardinet. In 1427, Martin de Vargas, a former monk in Piedra, daughter of Poblet, wanted to introduce more rigour in the Castilian monasteries, which in 1438 joined "the Regular Observance of Saint Bernard". Through the bull *Plantatus in agro* of 1496, Alexander VI united the abbeys of Tuscany and

Melrose cloister

Monks' lavatorium in Poblet

Cardinal Richelieu

THE ABSTINENTS

During the 17th century, the two observances diverged over the question of eating meat. Behind this debate, two concepts of monastic life confronted each other. Asceticism remained a more important component for the abstinents than it was for the conservatives.

1570. The successive abbots at the head of the Order were dedicated reformers. In 1584, in its *Definitions*, the General Chapter reminded the Order what discipline was. In 1601, the Great Chapter called together one thousand abbots and monks to define a great project of restoration that failed immediately. It was then that, with the support of Nicholas II Boucherat, the abbot of Clairvaux, Denis Largentier, with several abbots of its daughters, like La Charmoye, committed themselves in 1606 to "observe the Rule of Saint Benedict to the letter". They thus laid down the basis of what was to become in 1618 the Strict Observance, which was rapidly joined by abbeys like Longpont and Les Vaux de Cernay. Others refused to do so, while in still others, conservatives and reformers lived together. In 1623, with the support of Cardinal de la Rochefoucauld, placed in charge of the issue by the pope, the reformers, called *abstinents*, tried to constitute a separate congregation but the General Chapter was opposed. In Clairvaux, Claude Largentier succeeded his uncle in 1624. He opted for a conservative position called the Common Observance. There was disagreement between the two observances and Cardinal Richelieu was approached by the conservatives to put an end to it. The cardinal even took the head of the Cistercian Order in 1636 and named Charles Boucherat, a proponent of Strict Observance, vicar general. At Richelieu's death in 1642, divisions appeared once again and lasted until 1666, when Alexander VII, in his bull *In suprema* legitimized the existence of both obser-

The last meal of St Benedict and St Scholastica

Abbey church façade in Alcobaça

Baroque Art

The term *Baroque* comes from the Portuguese term *barroco* for an irregular pearl. Born in Italy at the end of the 16th century, the Baroque style had its roots in the Renaissance, which it expanded. It flourished during the 17th and 18th centuries, at the time that new discoveries, from Kepler to Galileo, revolutionized the concept of the universe by putting an end to geocentrism. The human dimension diminished before the feeling of the infinitely great. The weapon of the Catholic Counter-Reformation, the Baroque style was intended as the expression of the unmeasureable divine design that conceived the universe. Faced with the sobriety of Protestant temples, it offered churches with exuberant and spectacular decoration, made to provoke emotion and praise the greatness of God. On the ceilings, luxuriant frescoes overwhelmed the viewer by changes in perspective, by trompe-l'oeil. Sculpture, painting, and richly decorated furniture took up all the space. On the facades, often with several storeys and topped with domes, the architect let his fantasy take over and used curved lines. The Baroque was popular particularly in Austria, Germany, Belgium, Hungary, Spain, Portugal and Latin America, territories subject to the House of Hapsburg, a Catholic bastion in the face of Protestant expansion. Exalting feeling rather than reason, Baroque was opposed to the voluntarily materialistic thought of the Enlightenment.

Saint Bernard, St Urbain's Abbey

Sacristy in Poblet

vances under the authority of Citeaux. By that time, Armand Jean Le Bouthillier de Rancé had been abbot of La Trappe for two years. A member of the Strict Observance, he distinguished himself by his ardour and his austerity after 1675. The sprit of La Trappe soon influenced other monasteries, such as Perseigne, Barbeaux, Châtillon and Hautefontaine in France and Casamari in Italy.

However, these efforts at reform, while preserving the essential of the Order and the spirit of Citeaux, did not prevent the decline of abbeys that did not take part. In the latter, recruitment decreased and discipline was often lax. Their abbots were often named by the pope or by kings, despite rules of free elections. Some of these commendatory abbots confiscated the abbey's revenues and built themselves sumptuous outbuildings. The abbeys were rebuilt according to the canons of classical architecture in France, Baroque in the Germanic countries or the Iberian peninsula. The Kings' Hall in Alcobaça and the sacristy of Poblet date from this period. In France in 1766, King Louis XV put in place the Commission of the Regulars, which controlled two hundred and twenty abbeys of both observances. The report was severe except for those that had joined the movement started by Rancé a century earlier. Of the sixty bishops on the commission, thirty-six were in favour of abolishing the Order. Although no sanctions were pronounced, the French Revolution was soon to pose a new threat to a weakened Cistercian Order.

THE SPLENDOURS OF ALCOBAÇA

In 1762, Alcobaça (*below*) contained one hundred and thirty-nine professed monks. The English traveller William Beckford visited the abbey in 1794. In his account, he mentioned that the monks of Alcobaça organized concerts and put on plays within the confines of their abbey.

Azulejos in Alcobaça

Armand Jean Le Bouthillier de Rancé

The Founder of La Trappe

Born in Paris into a great family, after studying the humanities in 1651 Armand Jean Le Bouthillier de Rancé began his ecclesiastical career, although he continued to lead the worldly life associated with his social rank. He was in charge of several ecclesiastical benefices, including that of abbot of La Trappe Abbey, which he held in commendam. In 1657, the death of his friend, the Duchess of Montbazon, then in 1660, that of his protector, Gaston d'Orléans, hastened his conversion and led him to renounce the world. In 1663, he entered Perseigne as a novice, pronounced his vows the following year, then retired to La Trappe, of which he became the regular abbot. He joined the Strict Observance and, over a period of about ten years, reflected on monastic life. He presented his ideas in a book called *On Sanctity and the Duties of Monastic Life*. In 1675, he decided to reform his monastery according to the Rule of the first Cistercians – he re-established full monasticism, free elections of the abbot and Visits, abolished studies, imposed silence, penance and manual labour. Mortification of the flesh became even more extreme than at the time of Saint Bernard, Offices became longer. Very rapidly, the abbey began to enjoy unquestionable prestige. In 1700, at Rancé's death, it contained ninety professed monks, whereas it had had only six in 1642. Bossuet, Cardinal de Retz, Bishop Le Camus, and other religious personalities went to La Trappe for retreats.

Family tree of Citeaux's male monasteries

THE CISTERCIAN ORDER IN THE IBERIAN PENINSULA

"Citeaux is a monastery that has given its name to the Order of the White Monks, placed under the Rule of Saint Benedict. The early days of this order were lived in the greatest poverty. For this reason, the Church of Rome granted it many advantages..."
Alfonso X, King of Castile (1252-1284) *Las Siete Partidas*

The first Cistercian abbey founded in the Iberian peninsula was probably that of Sobrado, in Galicia. The event took place in 1142. By that year, Citeaux included nearly one hundred and fifty male establishments in Europe. There were about fifteen in Britain, and about a dozen each in Germany and Italy. At the death of Bernard of Clairvaux in 1153, there were 343 of which only about fifteen were located south of the Pyrenees mountains. These included Cántabos, which moved to Huerta in 1162, Fitero, La Espina, La Oliva, Moreruela, Oseira, Poblet, Santes Creus, Sobrado, Tarouca, Valbuena, Valparaiso, Veruela. This means that the Cistercian Order was implanted in the Iberian peninsula rather late. Several decades earlier, Bernard of Clairvaux had appeared reticent about extending to the region, perhaps because of worries about the dangerous situation linked to the *Reconquista*, taking place at the time. In any case, about 1127, he advised the abbot of Preuilly against it. It must also be taken into consideration that a wave of eremitism was washing over the north of the Iberian peninsula during the first half of the 12th century, responding, just like Citeaux but through different means, to the desire for a life of prayer, asceticism and poverty. In the hundred years following the death of Bernard, this wave was to the advantage of Citeaux, who harnessed it and directed it. From 1153 to 1250, the Order saw the number of its abbeys in the Iberian peninsula increase by nearly ninety, with over a third of them being houses for nuns. There were foundations, like Piedra in 1194 or Rueda in 1202, but also incorporations, like that of Carracedo in 1203, which was affiliated with Citeaux along with the ten monasteries it controlled. The first abbey for nuns was Tulebras in Navarre, in 1157. Others followed: Gradefes in 1168, Cañas in 1170, Vallbona in 1176. In 1187, the king of Castile, Alfonso VIII (1158-1214) and his wife, Alienor, entrusted the royal monastery of Las Huelgas in Burgos to the abbess Misol. The Iberian sovereigns favoured the development of Citeaux in their kingdoms. They donated lands to abbeys, granted them privileges, and allowed them exemptions. This interest in Citeaux developed as much from the monarchs' political understanding of their role, as from the ever-present religious feeling. Some made a great Cistercian abbey into the pantheon of their dynasty. Examples are Poblet for Alfonso II of Aragon (1162-1196), Las Huelgas of Burgos for Alfonso VIII of Castile, and Alcobaça for Alfonso II of Portugal (1211-1223). Strengthened by this royal support and members of a powerful religious order, the Iberian Cistercian abbeys did not undergo the difficult beginnings of the *Novum Monasterium*. They became wealthy landowners whose powers extended over vast properties. Most of them had rights over churches. They exploited granges. Some, like Poblet, Las Huelgas, Alcobaça or Sobrado, administered hospitals. They had great abbey churches built of stone, as well as large monastic buildings, able to contain important communities. They took on hydraulic works in order to provide drinking water, the evacuation of liquid waste, irrigation of land, and water energy for mills. The *armaria* of some abbeys turned into rich libraries, and Alcobaça, Huerta and Poblet had their own *scriptoria*. Their wealth was further increased by donations from benefactors. These gifts could be precious objects, such as the reliquary cross offered to Carrizo at the end of the 12th century, or the three gilded silver chalices given during the same period by Queen Dulce, the widow of Sancho 1st (1185-1211), to Alcobaça. This prosperity led to a relaxing of the Rule and of discipline, and created a distance between these abbeys and a General Chapter in which they did not always participate and which occasionally reminded them of their duties. Hence, in 1191, Fitero and Rioseco received visitors sent by the General Chapter to restore discipline. The Iberian Cistercian abbeys founded or incorporated before the end of the first half of the 13th century were implanted in areas controlled by the Christian kingdoms – in Galicia, north of the Tagus River in Portugal, in the valley of the Ebro in Castile and Leon, and in the Ebro valley and the areas of Zaragoza and Tarragona in Aragon. It should be noted that at the end of the 12th century, with the exception of Iranzu, they were all affiliated with Clairvaux and Morimond, with a clear geographical division between the two lineages. Clairvaux had spread in the north-western quarter of the peninsula, particularly in Portugal and the kingdom of Leon; Morimond had invested the kingdoms of Navarre, Aragon and Castile. However Santes Creus and Poblet, in the Clairvaux lineage, were installed in Catalonia, and Piedra, a daughter of Poblet, in Aragon. Citeaux also played a ıportant role in the organization of mil-ıry orders. In 1158, the abbot of Fitero ·unded the Order of Calatrava which, 1186, was attached to Morimond. nd it was with the help of some of ıese soldier-monks that, in the middle ' the 13th century, Ferdinand III of astile (1217-1252) re-conquered a ırge part of Andalusia and James 1st of ıragon (1213-1276) recaptured Valencia om the Moors. The new abbeys could

The Christ of Carrizo

ıen settle in the centre and south of the eninsula. Male abbeys were established Valencia in 1287, in Valldigna in 1297, ear Sevilla in 1301, Toledo in 1427, and sbon in 1429. Establishments of nuns 'ere also installed near cities, like Zaidia 1265, Alzira in 1273 – both of them ose to Valencia. But the rate of founda-ons slowed. Twenty-five took place in ıe second half of the 13th century, only ıree in the 15th. The Spanish kingdoms ːmained concerned by the process. In *ıs Partidas*, the new legal code of his ngdom that the king of Castile Alfonso I ıe Wise (1252-1284) had written up om 1256 to 1263, Citeaux was evoked. Although the text emphasized the enrichment of an order that had somewhat moved away from its founding principles, he nonetheless held it up as an example. In 1296, Saint Bernard Abbey near Guadalajara was created at the initiative of two of Alfonso Xth's daughters. Queen María de Molina founded Las Huelgas de Valladolid, where she was buried in 1321. Her father, the Infant Alfonso de Molina, brother of Ferdinand III, was already buried in La Espina because Cistercian monasteries continued to be the burial places of choice for nobles and monarchs. The Count of Barcelos chose to be buried in Tarouca in 1354. The tombs of Pedro 1st of Portugal (1357-1367) and Inès de Castro were placed facing each other in Alcobaça. Maria of Portugal, the wife of Alfonso XI, King of Castile (1312-1350) has her tomb in San Clemente in Sevilla. As for Pedro IV of Aragon, he had the pantheon of the kings of Aragon built in Poblet in 1340. The treaty of Alcañices in 1296 set the borders between Castile and Portugal; the treaty of Torrellas in 1304, set the borders between Castile and Aragon. Consequently, the map of dioceses had to be redrawn. There was also the birth of nationalism, of which abbeys were the occasional instrument. Military orders were organized by country. During the Great Schism of the West (1378-1417), the divisions within the Church caused cleavage too, sometimes between Iberian abbeys in different kingdoms and, often, between the latter and their French mother abbeys. The monasteries' economic systems deteriorated starting in the 13th century, when they had to progressively abandon direct exploitation of their lands. And missions to collect contributions, organized by the General Chapter, multiplied. In the 15th century, the institution of the commendam system aggravated the situation. In 1425, Martin de Vargas tried to reform the system and, against the advice of the General Chapter, founded the Congregation of Castile which, by in the middle of the 16th century, included over forty member establishments. It also set up a college in Alcalá de Henares in 1505, and another in Salamanca in 1514. In Portugal, in 1567, Alcobaça took the head of the Congregation of Saint Bernard. The Congregation of the Crown of Aragon was created in 1616, joined by Navarrese abbeys in 1634. However, the institution of these congregations did not cause a complete break with the Order's General Chapter. It did, nonetheless, put an end to the commendam system and, during the 16th and 17th centuries, gave a new spiritual and material impetus to member abbeys, which continued in the 18th century. But in the 19th century, the Cortes de Cadix of 1812, the Liberal Triennium (1820-1823) and, especially, the *Desamortización* of 1835, dealt a fatal blow to the Spanish regular orders and to the white monks in particular. Many of their abbeys were abandoned, and some completely ruined. In the 20th century, monks and nuns returned to occupy some of them to provoke a renaissance of the Cistercian ideal. In December 1936, the prior of Viaceli, Pío Heredia, along with eleven monks died as martyrs for their faith. Today, there are sixty-nine Cistercian establishments in Spain: twelve of monks, three of them belonging to the Cistercian Order and nine to the Cistercian Order of Strict Observance; and fifty-seven of nuns, of which twenty-four are members of the Cistercian Order, nine belong to the Cistercian Order of Strict Observance; and twenty-four to the Cistercian Congregation of Saint Bernard of Spain.

Nuns praying

Cistercian Nuns

The very first monks of Citeaux do not seem to have been very concerned about female vocations. However, in their former monastery of Molesme, Abbot Robert had taken women under his spiritual direction. These women were often related to the monks and, having taken vows of chastity and obedience, lived in communities in little houses near the abbey. But in 1098, there was no mention of nuns in the *Novum Monasterium*, where the intention was to live a rough life working the land. Furthermore, any female presence was excluded: "Because they did not read in the Rule nor in the life of Saint Benedict that the same Master had possessed churches and altars [...] neither that women had had access to his monastery [...], they rejected all these abuses", said the *instituta* written up after Robert's return to Molesme by Abbot Alberic (†1109) and his brothers.

It seems that the problem of nuns arose later in Citeaux, during the year 1112, with the arrival of Bernard and his thirty companions. Several female relatives or wives of these companions also wished to enter into monastic life but there was no existing structure able to accept them. Bernard then turned to Molesme Abbey, of which his family was the benefactor. Through his intermediary, a nuns' priory was created in Jully, where Molesme had a church and where Count Milon de Bar donated a castle. The nuns of Molesme were transferred there, and that was where the relatives and wives of Bernard and his companions took the veil. The first regulations of the priory – whose foundation was approved by the bishop of Langres in 1118, then by Pope Eugene III in 1145 – were provided by the successor of Robert of Molesme (†1111), Abbot Guy de Châtel Censoir. The nuns were to live a

Hombeline enters Jully

On the Hill of Jully

After the glorious times of the 12th and 13th centuries, the castle-priory of Jully, the burial place of Saint Hombeline, was greatly impoverished by the Hundred Years War. Suppressed in 1413, its goods were gathered at Molesme Abbey in 1420. Today, an association for the protection and activity of the castle of Jully brings its history back to life.

The castle-priory of Jully

Nuns, tomb in Cañas

THE BEGUINES

At the end of the 12th century, Belgium saw the birth of the spiritual movement of "holy women", gathering together laywomen wishing to lead a life in the image of the first Christian community described in the Acts. Spread throughout the Rhineland, the Netherlands, Flanders, and the Hainaut, despite the anarchy of its beginnings the movement joined together women of varying social status: virgins, widows, married women with growing children. They called themselves Beguines – a name of uncertain origin. Often coming from a good social background, alone in their homes or else in small groups, they led a life devoted to God, in poverty and chastity, practicing fasting, vigils and prayer, working with their hands or else begging for a living, and contributing to works of mercy – hospitality, care of the poor and the ill. In 1231, Pope Gregory IX prescribed their being grouped in enclosures, leading to the appearance of large Beguine convents provided with their own churches, where hundreds of holy women lived in private houses. At the beginning of the 13th century, hundreds of these communities requested their incorporation into the Cistercian Order. Lutgarde d'Aywières (1182-1246), a former Beguine, became one of the Order's great saints.

communal life, particularly concerning food and clothing that they were supposed to obtain with their dowries, through work or alms. Furs were forbidden, except as bedcovers. They were to possess neither servants, nor churches, nor farms. The lands that were given to them and that they could not exploit alone were to go to Molesme Abbey. Jully was placed under the authority of Molesme Abbey, which would send over four clerics, one of whom would take up the direction with the title of prior. The latter would assist and counsel the prioress, the first of whom was Elizabeth, the wife of Bernard's brother, Guy, who entered Citeaux at the same time as Bernard. Elizabeth was in charge from 1116 to about 1130, when Hombeline, Bernard's own sister, succeeded her and remained in charge until her death in 1141. Very rapidly, the priory of Jully seems to have welcomed several relatives and spouses of monks from the abbeys of Clairvaux, Pontigny, Morimond and Fontenay. And it was with the help of the abbots of these four Cistercian abbeys that Guy de Châtel Censoir wrote a second set of regulations for the priory between 1118 and 1132. Enclosure was strictly established, as well as abstinence from eating meat. Furthermore, the maximum number of nuns allowed in the community was sixty, along with four lay sisters. Jully was a flourishing establishment and starting in the 1130's, it became the mother-house of several other priories of nuns.

Although it was considered by many historians as the first Cistercian establishment for cloistered nuns, the priory of Jully, attached to Molesme Abbey according to a Cluniac type of organization, was not in fact the first, although the history of its origins is intimately linked with that of Citeaux. The 1985 Menology of the Cistercian Order more accurately defined it as a "monastery of Benedictines". Nonetheless, its role in the formation of the female branch of the Order remains undeniable, since the first abbess of Tart, the first Cistercian abbey for nuns founded between 1120 and 1125 by the Abbot of Citeaux, Stephen Harding (1109-1133), was a former nun from Jully.

The causes that inspired Stephen Harding to create Tart remain obscure. Was the solution offered by the foundation of Jully and her daughters to resolve the problem of female vocations not sufficient? What is known is that the birth of Tart was the result of a series of agreements between Bishop Josserand of Langres and his successor, Vilain, the abbot of Citeaux, the Duke of Burgundy and the de Vergy family. This lineage played quite an important role since it was Arnoul Cornu, a vassal of the lords of Vergy, who ceded the lands of Tart, located three leagues from Citeaux, and that the community's first abbess, Elizabeth, a former nun in Jully, was the daughter of Savary de Donzy and Elizabeth de Vergy. A benefactress and great admirer of Citeaux, the latter seemed to be especially interested in founding a monastery for nuns according to Cistercian customs. The observances of Tart, an abbey that very quickly found itself at the head of a congregation, became known through a charter of the abbot of Citeaux, Guy de Paray (1194-1200). The nuns lived according to the *instituta* of the

Cistercian Order, in other words, the Rule of Saint Benedict, the Charter of Charity and the statutes of the General Chapter. The abbey and its daughters remained under the responsibility of the abbot of Citeaux, who had "full power to correct and regulate all that is necessary, either in the head, or in the members". The abbot of Citeaux could also name or depose the abbess of Tart according to the Order's rules. Tart's daughter abbeys, of which there were eighteen at the time the Charter was written, had to meet annually, on Saint Michael's Day, in a General Chapter in Tart, under the double presidency of the abbot of Citeaux and the abbess of Tart.

Starting in the first third of the 12th century, and especially in the 13th century, foundations of Cistercian abbeys for nuns multiplied, both independently of the Congregation of Tart and within its circle, while simultaneously many requests for affiliation arrived at the Order from non-Cistercian female abbeys. Thus, in the Netherlands, Belgium and northern France, many communities of Beguines asked to become Cistercian. Furthermore, among the religious congregations that were allowed to unite with Citeaux, several included abbeys of both men and women, like the congregations of Savigny and Obazine, attached in 1147. In most cases, these female monasteries were placed under the supervision of a Cistercian abbot and adopted Cistercian customs, while remaining under the jurisdiction of the bishop of their diocese. Their status remained ambiguous for a long time; they were "affiliated" but were nonetheless not incorporated into the Order and the existence of a female Cistercian branch stayed unofficial. Until the 13th century, Citeaux's General Chapter was reticent and maintained a pointed silence about nuns. However, given how widespread the phenomenon was becoming, it was obliged to intervene and legislate, thus accepting the official existence of the Order's female branch.

The Chapter General's first intervention on the subject of an abbey of nuns concerned that of Las Huelgas, near Burgos in Spain, that it authorized in 1187 to become the mother-abbey of a congregation including nuns from Castile, according to the wishes of its founder, King Alfonso VIII of Castile. However, it was not until the beginning of the 13th century that Citeaux's General Chapter proposed measures concerning all Cistercian nuns. In 1213, it imposed strict enclosure on them, a *sine qua non* condition for being incorporated into the Order. In 1218, it decided that abbeys of nuns had to be built more than six leagues away from men's abbeys, and that they had to be separated from each other by at least ten leagues. Starting in 1224, it authorized Cistercian nuns to have lay brothers, who had to wear a habit, a tonsure and a beard. On several occasions – in 1221, 1228, 1239 – the General Chapter attempted to stem the flood of incorporations by prohibiting them. In 1251, it even managed to obtain a bull by which the Holy See renounced imposing any incorporation on the Order. But these decisions were not always easy to impose on the ground. Progressively, a procedure of incorporation was put into place: any candidate abbey was subjected to an

Chapter house in Fontaine Guérard

The Heiresses of Port Royal

The nuns' abbey of Port Royal was attached to Citeaux in the 12th century. In the 17th century, it was reformed by Mother Angélique, and passed into the jurisdiction of the archbishop of Paris. Its success was such that its nuns soon filled two houses – the original abbey, Port Royal des Champs, and Port Royal of Paris. A principal centre of Jansenism, the original abbey was suppressed by Louis XIV.
As for the Paris community, it survived the French Revolution. Transferred to Besançon in 1841, it obtained its reintegration into the Citeaux order in 1921, and in 1927 the nuns settled at the ancient abbey of La Grâce Dieu, that still today welcomes the spiritual heiresses of Port Royal.

Cloister, Las Huelgas Reales

The Spanish Recoletas

In 1591, several Cistercian nuns from Gradefes adopted the reform preached by Dom Álvaro de Salazar, who had re-established Strict Observance of Saint Benedict's Rule in his abbey of San Millán de la Cogolla. Named in 1593 to head the abbey of Perales by the abbess of Las Huelgas, Catherine of Castile decided to introduce this reform into her abbey, to which the abbess of Las Huelgas brought nuns from various monasteries. The *recolección* y *reformación* in the heart of the Cistercian Order were approved by the papacy in September 1595. In December of the same year, with the authorization of the abbess of Las Huelgas, Catherine of Castile transferred her community from Perales to Valladolid, where the monastery of San Joachim y Santa Ana was created. This is the origin of the Congregation of Recoletas of Valladolid. The term "recoleta" came from the Latin *recollectus* for someone who worshiped through contemplation, and who lives in spiritual retreat. Their constitutions, written by two Cistercians from Valbuena, were approved by the papacy in 1606: rising at two in the morning, two hours of mental prayer daily, discipline on Wednesdays and Fridays, abstinence from wine and meat, private work in the rooms.... This austere life did not prevent vocations from flooding in and foundations succeeded each other rapidly – El Cister de Malaga between 1599 and 1604; Nuestra Señora de la Asunción in Toledo in 1605; the Encarnación de Talavera in 1608; the Santo Sacramento in Madrid in 1617. The abbey in Valladolid was the only one of the congregation to be placed under the jurisdiction of the abbey of Las Huelgas, the others remained under that of their diocese bishops.

enquiry led by two of the Order's abbots, sent to the site by the General Chapter. They were supposed to check if the location of the abbey conformed to the rules, if it had sufficient resources, and finally, if enclosure was properly respected. If these conditions were fulfilled, the abbey's incorporation into the Order remained subject to the approval of the General Chapter which, if it gave a favourable decision, designated the father-abbot who would supervise the new community of Cistercian nuns.

According to the expression of Jean de la Croix Bouton, the 13th century was "the great century of nuns". According to repertories, between 752 and 873 monasteries of Cistercian nuns were counted in Europe and the Near East. Vocations were particularly numerous in the Germanic countries. Nuns' lives were lived to the rhythm of work and prayer, in conformity with the Rule. They received regular visits from their father-abbot and were subject to the decision of the General Chapter. Their spiritual life was structured by Cistercian confessors, almoners, and chaplains attached to each of their abbeys. Their work consisted of making ornaments for the church or ecclesiastical vestments, copying and illuminating manuscripts, teaching children – only girls, following the General Chapter's decision. But after the religious and moral crisis provoked by the Great Schism (1378-1417), after the Hundred Years War (1337-1453), many nuns' abbeys disappeared at the end of the Middle Ages and their possessions often went to enrich male communities. Generally, religious life seemed to be slacker, parents placed daughters with no vocation in the monasteries, in order to provide a bigger dowry for the daughters intended for marriage. In the Germanic countries, starting after 1525, the Protestant Reformation dealt a fatal blow to monastic life, while in England after1515, monasteries were progressively closed during the reign of Henry VIII (†1547). However, under the impetus of the Council of Trent, which met in several sessions between 1545 and 1563, the 1601 Citeaux General Chapter made an attempt at reform and, among other things, reminded nuns of

Chevet of Gradefes abbey church

the obligations of enclosure, poverty, and that they were forbidden to have servants and obliged to wear the Order's regular habit – a white tunic and cowl, black veil and scapular, with no silks or pleated wimples. These prescriptions were not completely ignored since there was a real desire for reform among many Cistercian nuns. In Spain, some nuns in Gradefes and Perales were at the origin of the Congregation of the Recoletas, officially recognized in 1595. In France, the female branch of the Congregation of the Feuillants was created in 1588, while the Bernardines were a product of the reform in the Cistercian abbeys of Rumilly and Les Ayes. In most countries, the 17th and 18th centuries saw the regrouping of Cistercian male and female monasteries into congregations. Some, like the Congregation of Upper Germany, remained closely linked to Citeaux; others, like the Congregation of Castile founded by Martin de Vargas, or the Italian Congregation of Saint Bernard, moved away. In France, where the effects of the Tridentine reform were delayed by the Wars of Religion (1562-1598), the great abbesses, such as Jeanne de Courcelles in Tart, or Jacqueline Arnauld in Port Royal, wished to restore monastic life. Transferring their communities into towns, according to the prescriptions of the Council of Trent, these two abbesses nevertheless preferred to break with a Cistercian Order divided in 1618 between Strict and Common observances, and placed their abbeys under the supervision of their diocese bishop.

Further changes were made during the Enlightenment, which raised the question of the social utility of contemplative orders. In France, Louis XV charged the Commission of Regulars with suppressing decadent establishments. In Austria, the "enlightened despot" Joseph II in 1782 suppressed all the nuns' monasteries that did not devote themselves to teaching or caring for the sick. These actions prepared the way for the persecution of monks and nuns during the French Revolution and the Napoleonic period. It was not until the fall of Napoleon that Cistercian religious life was totally restored, at least in France and in Italy. In Spain, the first third of the 19th century was a particularly dark period for monastic life, with the ravages of the War of Independence (1808-1813), then the measures of *Exclaustración* of the Liberal Triennium (1820-1829) and, above all, Mendizábal's *Desamortización* in 1835.

Today, Cistercian nuns are divided into several observances. The Cistercian nuns of Strict Observance, descended from the Trappist nuns gathered by Dom Augustin de Lestrange in Sembrancher, Switzerland in 1796, have 66 monasteries on five continents. The Cistercian nuns of the Order of Citeaux comprise, in 64 monasteries installed all over the world, communities that are part of a congregation or a federation, or that were directly integrated into the Order. The Bernardines of Esquermes, with 8 monasteries, are charged with teaching, like the Bernardines of Oudenaarde with 18 monasteries. The Cistercian Congregation of Saint Bernard in Spain, known by the name Las Huelgas, consists of 24 monasteries. All the nuns participate, every day, in the life, the decisions and the advancement of the great Cistercian family.

Jacqueline Arnauld

A Haven of Peace in the City

In 1816, ten Trappist nuns of Darfeld Monastery in Westphalia settled by the Mayenne River in France, at the old priory of Saint Catherine of Laval, not far from the monks of Port du Salut. In 1859, lack of space forced the nuns to move to the edge of the town, in a place called La Coudre, from the wild hazelnut bushes, *coudriers*, there – the name given to their new abbey. Today, a few hundred metres from the busy urban streets and housing developments, the fifty Trappist nuns of La Coudre continue to live in silence and contemplation, dedicated to prayer and manual work.

In particular, they produce powdered desserts and, in their cheese factory created in 1868, a cheese called "veritable Trappe", from Mayenne milk according to a recipe from the monks of Port du Salut. To welcome ever-increasing numbers of visitors, on January 25, 2003, the sisters inaugurated their new monastic Gallery: around a shop offering a wide range of monastic products, an itinerary leads to a discovery of community life through an exhibition and video-projections.

La Trappe

Fire Smouldering under the Ashes

In 1789, the French Revolution did not spare the Cistercians any more than it did other congregations. In November 1789, their goods were confiscated and then, in February 1790, the National Assembly suppressed the Order because it was considered useless. The monks went into exile. Only the Trappist community, directed by Dom Augustin de Lestrange, managed to sustain itself while fleeing from revolutionary troops. Starting in 1796, under the influence of revolutionary conquests and, after 1803, with the Napoleonic occupation, secularism spread throughout Europe. At the beginning of the 19th century, despite the courage of exiled monks or nuns, the Order was barely visible. It did not really reappear until 1815 and the fall of Napoleon's Empire. This revival occurred independently within the framework of each individual observance, but under the common authority of a General President, an abbot of the Order put into place by Pope Pius VII in Rome in 1816.
Within the Strict Observance, in 1814 during the Restoration Louis XVIII authorized the abbot of Darfeld, Eugène de Laprade, to return to France and install a community in the new monastery of Port du Salut. In 1815, after the interruption of the Hundred Days, Lestrange settled in Aiguebelle and the Abbey of La Trappe was restored. In France many abbeys, both of nuns and monks, came back to life, some of them following the Rule of La Valsainte,

Reference Dates

The National Assembly suppresses the Order of Citeaux	**1790**
Foundation of La Valsainte by Lestrange, from La Trappe	**1791**
Foundation of Port du Salut by Laprade	**1815**
Dom Augustin de Lestrange settles in Aiguebelle and La Trappe is bought back	**1815**
Pius VII names an Abbot General for the Order	**1816**
Foundation of the Cistercian Order of the Common Observance	**1816**
Foundation of the Cistercian Order of the Strict Observance	**1892**
Constitution *Haud mediocri sane*	**1902**

Aiguebelle

THE TRAPPIST EPIC

In 1790, several monks from La Trappe, directed by Augustin de Lestrange, the abbey's master of novices, decided to settle abroad. In May 1791, they moved to Switzerland, where they established a monastery in the former charterhouse of La Valsainte. The community, of which Lestrange was elected abbot and which followed a rule that was even stricter than that of Rancé, attracted many monks and nuns fleeing persecution. In 1793, some of the latter settled in the locality of Westmalle, near Antwerp, then, forced to flee once again because of invading French troops, they emigrated to Darfeld in Westphalia. In England, the Trappists settled in Lulworth. They also spread to Italy, Spain, and the Balearic Islands. In Switzerland, Lestrange created schools within the abbeys in order to welcome children of exiled French families. When the French political authorities demanded the return of these pupils, in 1798 Lestrange and his disciples left Switzerland, taking their young charges with them. Crossing Austria and the countries of Central Europe, they reached Russia where, during the early 1800's, they ran six establishments. Soon chased out by the Tsar, they returned to La Valsainte in 1802 because the situation had become less hostile since the signing of the concordat in 1801. Lestrange pursued his work and founded new "*trappes*" in Switzerland and Italy. However, in 1801 the abbot of Darfeld, Eugène de Laprade, approved neither the austerity of the changes Lestrange had made in Rancé's Rule, that he judged contrary to the harmony of the Benedictine Rule, nor of the monks taking charge of the schools. Laprade broke with the father-abbot and became the autonomous abbot of Darfeld, where he wished to bring back the spirit of Rancé. He was supported in this undertaking by the pope in 1808. Meanwhile, starting in 1807, the conflict between Napoleon and Pope Pius VII envenomed. The emperor having invaded the Papal States, the Holy See replied by excommunicating him. Napoleon then ordered the pontiff to be locked up and religious persecution began again. In July 1811, an imperial decree demanded the closing of all the Cistercian convents. After visiting Lulworth, Lestrange took refuge in the United States, where he found disciples established there since 1803. When the Empire collapsed in 1814, Eugène de Laprade took the initiative of re-establishing the Order in France. In February 1815, he founded the abbey of Port du Salut before dying in 1816 in Borsut, in what is now Belgium. In 1818, faced with the hostility of the Prussian government, Darfeld was transferred to Picardy, to the former Cistercian abbey of Gard. During the same period, Lestrange, back from the United States in 1815, took back the former abbeys of La Trappe and Aiguebelle. His disciples who had emigrated to the USA settled at Bellefontaine in 1816, while those of Lulworth settled in Melleray in 1817. That same year, Dom Huvelin, a former monk in Sept Fons Abbey, earlier reformed by Dom Eustache of Belfort, repopulated Bellevaux Abbey with some of his former brothers. These various Trappist families continued to spread and, in 1828, in France, seven male abbeys followed the La Valsainte Observance, five, those of Rancé. After thirty years of trials, the essentials had been saved.

Casamari, cloister and abbey church

THE MIRACLE OF HONORATUS

The monastery of Lérins (*opposite*) that, in 1872, became the seat of the Congregation of the Immaculate Conception, was founded in the first decade of the 5th century by Honoratus, the son of a Roman consul in Trier. Legend has it that when Honoratus, accompanied by Capras, arrived on the island of Lerina the island was infested with snakes. Honoratus prayed and the snakes died. But their numbers were such that their dead bodies made the air oppressive. Honoratus turned to Heaven and a tidal wave cleaned the island's ground, which lacked water. Honoratus tapped his stick three times on a rock and clear water sprang forth.

the abbey run by Lestrange during his exile; others followed that of Rancé. In 1824, Lestrange elaborated a project to unite the two groups, but another ten years passed before Gregory XVI gathered all the French Trappists into the congregation of the Cistercian Monks of Notre Dame de la Trappe. In 1847, Pius IX changed the papacy's position and ratified the existence of two congregations, which nonetheless remained very similar in their search for isolation and their practice of austerity. In fact, under the authority of Leon XIII, in 1892 they joined together once again in an independent order run by its abbot, which in 1902 through the constitution *Haud mediocri sane* took the name of the Cistercian Order of the Strict Observance.

In the ranks of the Common Observance, regional or national congregations were reorganized. In Italy in 1820, Pius VII resuscitated the Italian Congregation of Saint Bernard, which joined Hautecombe. In 1846, the Belgian abbeys formed a national congregation, and the Austrian ones followed in 1859. In 1854, in France, Abbot Barnouin bought Sénanque to establish his community there and in 1867 it became the Congregation of Sénanque, sometimes called of Medium Observance, joined by Fontfroide, Lérins and, after the union of Savoy with France, Hautecombe. In Portugal in 1834 and in Spain in 1835, the Cistercian abbeys were closed by political authorities. In 1869, the congregations of Italy, Belgium, Austria and France joined together in the Cistercian Order of the Common Observance.

Capital in apse, Sénanque

The Law of 1901

In 1900, the Ministry of Waldeck Rousseau suppressed the Assumptionist Congregation, which was violently anti-Dreyfus. Then, with the law of 1901, congregations became the only associations subjected to the control and authorization of the State.

Lérins Monastery

Charles de Foucauld

During the 20th century, the two orders progressed despite wars and despite the 1901 French law on associations that, rather unfavourable towards congregations, led to the expulsion of monks from Sénanque and Fontfroide. The Cistercians of the Strict Observance submitted to the Rule, respected the hierarchy of affiliations, lived retired from the world, and devoted themselves to manual and intellectual work. They created the review *Collectanea ordinis cisterciensis reformati* in 1933 and, later, the collection *Comentarii cistercensis*. Present on all the continents, the Order includes two thousand six hundred monks in ninety-six abbeys, among which are: Citeaux, Orval, Aiguebelle, Sept Fons, Acey, La Trappe, Notre Dame des Neiges, Tre Fontane, and a thousand, eight hundred and eighty-three nuns in sixty-six abbeys. The Cistercian Order of the Common Observance, known as the Order of Citeaux, includes monasteries with diverse customs – autonomous abbeys or congregations with principal abbeys and dependent priories, living a totally enclosed life or else with pastoral or educational duties or doing charitable work. It federates thirteen congregations, eight of which have a female branch, consisting of thirteen hundred and twenty-seven monks living in eighty-eight houses, including Lérins, Sénanque, Chiaravalle, Casamari, Himmerod, Poblet. The nuns, of whom there are about a thousand, live in sixty-four establishments. Despite their differences, these spiritual children of Robert, Alberic, Stephen and Bernard, united by a common history, form a single family, the Cistercian family.

Charles de Foucauld

Born in 1858 into a family of ancient nobility, Charles de Foucauld (*above*) entered the officer school of Saint Cyr in 1876. In 1883, he undertook an exploratory voyage to Morocco where, disguised as a rabbi, he covered over two thousand kilometres. After a religious conversion in 1886, wishing to live in the humility of Christ, he entered Notre Dame des Neiges (*opposite*) as a novice in 1890. After several stays in Syria, Palestine and Algeria, he was ordained a priest in 1901. He then left to live as a hermit-missionary in the Hoggar, where he shared the life of the Tuaregs, learning their language and studying their literature. He died in 1916, assassinated by members of a rival Tuareg tribe.

Notre Dame des Neiges

Parity and Universality

The Order of Cistercians of the Strict Observance (O.C.S.O.) has undergone great changes since the 1970's. Currently, it tends to develop outside Europe, particularly in Central and South America, Africa and Asia. This is especially due to nuns, who have made nineteen foundations since 1980; the monks have founded fifteen abbeys. A mixed order formed of two branches – one male, the other female – subject to the authority of the abbot general, the O.C.S.O. had to grant its nuns independence and the right to participate in the governing authorities as they deserved. A first step was taken in 1970, when nuns were allowed to hold their own General Chapter, presided by the abbot general. Today, the O.C.S.O. is governed by both General Chapters of abbots and abbesses. Both are sovereign although interdependent in certain fields.

The chapters are held at the same time and have common sessions, with votes concerning each branch remaining separate. Furthermore, in 1987, the Holy See granted the O.C.S.O. nuns the right to participate in electing the Order's abbot general, in the same way as the abbots. Their first vote took place in 1990, during the election of the Argentine Dom Bernardo Olivera. And since 1996, the abbot general's permanent council, whose seat is its Rome headquarters, accepts nuns in residence.

In September 2002, the possibility was considered that the Order would move towards a single mixed General Chapter, within which each abbot and each abbess would have equal rights. Today an abbess can accompany the visiting abbot during a regular visitation to both monks and nuns. She can also be chosen to carry out a regular visitation to nuns, either alone or else accompanied by another abbess or an abbot.

Hence, the O.C.S.O. provides a fine example of modernity within the Catholic Church.

Monks in Aiguebelle in a cloister gallery

2

ABBEYS

1

Clairvaux and its Lineage

On June 25, 1115, Clairvaux, the third daughter of Citeaux, was founded. Bernard became its first abbot. Thanks to his charisma and influence, the entire Cistercian Order enjoyed immense prestige and developed considerably. Clairvaux played an essential role in this development by giving birth to numerous daughters and by incorporating several monasteries. At Bernard's death in 1153, the Clairvaux lineage of the Cistercian Order included nearly one hundred and seventy abbeys throughout all of Western Europe, in France, Belgium, Germany, England, Ireland, Scotland, Spain, Portugal and Italy. Some of them withstood time and trials. Several are still living and all are witnesses to Cistercian art and history.

Lay brothers' dormitory

Clairvaux

On June 25, 1115, the young Bernard settled with several other monks on family property, south-east of Bar sur Aube, in the Absinthe valley, the light valley of the Langres Diocese, *Clara vallis*, that provided the name for the abbey of which he became the abbot. The *Monasterium vetus*, Clairvaux I, was built 300 metres west of the current abbey, at Petit Clairvaux. Only a few walls remain. In 1118, Clairvaux founded Trois Fontaines (3 Fountains) and Fontenay, the first daughters of the most prolific Cistercian line, which included about 360 daughters and granddaughters by the end of the Middle Ages. Its founder's prestige was such that, receiving donations from sovereigns and lords, Clairvaux became a real economic power, besides its spiritual and intellectual influence. Its library collection, now at the Troyes library, with its 1,400 manuscripts remains one of the biggest French medieval collections. During the 14th century, the abbey had 25,000 hectares of lands, 41 granges and 43 mills. The monks exploited forests, arable lands and vineyards, as well as rearing animals, particularly sheep. They had salt mines in the Jura, owned other mines and forges and were the master ironsmiths in Champagne. In 1135, during Bernard's lifetime, the construction of a larger abbey, Clairvaux II, was undertaken. Located on the site of the present monastery, it had an abbey church with a flat chevet. After Bernard's death in 1153, it was given a choir with an ambulatory with radiating chapels containing the relics of Saint Bernard, canonized in 1174. Clairvaux II, where 800 monks and lay brothers were living in 1153, was partly destroyed during the Hundred Years War, then again during the Wars of Religion. In the 17th century, it became one of the principal abbeys of the Strict Observance, under Dom Denis Largentier (†1624). It was rebuilt starting in 1708 although Clairvaux III retained only the abbey church and the lay brothers' buildings from the medieval period. Sold as a state property in 1792, the abbey contained a paper-works and then a glass-works. Bought by the State in 1808, it was transformed into a prison and lost its abbey church. Clairvaux held famous prisoners: Claude Gueux who inspired Victor Hugo's Jean Valjean, Blanqui, or Maurras. It still belongs to the Ministry of Justice, but the present abbey contains only the penitentiary's administration, the prison itself was built in 1971 away from the monastic buildings.

Entering the monastic area through the Southern Gate, on the left the visitor discovers the 16th century Ladies' Hostelry, the gardens and buildings of Petit Clairvaux. The abbey is on the right, in Haut Clairvaux. The gateway has two wings at right angles, the southern wing containing the abbey's dwellings. The gateway also provides access to the main courtyard, lined with stables, at the end of which the church used to stand. To the south of this courtyard, a passage opposite the hostelry leads to the lay brothers' building. The only remnant of Clairvaux II, the ground floor of this rectangular building held the friars' storeroom and refectory; on the second floor, the dormitory lay below the beautiful groined vaults of white stone. The professed monks lived further to the east, around the great cloister.

The *Vera effigies* of St Bernard

Clairvaux's Furnishings

In 1808, Clairvaux Abbey became a workhouse and a prison. The latter operated starting only in 1814. As for the workhouse, it opened in 1809 and was closed in 1816. Men and women from the entire Aube department were lodged in the monastery's hostelry, workshops were set up in the stables, where looms were later manufactured using the wood from the abbey church's roof beams, the remarkable remains of Clairvaux II, probably destroyed in 1810. Although not a single stone remains of this church, its furnishings have been scattered: its high altar is in St Peter's Church in Bar sur Aube; part of its treasure, as well as two reredos and two 17th century portraits are in the parish church of Ville sous la Ferté; Troyes Cathedral contains the great 18th century organ, its stalls, the reliquary containing Saint Bernard's head, as well as several portraits including the *Vera effigies* of Saint Bernard, from the 16th century.

The cloister

Fontenay

Blazon

In 1119, three years after the foundation of Trois Fontaines, Clairvaux's first daughter, Bernard sent a second group of monks, under the direction of his cousin Godefroy de la Roche Vanneau, the prior of Clairvaux, to a place located not far from Montbard, now the Côte d'Or department. The monks raised their first buildings in the heart of a small valley, on the site of a hermitage of two brothers, Martin and Milon, near a spring and a pond. In 1130, the community having become too big, it moved to a lower, but damp and swampy, location provided by Raynard de Montbard, Bernard's maternal uncle. A lot of work draining, stabilizing and clearing the ground had to be done before construction of the new abbey could start. It was called Fontenay, from the Latin *Fontenaium* "that swims in fountains". For his brothers in Fontenay, Bernard wrote his first great work, *De Gradibus humilitatis et superbiae*. In 1139, Ebrard of

Abbey milestone

World Heritage

Since 1981, Fontenay Abbey has been listed as a Unesco World Heritage Site. The natural surroundings of the abbey, the valley and forested range, were named a "protected site" by the French Ministry of the Environment in 1989.

The fountain

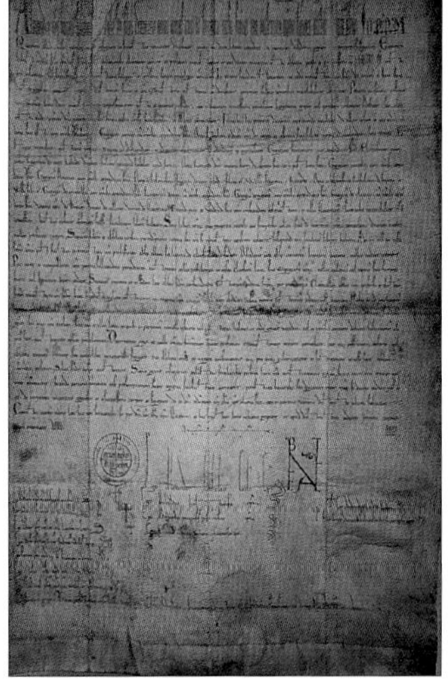

Papal bull of Alexander III

Cistercian Chants

When Saint Bernard specified in his Rule the prayers that were to be chanted at each Hour, among the psalms, antiphons and responses, he mentioned the Ambrosian hymns. These were chanted poems introduced into the liturgy of his church in the 4th century by Ambrose, Bishop of Milan. In the 6th century, Pope Gregory 1st codified and standardized the use of the texts chanted during holy offices, giving them the name of "Gregorian Chants". In a desire to return to the strict observance of the Rule, Stephen Harding sent monks to Milan, to recopy the chants attributed to Ambrose, and to Metz – places he considered as the authentic, because the most ancient, sources of Gregorian chants. But the use of these old forms was not accepted and the General Chapter entrusted the abbot of Clairvaux with making corrections. With the help of the abbot of Cherlieu and the monk Gui d'Eu, between 1141 and 1147 Bernard composed the *Treaty of the Chant*, in accordance with 12th century usage, to be followed in all the Order's abbeys. Bernard wrote, "I would like the melody to be above all serene, that it avoid feebleness as much as rusticity; through its sweetness it should please the ears in such a way that it may touch the heart, dispel sadness, and calm anger."

Arundel, Bishop of Norwich, a victim of royal persecution, found refuge in Fontenay and offered his fortune to build a monastery. At his death in 1149, he was buried according to his wishes in Fontenay abbey church, which had been solemnly consecrated in 1147 by Pope Eugene III. During the 12th and 13th centuries, provided with gifts, protected by popes and kings, Fontenay in its turn founded new abbeys, such as Les Écharlis, in the diocese of Sens, in 1131; Sept Fons, in the diocese of Autun, in 1132; or Chézery, in Savoy Bugey, in 1140. However, in 1359, during the Hundred Years War, the abbey was captured and sacked by the English, who left the place only after receiving a large ransom. Subsequently, the hordes of the Grandes Companies arrived and it was in vain that Abbot Nicolas (1378-1415) fortified the abbey to protect it from looting and exactions. In a final spurt of prosperity before the troubles of the Wars of Religion, the abbacy of Jean Frouard (1459-1483) returned its strength and fervour to Fontenay. Given into commendam in 1557, the abbey suffered from financial difficulties and its buildings were no longer maintained. The refectory, falling into disrepair, was demolished in the 18th century. The monks had to flee during the French Revolution. The property and the monastic buildings were put up for sale and bought by a paper manufacturer, attracted by all the water nearby. Transformed into a paper factory, in 1820 the abbey passed into the hands of the Mongolfier family, which created three other factories in the valley. At the dawn of the 20th century, the industrial operations came to an end. Starting in 1906, the new owners, Édouard and René Aynard, began an exemplary restoration of the site, giving Fontenay the look of its early days.

The church of Fontenay, in the shape of a Latin cross, with a flat chevet, is striking because of the extreme simplicity of its architecture and its majestic proportions. The nave, which communicates with the side aisles by large arcades, is covered with pointed barrel vaults whose ribs descend onto capitals decorated with leaves.

Ambrosians at the foot of Our Lady of Fontenay

The abbey church

Four chapels with flat chevets open onto the transept. A statue of the Virgin with Child, dating from the 13th century, stands in the northern arm of the transept. The sanctuary, rather shallow and lower than the nave, contains a reredos of carved stone from the end of the 13th century. Adjoining the church in the south, the cloister has remained intact. Each of its galleries contains eight semi-circular arcades, held up by clustered columns whose capitals are delicately sculpted with floral motifs. The tympana contain oculi in some places. The western gallery has groined vaulting, the others have Gothic barrel vaults. Large and bright, the chapter house, opening onto the eastern gallery of the cloister through a large doorway framed by two gemel openings, is vaulted on intersecting ribs like the monks' room, which is more austere and located beyond the parlour and the passage leading to the garden. Upstairs, the dormitory, partially rebuilt in the 15th century, has fine 16th century beams of chestnut wood. The southern gallery contains the warming-room, the monastery's only heated room. Its two tholos chimneys, from the 12th century,

The forge

Exploiting Iron

In their mine on the plateau of Munières, the monks of Fontenay extracted iron ore that they treated in their great forge (*opposite*), producing ploughshares and hoes, but also swords, daggers and glaives.

The abbey

A cloister capital

still stand on the roof. The western wing contained the buildings of the lay brothers. Inside the enclosure were the various buildings and workshops needed for a self-sufficient life. To the east, in the garden grew medicinal plants used in the infirmary. To the south, the mill run fed the fishpond and the monastery, as well as supplying power for the mills and the grand forge. To the north, beside the visitors' chapel, today containing a museum, a bakery produced bread. Welcomed at the gate, visitors stayed in the hostelry, to the right of the entrance. The abbey even had a prison, the *enfermerie,* built in the 16th century, in which monks guilty of serious sins were imprisoned, as well as occupants of the abbey's properties who were guilty of crimes or theft and over whom the abbot of Fontenay exercised justice.

THE ORGANIZATION OF SPACE IN AN ABBEY

"The Oratory will be what its name indicates. One will do nothing, nor put anything there that does not match its purpose."
The Rule of Saint Benedict

Cistercian monasteries, of which Fontenay Abbey is a nearly complete example, all adopted the same layout, in order to allow the monks to live in perfect harmony with Saint Benedict's Rule. The main entrance of the abbey was

The dormitory (e+)

through the gateway, set at the edge of the monastic enclosure and guarded by a friar. Next to the gate, the hostelry was intended to welcome guests. The regular buildings were set around the cloister (a). This inner courtyard, usually square in shape, open to the sky, appeared as a symbol of heavenly Jerusalem. A place of meditation and worship, talking was forbidden there. All around ran the cloister's galleries. The church (b) or oratory occupied either the southern or northern wing. It was in the gallery beside the church that, at the end of the day, the *Collatio* or communal reading preceding Compline took place, and on Saturdays, the ceremony of washing the feet. Inside the abbey church, the stalls of the professed monks were set up on either side of the chancel, with the infirm taking their place in the rear choir. As for the lay brothers, they entered the church through a different doorway than the monks, which gave onto the courtyard parallel to the cloister's western gallery. Their stalls were placed along the bottom of the nave and separated from the rear choir by a partition-wall. The cloister's eastern gallery, parallel to one of the arms of the transept, served the monks' wing. The ground floor contained, after the library, also called the *armarium* where books were kept, the chapter house or council room (c), square or rectangular, generally with three openings to the east and

Cloister capitals and columns (a)

opening onto the gallery through a doorway framed by openings. The friars met there every morning, after Terce in winter or after the chants of Prime in the summer, at the moment that it was

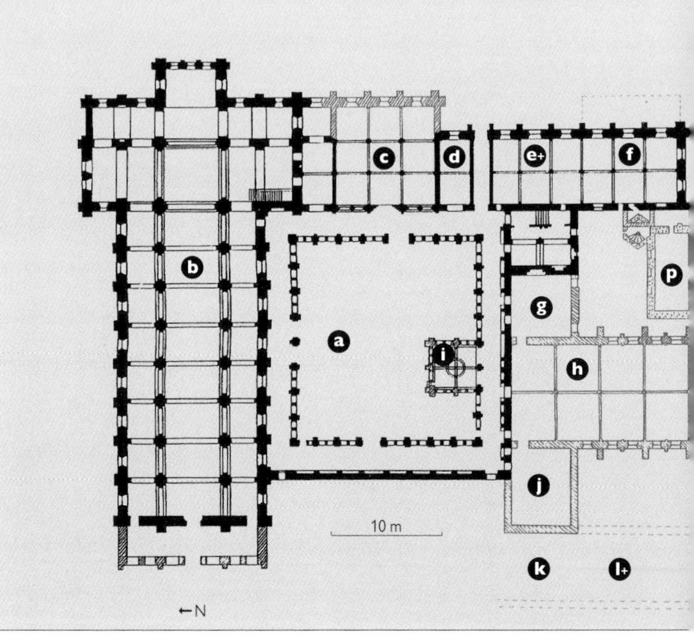

Plan of Fontenay Abbey

rightest. Meetings always started by reading and commentary of a chapter f the Rule, hence providing the room chapter house – with its name. Then, ach monk confessed his sins and his pses or failings. The lay brothers and ovices, who did not participate in the neeting, could nonetheless hear the bbot's sermons from behind the openngs framing the doorway. Next lay the arlour or auditorium (d) where oral ommunication took place. Beyond the tairs leading to the dormitory (e+), there was a large room originally used for the oviciate or as a work room (f). Upstairs, ne common dormitory took up the ntire length of the east wing. Stairs leadng directly to the transept of the abbey hurch allowed the friars to reach night Offices without being late. Overhanging ne canal that provided the abbey with water, the latrines occupied the far end f the building. The heating room (g)

Monks' room (f)

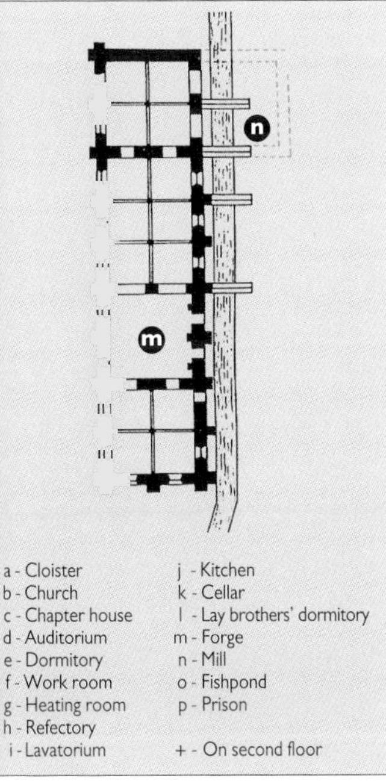

opened onto the gallery opposite the church. It was the only warm room in the monastery and here ink and wax, as well as polish for shoes, were maintained in a liquid state. Speaking and reading were forbidden here. The refectory (h) was located opposite the lavatorium (i) where monks washed before meals. The tables were set in a U-shape along the walls and the monks sat in order of seniority, with the prior and the eldest monks taking their place at the head. The refectory generally contained a water supply. The week's reader climbed up to the pulpit by a hidden staircase set in the thickness of the wall. The friars ate in silence, listening to the holy readings. The refectory communicated with the kitchen (j) through a serving hatch. The cloister's western wing, reserved for the lay brothers, was separated from the inner courtyard and the monastic buildings by a wall, behind which lay a rectangular courtyard called the lay brothers' walk. The cellar (k), opening onto the outside and near the kitchen, extended parallel to the courtyard. The refectory and the lay brothers' dormitory (l+) were located in its extension. The monastic enclosure thus contained all the buildings necessary for economic life like the mill, the bakery, the stables, the hayloft, and various workshops. As for the infirm monks, they lived separately near the cloister.

Abbey church nave (b)

Abbey church choir

The ambulatory

Ourscamp

In 1129, at the request of the bishop of Noyon, Simon de Vermandois, monks from Clairvaux led by Waleran de Baudemont settled at Ourscamp, on the left bank of the Oise River, where a monastery of regular canons already stood. The new abbey, which rapidly possessed several granges, spread to Beaupré in 1135 and to Froidmont in 1140. In 1137, it took over the supervision of the abbey of Mortemer in the Eure. The first Ourscamp abbey church, consecrated in 1134, soon became too small. Starting in 1154, the monks built a second one, communicating with the first through the north end of its transept. Raised thanks to the donations of Ode de Roye, this huge abbey church, 102 metres long and vaulted on intersecting ribs, was consecrated by the bishop of Noyon in 1201. In 1254, its flat chevet was replaced by an apse with an ambulatory and radiating chapels. Ourscamp was badly damaged during the Jacquerie, the peasant insurrection of 1358. The abbey was looted, partly burnt and several monks were killed. But the community tried to recover from this disaster as well as it could. In 1490, the abbey received the relics of Saint Anne – today kept at Chiry – brought from Hungary after the defeat at Nicopolis, by Matthieu du Plessys de Roye, a descendant of Ode de Roye. Placed into commendam under Francis 1st (1515-1547), Ourscamp was highly profitable. In 1677, its commendatory abbot, Prince Louis of Lorraine, had the conventual buildings rebuilt to the south of the church. In 1745, a Doric colonnade was put up to hide the façade of the medieval abbey, and three years later Cardinal de Gesvres, the commendatory abbot, had the abbey dwellings rebuilt to the north. At the Revolution, the abbey was used as a military hospital (1792-1797). Sold to private investors, it was transformed into a country villa and its two churches were demolished. The owner

Bear on pediment of the abbey church façade

The Bear's Field

According to tradition, in 641 Saint Eloi, the bishop of Noyon, laid the first stone of Ourscamp Oratory, set in the valley of the Oise River where he liked to retire to, and where Cistercians installed an abbey nearly five centuries later. There are several hypotheses about the origin of the name Ourscamp. Perhaps the site was occupied during the Gallo-Roman period by a certain Ursus. It would then have taken the name of *Ursi campi* (the bear's field) and become Ourscamp. But there is also a beautiful legend to account for the name. At the time that Eloi was building his isolated oratory in the Oise valley, the ox hauling the stones intended for the chapel's construction was attacked by a bear coming out of the woods. The ferocious animal was about to devour his prey when Eloi arrived and tamed it with a few words. He attached the bear in place of the dead ox, and kept it yoked up until the chapel was completed. Hence the name of "the bear's field". The abbey's coat of arms, "azure seme with gold lilies with two crosses addorsed the same way, to the sable bear passant its mouth muzzled ", is a reminder of this old story.

The chevet

kept the ruins only for their romantic appearance. Starting in 1810, Ourscamp passed to successive industrialists who installed their factories there. Occupied by the Germans in 1914, the former abbey was bombarded in February 1915 by French artillery. It has now been restored to its religious vocation by the Apostolic Congregation of the Servants of Jesus and Mary, which has occupied the monastery since 1941.

The visitor enters Ourscamp through the former hostelry. The great courtyard's central walk leads to the "classical façade". The Gesvres wing to the north holds lodgings for the monks; the Lorraine wing to the south was not restored after 1915. In the centre, a two-storey pavilion topped with a pediment, and whose entrance is framed by four columns, provides access to the church, of which ruins of the choir and transept remain. South-west of the nave, the coping of a well shows where the cloister used to be. At some distance to the east, the former infirmary from the 13th century, also called the Hall of the Dead, has been transformed into a chapel. With its three naves, well-lighted and vaulted on intersecting ribs, it contains a fine marble reredos framing a painting by Gaspard de Crayer – *Mary, Mother of Citeaux* (1640).

The infirmary

SIC TRANSEUNT

Built in about 1220 to the east of the abbey church, Ourscamp infirmary is positioned north-south, and measures 46 metres in length and 16 in width. On its south side, it was extended by an annex opening onto a garden. The ground floor of this annex contained the apothecary and the "fat kitchen", so called because the dishes prepared there were for the ill and could contain meat. Rooms for convalescing patients were located upstairs. Today converted into a chapel, the infirmary, vaulted on intersecting ribs, consists of a large hall divided into three naves by two lines of eight columns. It was well illuminated by the six openings – three small windows topped by two twin openings above them, those in turn surmounted by a rose window – along each of the walls at the level of the building's nine bays. According to Viollet le Duc, this room could contain over a hundred beds, with a row of 27 beds in each side aisle, and with two rows in the wider, central aisle. This number seems rather high. It is more likely that the infirmary, used solely by the community, never contained more than about thirty beds. At its north end, the great hall contained an altar that allowed the patients to attend holy offices without leaving their beds. In the south wall, a large fireplace provided heat. Finally, in the middle of the central nave, there stood a stone base on which monks' bodies were placed just after their death, according to Cistercian custom. No longer there today, this base gave the Ourscamp infirmary its name of "hall of the dead". The funeral rites used by the Cistercians are known thanks to monastic customaries. When the hour of death approached, the monk, after confessing and receiving absolution and extreme unction, was placed on the ground on a bed of ashes covered with a hair shirt, where he died in the presence of the entire community, called to the infirmary by the sound of a wooden tablet. Once the death had been confirmed and the deceased's eyes closed, his body was placed on the above-mentioned stone base, sprinkled with holy water, incensed, then washed and dressed in clean clothes. In the south-west corner of Ourscamp infirmary stands a basin that was probably used for these final ablutions. The deceased's arms were crossed in front of him, and his body was carried into the abbey church's chancel for the funeral, which had to take place no more than 24 hours after the death. This deadline was extended by several days in the case of abbots. After the mass, the whole community walked to the cemetery in a procession. The monk's body without the coffin was lowered into a common grave, with his feet facing east. In accordance with their poor and humble way of life, the first Cistercian abbots were also buried in common graves. Their bodies were placed inside a leather bag, with no insignia of their rank, and placed in the ground. At Clairvaux and Citeaux, the abbey grave was located in a recess, giving onto the cloister, made in the outside wall of the transept near the doorway leading to the church. In the 12th century, exceptions were made to the rule. Bernard of Clairvaux himself was buried in his abbey church, according to his wishes. Starting in 1180, new statutes permitted the abbey's tombs to be placed in the chapter house, following the practice of the Benedictines, and perhaps also already done in the Cistercian Order before that date. Hence, Cistercian abbots at the end of the 12th century were buried in the chapter house, under paving stones decorated only with an engraved cross, mentioning their name and date of their death. While facilitating religious devotion, this practice gave a new dimension to chapter meetings, which appeared to have the backing of the deceased. According to the original Rule of Citeaux, which forbade monks' profiting from burial revenues, only strangers to the Order dying within the Cistercian abbey could be buried there, as well as two laymen, at most, chosen among the monastery's friends. But these limits soon disappeared. The 1152 General Chapter allowed the burial of kings, queens and bishops in abbey churches, and soon the chancel of Ourscamp abbey church became the burial place of the bishops of Noyon. Then in 1157, the Orders' abbeys were authorized to contain the graves of their founders, most often placed inside the churches or in the chapter house. After those of the founders, ordinary benefactors' graves were soon admitted inside the abbeys, so that by the second half of the 13th century, the abbey's tombs had to be removed from the chapter house – already full of laymen – and be placed inside the church. Abbots were still buried without insignia, but in coffins and in sarcophagi. Starting in the 14th century, their tombstones carried epitaphs and were decorated with figurative portrayals.

South side of abbey church

The heating room

Monks' room

LONGPONT

In 1132, at the initiative of Bishop Joscelin de Vierzy of Soissons, monks coming from Clairvaux settled several leagues south of Soissons, in a marshy valley at the edge of the forest of Retz. The Roman road "in the shape of a long bridge" (*long pont*) that crossed the valley gave its name to the new abbey. In 1143, Longpont benefited from the generosity of Count Raoul de Vermandois, who paid for the construction of the monastery to atone for his sins. In 1184, Jean de Montmirail, Constable of France and a loyal servant of Philip Augustus, entered Longpont with several of his knights. His reputation for sanctity had spread far and wide; formerly avid for glory, devoted to war, he had converted and transformed his castle of Montmirail into a hostel for pilgrims, travellers and the sick whom he cared for himself. After his death in Longpont in 1217, wearing the Cistercian habit, many miracles happened on his tomb, contributing to the abbey's renown. Longpont's new abbey church, its size worthy of a cathedral, was consecrated in 1227 in the presence of the young King Saint Louis, then aged thirteen. Damaged during the Hundred Years War (1337-1475), the abbey was given in commendam during the first half of the 16th century, before undergoing new destruction during the Wars of Religion (1562-1598). During the 17th and 18th centuries, abbots had part of the monastic buildings rebuilt, but a great fire in 1724 destroyed two-thirds of the monastery, subsequently restored in 18th century style. At the time of the Revolution, the last monks left the abbey in 1793 and it was then sold at auction. Used as a stone quarry, the church was reduced to ruins until the Montesquiou family, who had bought the monastic buildings in 1804, bought the church in 1831 and thus put an end to its dismantling. The abbey suffered during the First World War but today the Montesquiou family continues to maintain and preserve it.

Consecrated in 1227, the abbey church, whose façade gives onto the village square, is the same size as Soissons cathedral, with its 105 metre length and its 35 metres of height under the vaulting, which has a triple elevation: arcades, triforium, and high windows. Built according to the Gothic model, it had a nave with side aisles, a vast transept and a chevet with an ambulatory and radiating chapels. The present ruins allow the visitor to imagine it easily. The huge rose window in its façade, gaping open today, is topped with a gable 40 metres up, pierced with openings and oculi. The southern end of the church has only the southern gallery remnants of the cloister, with its basket-handle vault from the 18th century. The southern wing of the monastic buildings, rearranged during the 18th century, has kept its warming room from the beginning of the 13th century, with its large square chimney that provided heat to the room above, reserved for copyists. The west wing contained the lay brothers' building, and was transformed into an abbey palace in the 18th century. It has retained its 13th century cellar, vaulted on intersecting ribs, a part of which has contained the village of Longpont's parish church since 1801.

North aisle

The choir

ORVAL

The abbey of Orval was founded in 1070 in the dense Ardennes forest, in what is now Belgian Luxembourg, by Benedictine monks from Calabria. Called back to Italy at the beginning of the 12th century, they were replaced by regular canons. Because of economic difficulties, these canons soon requested to join Citeaux and, in March 1132, monks from the Champagne abbey of Trois Fontaines, Clairvaux's first daughter, arrived in Orval. The beginnings were difficult and a fire in 1251 only aggravated conditions. To remedy the situation, in 1316 the General Chapter decided to give the abbot of Trois Fontaines full powers. Orval was brought back on an even keel. However, during the 14th and 15th centuries, the commendam system and the wars between France and Burgundy, then between France and Spain, once more troubled community life. Remarkable abbots like Bernard of Montgaillard tried, nonetheless, to re-establish the Rule's discipline. But in 1637, at the height of the Thirty Years War, Orval was looted and burned. Abbot Charles of Bentzeradt (1668-1707) managed to rebuild the patrimony of the abbey, which he reformed under the inspiration of Rancé's work at La Trappe. Starting in 1760, the community in Orval recovered its former vigour and started to build a new, larger monastery. A new church was consecrated in 1782. However, revolutionaries burned the abbey in 1793 and scattered the community. In 1926, the de Harenne family offered the abbey ruins to the Cistercian Order and monastic life was reborn in Orval. The abbey was repopulated by monks from Sept Fons under the direction of a Trappist monk, Dom Marie Albert. A new monastery was rebuilt on the ruins of that from the 18th century, according to plans by the architect Henry Vaes. In 1936, Orval became autonomous and Dom Marie Albert was elected abbot. Reconstruction of the new abbey ended in 1948.

A capital

MATILDA'S FOUNTAIN

Legend has it that Countess Matilda of Tuscany, who owned the castle where Pope Gregory VII received a contrite Henry IV in 1077, one day accidentally dropped her wedding ring in a fountain in this Ardennes valley. She began to pray to God and a trout broke through the water's surface with the precious ring in its mouth. Dazed by this miracle, Matilda exclaimed, "Really, this is a valley of gold here!" and to show her thanks to the Lord, she decided to found a monastery in the place of the fountain.

The cloister

Rose window

Abbey church apse

Rievaulx

Cloister arcades

Located in North Yorkshire, near Helmsley, in the valley of the Rye, the river that gave its name to the abbey, Rievaulx was founded in 1132, the same day as Longpont. It was set on lands given by the lord Walter l'Espec, with the approval of King Henry II and under the patronage of the Archbishop of York, Thurstan. The archbishop had addressed Bernard of Clairvaux, who sent a group of monks to settle at the new site. The first abbot was an English monk, William, Bernard's secretary, but also a master of chants and novice master in Clairvaux. The abbey of Rievaulx, the oldest Cistercian abbey in Yorkshire, was one of the most powerful and most dynamic abbeys in England, so much so that within ten years it was at the head of an affiliation of eleven abbeys. In 1145, at the end of William's abbacy, the abbey contained three hundred monks. William was succeeded by Aelred who, although of fragile health, was the author of numerous spiri-

The Northern Saint Bernard

Aelred was born in 1110 in Hexham, Yorkshire. His family, aristocratic and Christian, sent him as a youth to the court of King David of Scotland, the son of Saint Margaret, to complete his education. There he acquired the culture and competence necessary to be a seneschal, that is, the steward of a court. At the age of twenty-four, during an ambassadorship, he met Archbishop Thurstan and decided to enter Rievaulx, where he received an education strongly influenced by Bernard of Clairvaux. Novice master starting in 1140, he took over the direction of the new foundation of Revesby in Lincolnshire in 1142, before becoming abbot of Rievaulx in 1146. A spiritual guide who influenced the Church of England, Aelred appeared to the Cistercians of his time as another Bernard. A prolific author, he was interested in the history of medieval England and wrote numerous spiritual works. In 1141, he composed his first work, the *Mirror of Charity*, soon followed by hagiographic essays on the saints of Northumbria, like the *Life of Saint Ninian*. In 1163, he published his *Sermons on Isaiah*, then his dialogue, *On Spiritual Friendship*, inspired by Cicero but penetrated with Christianity. For the benefit of his sister, he wrote *Life of a Recluse* and, for his friend Yves of Wardon, *When Jesus was Twelve Years Old*, ascetic works that influenced the elaboration of eremitic ideals in the Middle Ages. Aelred died at Rievaulx in 1166, after twenty-two years of abbacy.

Abbot William's tomb

The Cause of our Joy

Aelred wrote in his *Mirror of Charity*, "It is this veritable beauty enjoyed by the saints of heaven that is the object of our meditations and the cause of our joy, they are the spiritual ornaments that the saints possess in justice and sanctity, they are the hymns sung to the glory of God, tirelessly, it is the brightness that they contemplate on the face of God."

Nave aisle

tual and mystic works. The man his contemporaries called "the northern Saint Bernard" ran the abbey for twenty-two years and died in 1166.
Because of its location on severely sloping ground levels, the church had to be built on a north-south axis, and not the traditional east-west axis. Built starting in 1135, the abbey church had a square chevet framed by three chapels in each of its transepts. In 1230, a larger choir, the same width as the nave, replaced the previous one, with an ambulatory at right-angles and five chapels against its end wall. This choir is a prime example of early English Gothic architecture. The bases of the pillars and walls subsist from the nave and side aisles. The cloister's galleries have retained several arcades held up by clustered columns. The chapter house ends with a semi-circular apse and contains the tombs of several abbots, including that of William, Rievaulx's first abbot, who died in 1145.

Heating room

The refectory

Melrose's blazon

Melrose Abbey

Sweetheart Abbey nave

AFFILIATED TO RIEVAULX

In 1136, Melrose, in the diocese of Glasgow, became the first daughter of Rievaulx. The abbey had been founded at the beginning of the 7th century by the Irish monk Columba. When Cuthbert became its prior in 664, he introduced the Rule of Saint Benedict. In 1136 Rievaulx diffused to Wardon, in 1142 to Revesby where Aelred was the abbot for four years, and to Dundrennan which, in 1273, founded the abbey of Sweetheart.

Wine-press

Eberbach

Chapter house window

In 1135, a group of monks from Clairvaux settled in a monastery of regular canons, created in 1116 by Albert 1st, the Count of Saarbrück and Archbishop of Mainz, and united with the Benedictine abbey of Johannisberg in 1131. The abbey, Clairvaux's first daughter outside France, is located on the northern slope of the Rheingau, among the Taurus hills in the valley of Kisselbach. Eberbach developed under the impetus of the Cistercians. Its properties increased thanks to donations and, between the 12th and 13th centuries, it contained between two and three hundred monks. Coming from Burgundy, a land of vineyards, the Cistercians produced wine which became the abbey's principal resource. Transported on the Rhine River with their own boats, their wine was sold in cellars that they owned in Cologne, Frankfurt and Mainz. The monks also manufactured cloth and leather goods, as well as selling the products of their mills. In 1159, when Frederick Barbarossa supported the anti-Pope Victor IV, the monks of Eberbach took the side of the legitimate pope, Alexander III, despite the emperor's persecutions. Starting in the 13th century, community life was troubled by lay brothers' revolts. The abbot of Clairvaux in person had to intervene, but without really managing to re-establish the situation since, several years later, the abbot of Eberbach was murdered by one of the lay brothers. At the end of the 15th century, a lack of manpower led abbots to employ ever more lay workers and eventually to lease the abbey's lands. During the Peasants' War (1524-1525) the threatened abbey had to consent to the secularization of its goods. During the Thirty Years War (1618-1648), in the course of his victorious campaign in Germany (1630-1631) the Protestant King of Sweden, Gustavus Adolphus, offered the abbey to his chancellor Oxenstierna. The monks then took refuge in their house in Cologne. Most of the library, art works and monastery supplies disappeared, while a large number of its operations were destroyed. When the monks returned, their abbey was completely ruined. Eberbach attempted to recover over the course of the 18th century and great renovation works were undertaken in the period's Baroque style. In 1802, Eberbach was secularized. The princely House of Nassau obtained the abbey as compensation and the last monks were scattered. The Nassau continued the wine-producing operations of the properties without causing too much damage to the monastic buildings. The property was used variously over time: successively the ducal domaine of the Nassau, then a Prussian domaine in 1866, from 1813 to 1912 the abbey contained a penitentiary, then

Saint Bernard

Conrad *Exordium Magnum*

A monk in Clairvaux before entering Eberbach and becoming its abbot from 1213 to 1226, at the end of the 12th century Conrad wrote the first four books of the six that compose the *Great Exordium of Citeaux*. This text, much longer than the *Short Exordium* written by Stephen Harding, recounts the origins of the Order and the early days of Clairvaux and its affiliation. In this work, sometimes called the "*Fioretti* of the Cistercian Order", Conrad sharply reproached Robert for abandoning the *Novum Monasterium* to return to Molesme in 1098.

Abbey church nave

The abbey

Masculine-Feminine

In his *Dialogue of Miracles*, Cesarius of Heisterbach tells the story of Brother José, a novice at the abbey of Schönau, a daughter of Eberbach. During the final ablutions, the body of this friar deceased in 1188 turned out to be that of a young woman whose condition had not been noticed when she entered the abbey.

Stained-glass window

an asylum for the insane, before becoming a military convalescent hospital between 1913 and 1918. In 1926, restoration work was begun to give Eberbach its medieval appearance once again. When Hesse was created in 1946, the administration of national vineyards took charge of operating the abbey's former wine-producing properties. Auction sales of wine take place nowadays in the lay brothers' dormitory and concerts are organized within the monastery precincts.

A hundred-metre long wall, built during the 12th century, protects the abbey's buildings. Although the outside of the church was modified in the 18th century, an example being the wooden steeple with a Baroque dome rising above the transept crossing, the interior has retained the Romanesque purity and austerity of its beginnings. Started in 1145, the construction of the abbey was interrupted in 1160 when troubles caused by the election of the anti-pope Victor IV led the abbot to take refuge in Rome. Work began again in 1170 and was completed in 1186. Facing east, in the shape of a Latin cross, the church consists of a long nave covered with groined arches, which communicates with side aisles through arcades with semi-circular arches. During the 14th century, six chapels were added in the south aisle which then received a vault on intersecting ribs. Six chapels open onto the wide transept. The sanctuary, with its flat chevet, is lit by five windows. At the end of the northern arm of the transept, a staircase leads to the monks' dormitory, in early Gothic style, built during the second half of the

13th century. This room, measuring seventy-three metres in length, takes up the entire upper storey of the cloister's eastern wing. A row of columns with decorated capitals supports the diagonal ribs of its vaulting. The ground floor contains the chapter house, covered with starred vaulting, whose ribs rest on a central pillar. The room opens onto the courtyard through a doorway framed by openings that are among the rare remnants of the Romanesque cloister of 1186. The present cloister was rebuilt during the 13th and 14th centuries, during the Gothic period. Only the western and northern galleries survived the demolition of the 19th century and retained their clerestory. The north wing, which contained the refectory, the kitchen and the warming room, was entirely rebuilt at the beginning of the 18th century. In the western gallery, a staircase tower provides access to the former library, arranged in half-timbering, today containing the abbey's museum. The lay brothers' buildings, separated from those of the regular clergy by a courtyard, extend behind the western wing of the cloister. Presses of Cistercian origin, the oldest of which dates from 1668, are stored in the former refectory. Upstairs lies the dormitory, ninety-three metres long, in which wine auctions are held nowadays. To the east of the regular clergy buildings, on the location of the former monastery of regular canons from 1116, an infirmary was built in 1220 by the monks. Its exterior has retained its Romanesque appearance. Inside, the groined arches rest on tall columns decorated with fine capitals.

Bebenhausen cloister

DAUGHTERS OF EBERBACH

In 1145, Eberbach founded Schönau which in 1190 repopulated Bebenhausen (*above*), founded in 1183 by the Palatine Count Rudolph 1st of Tübingen. About 1174, its monks replaced the Benedictines of Arnsburg (*below*).

Arnsburg chapter house

Ruins of the tower and abbey church

Fountains

In 1132, tension arose within the Benedictine community in Saint Mary's Abbey in York. Against the advice of their abbot, several of the monastery's monks, with their prior Richard at their head, wished to return to the strict observance of Saint Benedict's Rule, in all its authenticity. Accusing of wanting to make trouble, the thirteen dissidents were forced to leave the abbey. The archbishop of York granted them land near Ripon, in Skeldale. The little community, without an Order and without an abbey, armed only with its members' ideals, sheltered during the winter of 1133-1134 under an elm tree and built themselves a few rudimentary buildings. The monks chose Richard as their abbot before turning to Bernard of Clairvaux who sent one of his monks, Geoffroy d'Aignay, to teach them the customs of the Order. The construction of the great abbey of Fountains, directed by Geoffroy, an architect, was then undertaken. In 1135, Fountains became Cistercian as a daughter of Clairvaux. Thanks to the generosity of neighbouring lords, the abbey soon owned the town of Harleshows with some adjoining lands, the village of Caiton and the grange of Aldeburgh. The monks cleverly took advantage of these gifts and by 1139 Fountains was able to diffuse. Its affiliated abbeys, established as far away as Norway, numbered fourteen. Many of Fountains' abbots were known for their holiness, like John Grenewell, whose abbacy lasted twenty-seven years and who, in the middle of the 15th century, was charged with reforming the monasteries of England, along with the abbots of Wardon, Coggeshal and Furness. However, when King Henry VIII (1509-1547) had the Act of Supremacy voted by Parliament in 1534, designating him Head of the Church of England, the days of Fountains were numbered. Indeed, the king soon had convents and monasteries closed and their possessions seized. Rebellious monks were punished severely – with either death or expulsion. In 1539, the king offered Fountains Abbey to Sir Richard Gresham. Over the course of the years, the deserted buildings fell into disrepair and during the 18th century their stones were used to build the manor house Fountains Hall to the west of the monastery.

Construction of the church began in 1135 under the direction of Geoffroy d'Aignay. In the form of a Latin cross, originally it consisted of a nave with side aisles, a transept onto which six chapels opened and a small sanctuary with a flat chevet. The western façade contained a doorway decorated with voussoirs, topped with a large opening whose tracery has disappeared. The nave, originally covered with a barrel vault, communicates with the side aisles through large, slightly Gothic arcades, supported by imposing cylindrical pillars and topped with a row of semi-circular windows. Under the abbacy of John of York at the beginning of the 13th century, work was started on the abbey, which had become too small for the community. The previous chevet was replaced by a nave with five bays with side aisles, ending with a second transept at the end of which stood nine altars. The whole was entirely vaulted on intersecting

Guest house

A Much Requested Abbot

Ever since Bernard of Clairvaux, the papacy was used to entrusting Cistercians with a certain number of missions. William, the abbot of Fountains, had to carry out so many at the request of Lucius III that his monks complained to the pope. In a letter in 1185, the pope reassured them by promising not to call on their abbot again except in a case of extreme necessity.**

South aisle and nave

ribs and was called the Chapel of the Nine Altars, bringing the total number of altars in the church to twenty-seven. In 1483, the three openings in the chevet wall were replaced by a single large opening. The high, four-storey tower, with numerous openings, rising to a height of over fifty metres at the end of the north transept, was built during the abbacy of Marmaduke Huby (1494-1526). Fountains cloister, at the south of the church, burned during the 12th century, and was entirely demolished by the abbey's owner in the 18th century to make room for a vegetable garden. In the cloister's eastern gallery, three doors open onto the chapter house. The bases of the three rows of columns that divided the room into three bays are still standing. Along the walls stand rows of stone seats on which the monks used to sit. The first opening in the south gallery provides access to a staircase leading to the dormitory. Next was the warming room, vaulted with intersecting ribs, that has retained two large hearths, one of which is walled off. A doorway similar to those in the chapter house opens onto the refectory – a room thirty-five metres long and fifteen metres wide, divided into two bays. The stairs that lead to the pulpit are still there and at their bottom stands the *armarium* in which the abbey's books were kept, under the supervision of the cantor. On either side of the doorway, the monks' lavatorium, topped with arcades, was arranged within the thickness of the wall. The kitchen with its two hearths came next. The lay brothers' building, of which only the ground floor remains but whose unity is admirable, abuts the western gallery of the cloister.

Chapel of Nine Altars

CHAPEL OF THE NINE ALTARS

In the course of the 13th century, many Cistercian churches were equipped with supplementary altars, like those of the Chapel with the Nine Altars in Fountains (*below*), to allow the monks who were ordained as priests to celebrate their daily masses.

Lay brothers' refectory

THE SUPREME HEAD OF THE CHURCH OF ENGLAND

The son of Henry VII, the first Tudor sovereign, Henry VIII acceded to the throne in 1509, at the age of eighteen. A humanist king, Henry was the friend of Erasmus and Thomas More and, as a fervent Catholic, he published the *Asserio septem sacramentorum* denouncing Luther, leading Pope Leon X to give him the title "Defender of the Faith" in 1521. However, starting in 1526, his attitude towards the Holy See changed considerably. His marriage to Catherine of Aragon, his brother's widow, was a failure; of the royal couple's six children, only Mary, born in 1509, survived. Furthermore, he was in love with one of the queen's maids of honour, Anne Boleyn, who Henry believed would be able to provide him with the male heir he so desired. In 1526, he asked Pope Clement VII to annul his marriage. But the pope, fearing the animosity of Holy Roman Emperor Charles V, Catherine of Aragon's nephew, hesitated. After waiting six years, Henry VIII broke with the papacy and proclaimed himself Head of the Church of England. He had the Archbishop of Canterbury annul his marriage and married Anne Boleyn in 1533. The Holy See immediately responded by excommunicating the king. Henry VIII then had Parliament vote the Act of Supremacy in 1534, by which he was raised to be Supreme Head of the Church of England. To establish his authority, Henry VIII had his subjects take an oath of fidelity and did not hesitate to punish those who refused, like his Chancellor Thomas More, who was executed in 1535. In 1536, on the advice of some of his councillors who had adopted Protestantism, Henry dissolved the small monasteries, then all the others in 1539. Their often considerable riches were secularized. The most powerful abbeys were reserved for the royal domain, the others were sold or transformed into colleges. From October to November, 1536, an enormous revolt against the action took place; the "pilgrimage of grace", gathering together twenty thousand "pilgrims" against the "king's evil councillors". The insurrection was rapidly put down and the main leaders were executed in 1537. Personally attached to the Catholic faith, Henry was also influenced by his advisor Cranmer, a Lutheran sympathizer who, until his death in 1547, never stopped wavering between the two faiths. As for his married life, Henry's first divorce was only a prelude. After having Anne Boleyn executed, Henry VIII remarried four times – Jane Seymour died after giving birth to the future Edward VI; Anne of Cleves was repudiated; Catherine Howard was executed, and Catherine Parr survived Henry. After Henry's death, England was successively Protestant during the reign of Edward VI, Catholic under Mary Tudor, the daughter of Catherine of Aragon, then once again Protestant under Elizabeth I, the daughter of Anne Boleyn.

Tintern Abbey

Fountains' tower and west façade

Boatmen's grange

Notre Dame d'Aulps

Hautecombe

About 1101, monks from the Benedictine abbey of Aulps in the Chablais settled on Cessens Mountain, between Rumilly and the Rhône River valley, in the hollow of a coomb. The location inspired the monks to name their abbey Hautecombe (high coomb). After Bernard of Clairvaux's visit in 1135, Hautecombe joined the Cistercian Order, affiliated with Clairvaux. With the help of Sibaud of Clermont and Count Amadeus III of Savoy, the community moved to the western shore of Lake Bourget, a more favourable place for monastic life. However, since land access to the monastery was only possible by a long, steep path along the lake, to ease communication with the eastern shore the monks built a boat grange consisting of a large basin to hold the boats, a hangar and a loft. Hautecombe's rise was rapid. The lands it received from its benefactors extended to Savoy, around Geneva and Bugey, in the Lyonnais, the Dauphiné and as far as Tricastin. A veritable "Savoy pantheon", by the 12th century the abbey contained the tombs of the princes and princesses of the House of Savoy. However, Duke Amadeus VIII, as the anti-pope Felix V in 1439, placed it in commendam the following year. In the 18th century, the monastic buildings, suffering from disrepair, threatened to collapse, and the abbey palace did indeed do so in 1718. Reconstruction work was begun but the Revolution arrived. The abbey was ransacked twice before being transformed into an earthenware factory from 1799 to 1804. In 1824, King Charles Felix of Savoy undertook restoration of the abbey church containing the tombs of his ancestors. He then entrusted the abbey to Cistercians from the Consolata of Turin, then in 1864 to the monks of Sénanque. After 1922, Benedictines from Solesmes occupied it until their departure for Ganagobie in 1992. Today, Hautecombe is inhabited by the new religious community called Chemin Neuf (New Way).

The abbey

Guérin, Abbot of Aulps

In 1090, monks from Molesme spread throughout the Chablais, south of Lake Leman, and founded the Abbey of Aulps *(above)*. Among them was Guérin, elected abbot at the beginning of the 12th century. In 1135, Bernard of Clairvaux came to see him and on June 28, 1135, Aulps entered the Clairvaux line of the Cistercian Order. In 1138, aged seventy-three, Guérin became Bishop of Sion, a position he occupied for twelve years before returning to die in Aulps, where his remains are reverently kept in a reliquary *(below)*.

Aulps, Guerin's reliquary

Nave in the abbey church

FOSSANOVA

When Hautecombe became a daughter of Clairvaux in 1135, the Benedictine monks from Santa Pudentiana, about a hundred kilometres south-east of Rome, also wished to join thc Order. Their wish was fulfilled and Hautecombe became their mother abbey. The new Cistercian community immediately set to work and started to drain the water from the Pontine Marshes towards the sea by building a new canal, *fossa nova*, giving its name to the monastery. Reconstruction of the regular buildings and the church, begun in 1163 under the abbacy of Gerard, provided the first appearance of Early Gothic architecture in Italy. When it was completed at the end of the 13th century, Fossanova already had nine monasteries in its affiliation. In 1274, the abbey welcomed Thomas Aquinas, on his way to the Council of Lyons. Tragically, he fell ill and died at the abbey. The room he had occupied in the hostelry was transformed into a chapel during the 17th century. In 1456, the first commendatory abbot, James Lusitano, the nephew of the king of Portugal, arrived in Fossanova. He succeeded Jean Magdale, elected abbot of Fontfroide the same year to replace Pierre Ferrer. The latter had been deposed in 1445, revolted and regained possession of Fontfroide with arms. In 1623, the abbey of Fossanova, containing only six monks, was joined to the Congregation of Saint Bernard. Then in 1795, it was repopulated by monks from Casamari who had adopted the half-hearted reform of Buonsollazzo. Repressed by Napoleon in 1810, Fossanova was bought by Pope Leon XII (1823-1829) who entrusted it to the Carthusians of Trisulti. In 1936, the bishop of Terracino placed it at the disposition of conventual friars who turned it into a college for their monks. Fossanova was restored by the Superintendency of Monuments of Latium and, since 1950 its church, with its beautiful and very high nave characteristic of Cistercian architecture, is a parish church.

Mosaic tympanum over abbey church doorway

Abbey church façade

SAINT THOMAS AQUINAS

Born in 1225 into a noble family in the kingdom of Naples, Thomas was raised at the Benedictine abbey of Monte Cassino. At the age of sixteen, despite his family's opposition, he joined the Dominican Order and continued his studies in Cologne and Paris. Returning to Italy and Naples in 1259, he wrote the *Summa contra Gentiles*. From 1265 to 1268, he taught in Rome and began writing his major work, the *Summa theologica*, a synthesis of traditional thinking of the Fathers of the Church, particularly Saint Augustine, and contemporary demands for rational thinking, marked by the rediscovery of Aristotle. He stayed in Paris again in 1268, returning to Naples in 1272. In 1274, he attended the Council of Lyons, convoked to bring together Roman and Greek Catholicism, but on his way he fell ill and died in Fossanova. His remains were transferred to the Jacobins Church in Toulouse in 1368.

The abbey church

Acey

The abbey of Notre Dame of Acey is located in Franche Comté, not far from Dole, in the valley of the Ognon River. It was founded in 1136 at the instigation of the Archbishop of Besançon, Ansério, by a group of monks from the abbey of Cherlieu, a daughter of Clairvaux. They were joined by a group of hermits from Val Saint Jean who had settled a few kilometres from the new foundation. Great works of clearing and drainage were undertaken, a diversion canal was dug and work started on the abbey. Thanks to favours by the Count of Burgundy, Raynaud III, and work by the community, Acey rapidly prospered. In 1184, it founded an abbey at the foot of Mount Pilis in Hungary, which in turn started three other monasteries. However, because it was located in the Kingdom of Burgundy, a bone of contention between France and the Empire, Acey did not avoid the wars, looting and coalitions which impoverished and disturbed the life of its community from the 15th to the 17th centuries. Furthermore, starting in 1545, the commendatory abbots placed at its head neglected to maintain the buildings to the extent that, in 1650, part of the vault of the church's central nave collapsed. To cap it all, a fire devastated the monastery in 1683. Restoration work was started only in 1763. The nave of the church was closed at the level of the second bay of the chancel, and the monastery was rebuilt. At the Revolution, the monks had to flee and the abbey and its possessions were put up for sale. In 1829, Acey was home to a boarding school for girls. Starting in 1853, Benedictines from Solesmes, then Cistercians from Les Neiges and Les Dombes tried successively to re-inhabit the monastery. It was not until 1873 that Trappists from Aiguebelle Abbey settled in what was to become their mother abbey. In 1880, anti-clerical laws led to the expulsion of the monks but the community re-formed secretly. In 1937, Dom Eugène Court was elected abbot of Acey. During his abbacy the community was reborn and in 1938 Acey was once again entitled an autonomous abbey. The church was restored in 1971 and listed as a historical monument. Today, the Acey community lives according to the Rule and the spirit of the first Cistercians. The monks have installed an electrolysis workshop near their monastery and practice agriculture in the area. Since 1945 they have restored the hostelry and arranged a neighbouring farm to welcome groups of young people.

South of the monastery's façade, dating from the 18th century, the architecture of Acey church represents the purest Cistercian spirit. The vast entrance, forming a kind of narthex, comprises the beginning of the original nave which collapsed in the 17th century. The plain 12th century church, in which the architecture appears in all its austerity and beauty, contains a nave with two bays with side aisles, a large transept onto which four chapels open and a sanctuary with a flat chevet. The church's Romanesque windows are filled with modern stained glass, with neither colour nor images, taking their beauty from the characteristic sobriety of Cistercian art.

South aisle of abbey church

Working with their Hands

The monks of Acey divide their time between common and individual prayer, *lectio divina*, intellectual and manual work. To pay for their subsistence and the maintenance of their monastery, they have made good use of the heritage transmitted by their brothers of the 12th century. The waters of the Ognon, channelled in the Middle Ages, used to supply power for a mill and later a sawmill, and now for a turbine that feeds the electrolysis workshop where parts for the automobile and electronics industries are treated.

The Virgin with the mantle

The abbey

Cloister capitals

Cloister capital detail

NOIRLAC

Around 1136, a group of monks from Clairvaux founded a new monastery at the place called La Maison Dieu (House of God), on lands bestowed by the lord Ebbes V of Charenton. Contrary to the Rule, the new abbey was installed on the side of a very busy road, near the village of Saint Amand, and on the shore of the Cher River, which had heavy boat traffic during the Middle Ages. The community's first abbot was Robert of Châtillon, the nephew of Bernard of Clairvaux who, after fleeing from Cluny, had returned to the monastery where he had professed. At its beginnings, the small community lived in such destitution that, in 1149, Bernard applied to Suger, the distinguished abbot of Saint Denis and king's councillor, for the monks to receive a grant of wheat. Starting in 1180, the abbey began to develop thanks to donations. In 1276, it took the name Noirlac, from a swampy little lake located nearby and in which a son of the Lord of Charenton had drowned. In the 14th century, during the Hundred Years War, Robert of Knolles' Grandes Compagnies ravaged the Berry area and occupied the monastery. The monks sought protection from neighbouring lords who defended them and fortified the monastery. At the same time, community life was disturbed by sombre affairs implicating the monks. The General Chapter intervened to rehabilitate a renegade monk in 1459, and in 1476 even

SUGER

Born into a poor family, Suger was adopted as a young boy by the Benedictine abbey of Saint Denis, near Paris. This royal abbey, founded about 625 by Dagobert 1st, has contained the tombs of the kings of France since the 7th century. Under the Capetian dynasty, it also contained the coronation ornaments and the standard of the kingdom's armies. Suger studied in the company of the future Capetian monarch Louis VI, becoming first his friend and then his councillor when he acceded to the throne in 1108. Remaining a monk, Suger was elected abbot of Saint Denis in 1122, when he acted as a veritable prime minister to the king. Between 1135 and 1144, he had the façade and chevet of Saint Denis rebuilt, making them masterpieces of Early Gothic architecture. He inaugurated the art of great stained glass, using pictures for theological teaching. For Suger, nothing was too beautiful to raise the spirit towards the Lord, but it led to controversy between him and Bernard of Clairvaux, who was otherwise his friend. At the accession of Louis VII in 1137, Suger was maintained in his role with the king, who even entrusted him with the kingdom's regency when he left on the Second Crusade from 1147 to 1149. Suger then had to ensure order in the kingdom which was threatened by intrigues among the nobles and clerical insubordination. Upon his return, the king named him "Father of the Homeland". Suger died at Saint Denis in 1151, as he was about to leave for the Holy Land.

The cloister

The heating room

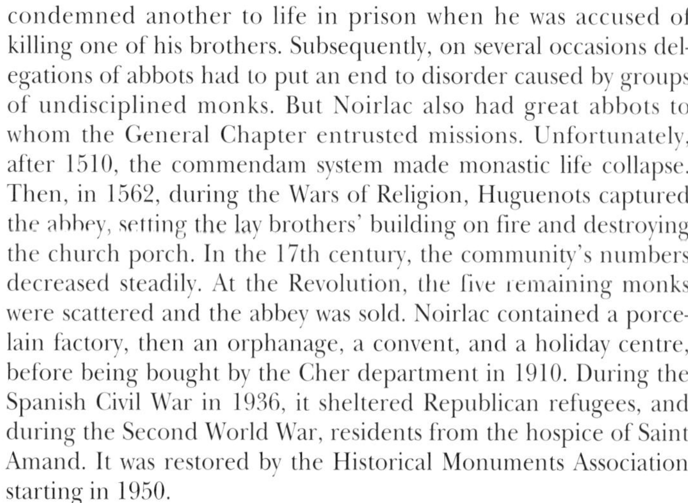

condemned another to life in prison when he was accused of killing one of his brothers. Subsequently, on several occasions delegations of abbots had to put an end to disorder caused by groups of undisciplined monks. But Noirlac also had great abbots to whom the General Chapter entrusted missions. Unfortunately, after 1510, the commendam system made monastic life collapse. Then, in 1562, during the Wars of Religion, Huguenots captured the abbey, setting the lay brothers' building on fire and destroying the church porch. In the 17th century, the community's numbers decreased steadily. At the Revolution, the five remaining monks were scattered and the abbey was sold. Noirlac contained a porcelain factory, then an orphanage, a convent, and a holiday centre, before being bought by the Cher department in 1910. During the Spanish Civil War in 1936, it sheltered Republican refugees, and during the Second World War, residents from the hospice of Saint Amand. It was restored by the Historical Monuments Association starting in 1950.

The cloister is located to the south of the church. The western and northern galleries from the 13th century open onto the garden through gemel arcades topped with oculi. The capitals are decorated with plant motifs. The 14th century eastern gallery has quadruple arcades, their tympana contain rose windows. During the 19th century, a grave was discovered in a funerary niche in a wall in this gallery. It contained the skeleton of a man dressed in a habit, wearing new sandals and holding a wooden crosier. This was probably Robert, Bernard's nephew and the first abbot of Noirlac. A Romanesque doorway framed by two gemel openings provides access to the 12th century chapter house. In the centre, two columns with decorated capitals support the vault's ribs. The monks' rooms lie beyond. Upstairs, the dormitory was entirely rearranged in the 17th and 18th centuries. The vast refectory, with its intersecting rib vaulting, opens onto the southern gallery. In the western gallery, the cellar is the sole remnant of the lay brothers' building that was burnt in 1562.

In Commendam

In instituting commendam, from the Latin *commendare*, to entrust, Clement VI (1342-1352) retained the right to name abbots, chosen from the secular clergy. This practice,caused by the Avignon papacy's need for money, spread throughout France where, after the Concordat of Bologna (1516), the king reserved the right to name commendatory abbots, sometimes even laymen. These abbots received their abbey's revenues and delegated spiritual power to the priors. Commendam often had disastrous effects since some abbots were more concerned with increasing their own revenues than with ensuring proper management of the monasteries.

Lay brothers' dormitory

East gallery of the cloister

Entrance to the chapter house

Abbey church nave

North transept

THE ABBEY CHURCH

Noirlac abbey church was built in three stages that lasted from 1150 until the first half of the 13th century. In the shape of a Latin cross, it consists of a long nave with ribbed vaulting and side aisles, a transept with four square-shaped chapels, and a small sanctuary with a flat chevet. There is no decoration to distract the visitor's eye from admiring the purity of the lines. The light alone emphasizes the pale colour of the stone.

West façade of abbey church

The chevet

Cloister side of abbey church

Medallion cloister

Oseira

The first mention of Benedictine monks settling on the right bank of the *Ursaria*, fifteen leagues south-east of Santiago de Compostela, was made in 1137. The region was mountainous and wild. The name of the river, derived from the Latin *ursus*, shows that bears had chosen this territory for their own. The name of Oseira that was given to the monastery had the same origin, and two bears are shown on the abbey's blazon, standing on their hind legs and leaning on a tree trunk. In 1141, the abbey of Sobrado, further north, had just been founded by monks from Clairvaux. In the same year, the community in Oseira was incorporated into the Cistercian Order in the same affiliation. Santa María de Oseira was not far from the roads taken by pilgrims going to Santiago and in 1142 one of them, Famiano, a German, stopped in the abbey, where he took the habit. He died in 1150 in Italy, in Galessa where he was buried. This saint's body remained uncorrupted. Don Lorenzo was elected abbot of Oseira in 1205. In 1223, he took over the running of Clairvaux. His successor in Oseira was Don Ferdinand Méndez who, from 1206 to 1215, had directed and restored Alcobaça, which had been sacked in 1195 by the Moors. In November, 1230, the king of Castile Ferdinand III (1217-1252) united the kingdoms of Castile and Leon. In the months that followed, Don Ferdinand Méndez was anxious to have the new political power confirm the privileges, titles and incomes that had been granted his abbey by the monarchs of Leon. Starting in 1498, at the request of the Catholic Kings, Sebastián de Padilla introduced the reformation in the Cistercian houses of Galicia. He began with Carracedo. His successors pursued the work in Melon and Oseira, then under the abbacy of Don Suero de Oca (1485-1512), the Archbishop of Tarse. In 1513, the abbey passed under the control of commendatory abbots, but in 1545 it joined the Congregation of Castile. In 1552, a great fire damaged the buildings and the monks had to be moved to the area of Valladolid. But Abbot Marcos del Barrio was opposed to this solution and restored Oseira, where much work was carried out until the end of the 18th century. During the 19th century, Oseira was a victim of the *Exclaustración* in 1820, and the *Desamortización* in 1835. On October 15, 1929, monks from the Cistercian Order of the Strict Observance arrived in Oseira and undertook the rehabilitation of this "Galician Escorial". They were rewarded in 1990 with the prize *Europa Nostra.*

Arriving in Oseira by the road from Cea, as he comes around a curve the visitor discovers the monumental size of one of the first Cistercian establishments installed in the Iberian peninsula. In the village next to the abbey, one of the houses is a former pilgrims' hospital. The entrance gate opens onto a vast courtyard, bordered in the east by the façade of the abbey church, and in the south by the monastic buildings. The abbey church's façade was built between 1639 and 1647. Above the gateway, framed by statues of Saint Bernard on the left, and Saint Benedict on the right, stands a statue of Our Lady. Between the two steeples, the frontispiece

Coat of arms of Castile and Leon

The Mother of Jesus

In the choir of Oseira abbey church, a 13th century polychrome statue of a Virgin and Child is placed on a monolithic column. This is a rare portrayal because Mary is using her right hand to give her breast to the Child, whom she is holding on her lap with her left hand. Jesus, with curly, blonde hair, dressed in a finely draped robe, is busy greedily drinking the milk of his mother with her gentle, dreamy look.

Virgin with Child

Medallion in chapter house

The Three Faces of the Soul

In an interesting study, "Oseira, Where the Phoenix Lands", published in 2001, Pablo Alonso Bermejo analyzed the meanings of the portrayals on the medallions in the former chapter house in Oseira. One of the medallions, on the north-eastern side, shows three faces. The author notes that the one on the left shows attention, the central one is rather sensuous, and that on the right shows anger. The artist thus wanted to express the three facets of the soul described by Plato in the *Timaeus*: intellectual, concupiscent, and irascible.

shows the sculpted coat of arms of Castile and Leon. The abbey has three cloisters: in the west, the cloister of the Knights; in the east, the cloister of the Pinnacles; and between the two, the cloister of the Medallions. The first was built between 1713 and 1759. Construction of the second one, which does not have a west gallery, was completed in 1629. As for the third, it occupies the location of the medieval cloister, on the southern flank of the church. Rebuilt during the 16th century, it was rearranged starting in 1760, with the medallions that gave it its name being re-used under the overhangs of the roofs of the upper galleries. The central fountain is a copy of the16th century original, which now stands in the Plaza del Hierro in Orense. The main staircase is located between the cloisters of the Knights and the Medallions. It leads to their upper galleries. The refectory, from the end of the 16th century and restored in 1987, opens onto the south upper gallery of the Medallion cloister. Work on the abbey church began in 1185. It is shaped like a Latin cross. The nave with its seven bays has side aisles. The transept crossing is topped by a dome on squinches, built in 1282. The chevet consists of three bays with side aisles, extended by a semicircular apse surrounded by an ambulatory with three radiating chapels. The central chapel contains the reredos of Our Lady, dating from the 18th century like the other reredos of the abbey church, as well as the painted décors of the apse and the dome. The door in the southern arm of the transept leads to the sacristy. This communicates with the former chapter house, built between the end of the 15th century and the beginning of the 16th. The Manueline influence is obvious. The ribs of the arches separate and develop into palm trees starting from four central pillars, twisted and decorated with floral motifs, and coming down onto twelve brackets that are supported in the side walls. Like the forty-five polychrome ceiling medallions, these brackets are carved with various designs: phoenix, doves, heads of people like those of a man and a woman joined on the central medallion.

Santa María la Real Abbey

Chapter house

Cloister and lavatorium

MELLIFONT

Ireland was not open to Benedictine monasticism until the 12th century, when a former monk of Bangor became archbishop of Armagh. This was Malachy, a friend of Bernard of Clairvaux. In 1142, Bernard and Malachy founded the abbey of Mellifont, the first Cistercian abbey set in Ireland, located north-west of Drogheda, on the shores of the Mattock River. Bernard sent French master masons to build the monastery right away. The church was consecrated in 1157. Despite the persistent traditions of Celtic monasticism, which did not facilitate the introduction of a new Rule in Ireland, the Cistercian Order set up as many as forty-three abbeys. The conflict between the lineage of Mellifont and the Order's other Irish abbeys, founded starting in 1171 by English mother abbeys, was deep. There was no communication between the two groups, even when it was a question of institutional operation. In 1228, Esteban Lexington, Abbot of Sawley, a granddaughter of Fountains in the English diocese of York, went to Ireland at the peril of his life since he was suspected of wanting to put an end to the *Mellifont conspiration.* He was simply able to note that, with the exception of Mellifont and Saint Mary's of Dublin, Cistercian principles were rarely respected. This antagonism persisted. In 1321, Edward II complained to the General Chapter that Mellifont refused to recruit Englishmen. In 1537, Henry VIII extended the Act of Supremacy to Ireland. He had proclaimed himself Supreme Head of the Church and included the Irish crown. From then on, Mellifont's days were numbered. The king ordered the dissolution of monasteries. In 1556, Mellifont was transformed into a private mansion and was completely abandoned in 1727. Today, only ruins remain. The abbey church had been built in the shape of a Latin cross, typical of Cistercian tradition. The chapter house, in the cloister's east wing, dated from the 14th century. The remnants of an imposing octagonal lavatorium stand opposite the refectory.

Lavatorium detail

BERNARD AND MALACHY

It was while he was on his way from Ireland to Rome that Malachy stopped in Clairvaux, where he met Bernard and became friendly with him. In October 1148, six years after Mellifont had been founded, Malachy stopped once again in Clairvaux during a new trip to Rome. Taken ill with fever, he died in the arms of Bernard, who wrote Malachy's biography. In 1626, Pope Urban VIII joined the Irish Cistercian monasteries together in the Congregation of Saints Bernard and Malachy.

Vestiges of the abbey

The lavatorium

Nenay

Bective

Jerpoint

THE DAUGHTERS OF MELLIFONT

The very powerful Mellifont founded eight daughter abbeys in Ireland. Among them were Bective in 1147; Boyle, Nenay and Baltinglass in 1148; and Hore in 1272. These daughters spread in turn, creating Abbeydorney in 1154, a daughter of Nenay; Jerpoint in 1180, daughter of Baltinglass; Knockmoy in 1190, daughter of Boyle. As for the monastery of Corcomroe, it was founded in 1195 by Inishlounaght, another of Nenay's daughters.

Boyle

Hore

Corcomroe

The abbey church

Convent building ruins

Moreruela

At the end of the 9th century, Froilan and Atilano, the bishops of Leon and Zamora, founded a monastery named for Saint James the Greater at the point of contact of their two bishoprics, on the right bank of the Esla River. Some time later, it was transferred to the left bank, on the lands of Moreruela that Alfonso VII of Castile (1126-1157) and his sister Doña Sancha granted to Bernard of Clairvaux to establish an abbey. About 1143, Peter and Sancho, two monks from Clairvaux, arrived in Moreruela. The original Benedictine monastery had been abandoned. Work on the new abbey church, dedicated to Santa María, began in 1163. It was completed at the end of the 13th century. The abbey, close to the *Via de la Plata*, a route used by pilgrims heading for Santiago de Compostela from the south, had a hospital for pilgrims. Named a national historical monument in 1931, the abbey is the property of the *Junta de Castilla y León.*

In a silence barely disturbed by the blowing wind and a solitude that may be broken by the presence of storks, stand the imposing and still stately ruins of what had been one of the greatest Cistercian abbeys in the Iberian peninsula. The visitor arriving from La Granja de Moreruela can only be impressed by the beautiful light-coloured stone and the regular structure of architectural elements that have withstood both time and man's folly. The 12th century chevet, with its three well-tiered sections, and the southern wall are perfectly preserved. The field of ruins remaining of the church nonetheless permit the visitor to understand its plan, that of a Latin cross, with a central nave, nine bays, with side chapels, a projecting transept and the choir. The apse of the choir, semicircular in shape, opens by a Romanesque arch. It is surrounded by an ambulatory with seven radiating chapels, with a semi-dome vault. Nothing remains of the cloister at the north of the church. Its eastern wing used to open onto the chapter house, with lancet arches, of which a small part remains.

The ambulatory

Abbey church choir

Chapter house

The cloister

Star of David, south transept rose window

Beaulieu

Located in the valley of the Seye River, north-east of Montauban, Beaulieu Abbey, *Belloc* in the Occitanian language, a daughter of Clairvaux, was probably founded in 1144 by Bishop Adhémar III of Rodez. Certainly destroyed during the Albigensian Crusade, its abbey church was rebuilt starting in 1272, thanks to donations by Bishop Vivien of Rodez. The abbey suffered during the Hundred Years War and again in the 16th century from the Wars of Religion, located as it was between Protestant Saint Antonin Noble Val and Catholic Caylus. Some of its buildings were burnt and its cloister destroyed. Having fallen into decline, Beaulieu was nearly closed down in 1768 when the Commission of Regulars found only three monks there. Sold as state property in 1781, the abbey was turned into a farm. Bequeathed to the town of Saint Antonin, its abbey church was named a historical monument in 1875, but for a long time it remained uncovered. In 1959, a couple of art lovers bought Beaulieu and began to restore it. This work was pursued by the National Fund for Historical Monuments and Sites, who has been the owner since 1973. A centre for contemporary art, Beaulieu today contains a renowned collection. In the summer, the abbey is the site of exhibitions, concerts and shows.

The Gothic abbey church, whose western doorway is decorated with a rose window, consists of a single nave, with intersecting rib vaulting and lit by tall windows. Its transept crossing is topped with an octagonal dome on squinches. The apse has seven tall openings, and its keystone is decorated with the Easter lamb. Abutting the church in the south, the east wing of the cloister, now disappeared, contained the monks' building with a dormitory on the second floor. The chapter house from the beginning of the 13th century is on the ground floor; the monks' bench runs along the walls and two pillars hold the ribs of its arches. The cellar stands opposite in the western wing of the lay brothers' building where, nowadays, the dormitory upstairs is used as an exhibition hall. The southern wing, which used to contain the kitchen and refectory, was transformed into abbey lodgings in the 17th and 18th centuries. The park contains a large fish pond for trout. Further on, Saint Anne's Chapel was used by lay brothers or travellers.

Abbey church nave

The Sacred Number

Built between 1272 and the beginning of the 14th century, Beaulieu abbey church, 56 metres long and 20 metres high at the transept crossing, is remarkable for its austerity. Its architects gave particular importance to the number seven, which is frequently alluded to in the Bible: seven days of the week, seven heavens where the angelic orders live… Symbolizing all of space and time, but also spiritual perfection, seven is the number of windows lighting up the chancel, as well as the seven rose windows in the abbey church. The rose window in the façade has seven points; the one in the transept's north arm consists of seven circles.

Keystone showing the Easter Lamb

Cloister and steeple

Fontfroide

In 1093, Aymeri 1st, Viscount of Narbonne, authorized the establishment of a group of Benedictine monks in a lonely valley of the Corbières range, containing a stream fed by the "*Fons frigidus*". In 1144, the community joined the obedience of the abbey of Grandselve, with the desire of strictly observing the Rule of Saint Benedict. In 1145, when Bernard of Clairvaux was passing through, Grandselve was allowed to join the Order, entering through affiliation with Clairvaux. The following year, Fontfroide also became Cistercian and was declared a daughter of Grandselve. Fontfroide founded its first daughter, Poblet Abbey in Catalonia, in 1149, at the request of the Count of Barcelona, Ramon Berenguer IV. Thanks to donations from neighbouring lords, the abbey's properties enlarged considerably and, by the 13th century, Fontfroide was the owner of twenty-five granges. Its affiliation also increased. Between 1194 and 1236, Poblet founded three daughters – Piedra in Aragon, Benifaza near Valencia, and Our Lady of Real on the island of Majorca. In 1203, Pope Innocent III named two monks from Fontfroide, Raoul and Pierre de Castelnau, papal legates charged with curbing the Cathar heresy. The murder of Pierre in 1208 by a vassal of Raymond VI, Count of Toulouse, who was suspected of sympathizing with the heretics, set off the Albigensian Crusade in 1209, during which Fontfroide appeared as a citadel of Catholic orthodoxy. The end of the 13th century was the most brilliant period in the abbey's history. In 1297, Arnaud Nouvel, a former monk of Boulbonne, was elected abbot of Fontfroide and directed it for eleven years. Named cardinal in 1310, he was the pope's legate to England before representing him at the trial of the Masters of the Temple. At his death in 1317, he was buried in Fontfroide, according to his wishes. He was succeeded by his nephew, Jacques Fournier, in 1311. As the bishop of Pamiers in 1317, he directed the court of the Inquisition during the trial of

Lay brothers' refectory and fireplace

Saint Anthony

Olivier de Termes

The castle of Termes in the Corbières, defended by his father Raymond, had had to surrender to Simon de Montfort in August, 1210, during the Albigensian Crusades. Olivier de Termes joined the ranks of lords called *faidits*, or dispossessed. He participated in all the battles against the northern lords and the king of France, but finally rallied to him in 1245. A fervent knight, he took part in the recapture of Majorca at the side of James of Aragon and won renown during the Seventh Crusade. He went to the Holy Land three times. He was at the bedside of Louis IX when the king died in Tunis in 1270. According to some, Olivier died on a crusade. Others believe that, after he died on his lands, his body was placed in Fontfroide of which he was a benefactor.

Fontcalvy Grange

Abbey rose garden

the last Cathars of Sabarthès. Then in December 1334, he succeeded Pope John XXII under the name of Benedict XII. As pope, he attempted to abolish commendatory practices, but unfortunately commendam was eventually put in place in Fontfroide in 1476. A foretaste of the difficult times ahead, the Black Death arrived from Marseilles and swept through Narbonne in 1348, decimating half the monastery's community. By 1764 there were so few monks that, with royal approval, Fontfroide lost its title of abbey and the abbey was attached to the bishopric of Perpignan. At the Revolution, the abbey and its lands became state property and its revenues were allocated to the hospices in Narbonne. However, monastic life was never totally extinguished in Fontfroide. In 1858, the community Father Barnouin had installed in Sénanque in 1854 bought and repopulated Fontfroide. Under the direction of Father John, the new community returned to its original ideals by leading a pious life, divided between prayer and manual work. The law of 1901 provoked the monks' exile to Spain. Upon their return, they merged with the community of Lérins. In the meantime, the abbey had been put up for sale and was bought by a family – still the owner today – who began extensive restoration work, thanks to which Fontfroide has recovered the beauty and majesty of its early days.

The lay brothers' refectory is the first room the visitor to Fontfroide discovers. This vast hall, with intersecting rib vaulting, opens onto a courtyard that was rearranged during the 18th century. Formerly, the lay brothers' workshops, carpenter's workshop, forge and bakery had

Father John

At the death of Abbot Barnouin in 1887 at Lérins, Father John was elected Vicar General of the *Cistercian Congregation of the Immaculate Conception*, with the authorization of keeping his residence at Fontfroide. He was promoted to the rank of abbot in 1889.

The Fontfroide Virgin

Arnaud Nouvel and Jacques Fournier

The Cistercian Abbey of Boulbonne, the "Graveyard of the Counts of Foix" received two future abbots of Fontfroide – Arnaud Nouvel and Jacques Fournier. Born about 1250 in Saverdun, in the county of Foix, Arnaud Nouvel began a successful career as a jurist at Toulouse University. Entering Boulbonne before 1295, he was elected abbot of Fontfroide in 1297. In 1306, Clement V charged him with replacing the Bishop of Albi, Bernard de Castanet, who had been suspended, and in 1308 he conducted the bishop's trial.

Jacques de Molay

In 1310, the Holy See raised him to a cardinalship. Nouvel used his judicial and theological abilities during the many missions that took him as far as England. In December, 1313, with other cardinals he was entrusted with judging the dignitaries of the Order of the Temple, Charnay and Molay, accused by Philip the Fair. The sentence handed down on the square of Notre Dame on March 18, 1314, condemned them to death at the stake and the accused died the same evening. However, Nouvel had not approved of this execution and the king's resentment led to his opposing Nouvel's election to the papacy in 1316. He died in Avignon in 1317, shortly after this failure. His body was transferred to Fontfroide and buried under the high altar of the abbey church. His nephew Jacques Fournier was to succeed where Nouvel had failed. Born in 1285, Fournier was also from Saverdun. He entered Boulbonne as a young novice and distinguished himself by his intelligence and rigour. He was sent to Paris, to Saint Bernard's College, where his brilliant studies ended with his becoming a doctor of theology. Welcomed by his uncle in Fontfroide in 1305, Fournier succeeded him in the abbacy in 1311. In March 1317, Pope John XXII named him bishop of Pamiers where, over the course of seven years, he ran the Inquisition's last trials of the heretics. In 1326, the pope transferred him to Mirepoix before naming him a cardinal in 1328. In 1330, he was called to join the members of the Curia, and became pope under the name of Benedict XII

Cloister gallery

in 1334. In 1335, he decided to build the Palace of the Popes in Avignon. In a desire to restore religious life, he cancelled the commendams put into place by John XXII and undertook reforms of monastic orders, beginning with the Cistercians in 1335, for whom he wrote the bull "*Fulgens sicut stella matutina*". However, his successors did not continue his work. Before his death in 1342, he donated all his books to Fontfroide.

Recumbent figure of Benedict XII

The chapter house

A capital

been located to the north of the courtyard and the noviciate stood to the east. The lay brothers' passage, with its semi-barrel vault, running along the cloister's east gallery leads from the courtyard to the abbey church. Construction of the Gothic cloister started at the end of the 12th century and finished in the 14th. The galleries are open on the garden side by semicircular arcades, supported by gemel columns whose capitals are decorated with leaves. These arcades are topped by large lancet arches, their tympana occasionally containing oculi. The south gallery provides access to the church, built during the second half of the 12th century. The oldest section is the nave. Twenty metres high, it is covered with a gothic barrel vault and communicates with the side aisles by large, partly lancet, arcades. Four chapels open onto the transept, which is vaulted on intersecting ribs. At the

end of the northern arm, a staircase leads to the monks' dormitory. At the transept crossing, the keystone has been replaced by a circular opening. The sanctuary ends by a five-sided apse, opened by three narrow semicircular windows that light up the altar. Fontfroide's stained glass windows were made at the beginning of the 20th century, after the discovery of a treatise on the manufacture of stained glass, written in the 12th century by a monk called Theophile. The visitor passes from the chapter house to the cloister's east gallery through a semicircular arcade, framed by two openings. The vault's diagonal ribs are supported by four columns whose capitals are decorated with flat leaves – the *cistels* from the ponds of Burgundy that gave their name to Citeaux. Above the northern gallery, whose buildings, *scriptorium*, kitchen, refectory, were rearranged during the 18th century, a standing gallery leads to the lay brothers' dormitory, covered by a large pointed barrel vault.

In the rose garden

Abbey church nave

Negotium pacis et fidei

"This pestilential contagion of heresy is so widespread that it has caused discord among those who were united [...] As for me [...], I recognize that I lack the strength to carry through such a vast and difficult affair, because the most noble in my lands are already affected by the evil of infidelity, taking with them a great multitude of people who have abandoned the faith..."
Letter of Raymond V to the Abbot of Citeaux

This confession of powerlessness by the Count of Toulouse showed the progress made in Languedoc by the Arian heresy since Bernard's passage in Toulouse and Albi in 1145. These heretics were Christian dualists for whom there were two creations: that of Good, the work of God, and that of Evil. For them Christ did not live on Earth to atone for original sin but to reveal to man the way of deliverance that would permit those souls led astray by Evil to return to the Kingdom of God. This way was Baptism, the only sacrament they practiced. They were particularly well established on the territories of the Count of Toulouse, but also in Italy, where they were known as Patarins, and in Germany, where in 1163 five of them were burnt at the stake in Cologne. On that occasion, Eckbert of Schönau, a canon of the cathedral, wrote, "These heretics do not hesitate to name themselves *Katharos*, that is, Pure." In 1178, the Abbot of Citeaux, Henry of Marcy, accompanied by a papal legate and the bishops of Poitiers and Bath, went on a pastoral mission to Toulouse. In Saint Sernin's Church, the papal legation managed to make a Cathar, Pierre Maurand, reconcile with the Church, and in Saint Stephen's Cathedral, two other heretics, Raymond de Baimiac and Bernard Raymond, were excommunicated. This had happened several days earlier in Albi to Roger Trencavel, Viscount of Béziers and son-in-law of Raymond V.

Les Vaux de Cernay

Named cardinal of Albano at the Lateran Council of 1179, Henry of Marcy returned in 1181 to Lavaur, in the Toulouse area where the two heretics and Roger Trencavel recanted their errors. At the beginning of his papacy in 1198, Innocent III was told of the vigour of the heresy by the bishop of Auch. The new pope immediately sent two new legates, the Cistercian monks Rainier and Guy. In 1203, he entrusted the legation to two other Cistercian monks from Fontfroide, Pierre de Castelnau and Raoul, who travelled throughout the lands of Languedoc. In 1204, they attended the pleading of Carcassonne, organized by Peter II of Aragon, gathering together representatives of the pope, Waldensians and Cathars. On May 31, 1204, Innocent III praised his two legates and the praise reflected on the entire Cistercian Order. He named a new legate to join them, Arnaud Amaury, the Abbot of Citeaux in person, former abbot of Poblet and Grandselve, daughter and mother of Fontfroide, respectively. Foulque, the abbot of Thoronet, had just been named Bishop of Toulouse and was to remain

Saint Gilles

his post for twenty-five years. In June
206, the Cistercian legates met and joined
ith Diego and Dominic in Montpellier.
Vhile Arnaud Amaury returned to
iteaux for the General Chapter of the
)rder during the autumn of 1206, Pierre
e Castelnau, Raoul, Diego and Dominic
t off on a round of preaching. Following
e advice of Diego and Dominic, they
ere barefoot and begged for their food
s they passed through Servian, Béziers
nd Carcassonne. In the heart of Cathar
ountry, they participated in colloquia at
erfeil, Montréal and Pamiers discussing
very inch of the way with Waldensians
d Cathars. In Pamiers, they were
ined by Arnaud Amaury who arrived
r the "Holy Preaching" accompanied
y twelve Cistercian abbots, including
uy, the abbot of Les Vaux de Cernay.
hese efforts were not in vain, but were
warted by the fact that the local lords,
mong them Raymond VI, Count of
oulouse, were influenced by the heretical
eses, when they did not support them
penly. On May 29, 1207, Innocent III
xcommunicated Raymond VI. An
ttempt at reconciliation was organized

Jacobins palm tree in Toulouse

in Saint Gilles at the beginning of January, 1208 between the Count of Toulouse and Pierre de Castelnau. The meeting was a failure and the papal legate was murdered on the banks of the Rhone River on January 14th. Raymond VI was accused of instigating the assassination. A year later, Innocent III launched his call for the Albigensian Crusade and Arnaud Amaury became its spiritual leader. Béziers was sacked on July 22, 1209. On this occasion, did the abbot of Citeaux really pronounce the terrible words, "Kill them all! God will recognize his own"? In any case, they were reported ten years later by Cesarius of Heisterbach, a Cistercian monk from Cologne. Later, Cistercian monks continued to influence events in the area. In 1212, Arnaud Amaury became Archbishop of Narbonne and Guy of Les Vaux de Cernay, Bishop of Carcassonne. In 1229, the abbot of Grandselve, Elie Garin, took part in preliminary talks of the Treaty of Meaux, which sealed the capitulation of Raymond VII of Toulouse before Louis IX and Blanche of Castile. As for Hélinand of Froidmont, a monk in the Cistercian abbey of Beauvaisis, in 1229 in Toulouse, at the side of Cardinal de Saint Ange, he was the papal legate charged with putting the clauses of the Treaty of Meaux into practice on the ground and,

Cathedral and bishops' palace in Narbonne

Montaillou Castle

in the framework of the council held in the capital of the Saint Gilles family, pronounced three speeches in Latin. And from 1318 to 1325, Jacques Fournier, the former abbot of Fontfroide and future pope under the name of Benedict XII, as Bishop of Pamiers conducted the interrogations of the last Cathar heretics of Sabarthès, in Montaillou, the "Occitan village" described by the historian Emmanuel Le Roy Ladurie.

The abbey

Lay brothers' building

Villers

The abbey of Villers is located south-east of Brussels, between Nivelles and Gembloux. Founded in 1146 by Judith of Marbais, it was offered to Bernard of Clairvaux who sent a group of monks under the leadership of Laurent, the first abbot. The monks settled in the Boverie woods, at the source of the Goddiarch. In January 1147, Bernard came to visit them, encourage them and advised them to move their monastery further north in the valley, on the shores of the Thyle. Construction of the permanent abbey started under the abbacy of Charles of Seyne (1197-1209) from Himmerod in the Rhineland. Villers soon began to develop, both materially and spiritually. In the course of the 13th century, thanks to gifts and the monks' labour, its properties covered about ten thousand hectares, farmed by about twenty granges. Villers had some eminent abbots like Conrad of Urach (1209-1214), the future abbot of Citeaux and legate of the Holy See; or William of Brussels (1221-1238), who would preside over the foundation of two of Villers's daughters – Grandpré, in Namur county, and Saint Bernard on the Scheldt, near Antwerp. Some contemporary chronicles praise the exceptional charity shown the poor by the monks of Villers. In 1258, Julienne du Mont Cornillon, who started the feast of the Holy Sacrament, was buried in Villers according to her wishes. However, for refusing to pay tribute to a duke, the monks had to flee in 1314, then again in 1315 because of a deadly famine. When expansion of the property stopped, the General Chapter decided to rent the granges and lease the farms. During the 15th century, the Dukes of Burgundy interfered in the abbey's elections, and in the 16th century Emperor Charles V received the right from the pope to intervene in naming abbots. However, Abbot Denis Van Zeverdonck (1524-1545) took the abbey's future in hand, restored discipline and tried to preserve the monastic patrimony. But conflicts during the reign of Philip II (1556-1598) provoked a new exile by the community, who had to take refuge in urban houses. After things calmed down, Abbot Bernard Van der Hecken (1653-1666) founded Villers College within the University of Louvain, in 1660. The Franco-Spanish Wars disturbed the community until the end of the 17th century. Starting in 1713, under Austrian domination, Villers' abbots undertook restoration work and tried to solve the abbey's financial difficulties. But the imperial yoke was a heavy burden and the abbey had to provide financing for the construction of an imperial palace in Brussels. Abbot Bruno Cloquette opposed Emperor Joseph II, who had promulgated an edict suppressing contemplative orders in 1783, and supported the Brabant Revolution of 1789. He did not return to Villers from exile until after the departure of the Austrians. However, after the short period of the Union of Belgian States, Austria returned to power in 1790. French revolutionary troops annexed Belgium and in July, 1794 they swept into Villers and sacked it over a period of two weeks.

Chapter house window

Conrad of Urach

In 1209, at the resignation of Charles of Seyne, Conrad of Urach succeeded him at the head of Villers. In 1214, Conrad was elected Abbot of Clairvaux and in 1217, Abbot of Citeaux. Soon a bishop and a cardinal, he became the legate of Pope Honorius III. As such, he confirmed the new Order of the Preaching Friars and supported the pope in his battle against the Cathar heresy. Refusing the papal crown at the death of Honorius III, on his death bed Conrad allegedly said, "May it please Heaven that I persevered until this day in Villers under regular discipline, and that I washed bowls with the kitchen servants".

Abbey church vestiges

In December, 1796, the last monks were expelled and the abbey was declared national property. After its sale in 1797 it was used as a quarry – a sad fate for Villers. The buildings were soon ruined and the final owner even allowed train tracks to pass through. When the State bought the abbey in 1893, a large amount of consolidation and restoration were needed to preserve the remnants that still today are evidence of its past splendour.

Except for the Romanesque narthex from 1197, Villers abbey church was built in stages between 1210 and 1267. Over ninety metres long, it has a nave with ten bays flanked by aisles, a huge transept and a sanctuary ending in a seven-sided apse. During the 13th and 14th centuries, seven chapels were added along the northern aisle. The nave, nearly twenty-three metres high, was covered with quadripartite ribbed vaulting. The sanctuary was lit by two rows of tall lancet windows, between which two rows of oculi were set. To the south of the church, several of the cloister's bays, rebuilt in the 13th century and with ribbed vaulting, subsist. In the eastern gallery, between the *armarium* and the church door, a funerary niche containing the recumbent figure of a monk dressed in a habit, lying in front of a fine rose window, draws the visitor's attention. This is the tomb of Gobert, Lord of Aspremont, a knight who participated in the Albigensian Crusade and the Sixth Crusade before retiring to Villers in 1237. Further on, one enters the chapter house. One of the twin Romanesque windows that framed the entrance still remains. In the southern gallery, beyond the *scriptorium* and the heating room, is the 13th century refectory which communicates with the kitchen. Entirely preserved, the former hostelry from the 13th century, in pure Romanesque style, provides a fine example of Cistercian architecture. It was later turned into a brewery. A large ventilation chimney is located near the entrance and, at the end of the room, a second chimney was used for drying grain, which was stored upstairs.

Former lay brothers' workroom

VILLERS BEER

Each monk in Villers was allowed, besides wine, about a litre of beer per day. In 1686, the annual production of the abbey's brewery (*opposite* and *below*) was thirty-three thousand litres. Nowadays, beer called *Old Villers* is still sold.

Tomb of Gobert of Aspremont

Inside the brewery

The brewery

West façade of abbey church

The chapter house

La Espina

Legend has it that Sancha, the sister of Alfonso VII, King of Castile (1126-1157) brought relics back from the Holy Land: a piece of the true Cross and Saint Peter's finger. On her way home, the king of France allegedly presented her with a thorn from Jesus Christ's crown. She supposedly met Bernard of Clairvaux and convinced him to establish an abbey on lands she possessed at the foot of the Torozos Hills, in the valley of the Bajoz, a tributary of the Duero River. And Bernard allegedly sent his brother, Nivardo, to found San Pedro de La Espina (thorn) where, at his death, Nivardo was buried. The reality was rather less colourful. The abbey's chronicle, written mainly at the beginning of the 17th century, specifies that in 1147, Sancha ceded to Clairvaux lands that she owned at San Pedro de La Espina to found an abbey there. The same chronicle says that at the donation date, there existed an original monastery that was perhaps abandoned, called San Pedro de La Espina and that it already contained the famous relics. But nothing is settled about this and the presence of the term *Espina* in the abbey's name is perhaps linked to thorny plants growing in the area. The first abbot was Baudouin (1147-1160). During the abbacy of the second, William (1160-1172), La Espina diffused to Sandoval in 1167, and under the third abbot, Juan de La Espina (1172-1195) to Valdeiglesias in 1177. In 1185, the abbey received a donation from the king of Leon, Ferdinand II (1157-1188), the husband of Apolonia, daughter of the founder of Cañas. Construction work on the abbey church began by the chevet but a lack of means prevented its completion. Donations from Martín Alfonso Téllez in 1285 and Juan Alfonso de Albuquerque in 1354 permitted the completion of the church and the cloister. In the 15th century, when Martin de Vargas organized the Cistercian Congregation of Castile, it was the abbot of La Espina, Alonso de Urueña, who, along with the abbot of Herrera, was charged by the General Chapter of Citeaux with curbing the initiative. However, at the death of this abbot in 1484, La Espina joined the Congregation, later directed by Marcos del Barrio who was abbot of La Espina in 1551, by then called Santa María. On September 28, 1559, during a hunting party in the Torozos Hills, in front of the abbey Philip II was introduced to his half-brother, the illegitimate son of Charles V and future John of Austria, the victor at Lepanto in 1571. In 1574, the abbey was surrounded by walls and, in 1635 a chapel was built in the southern arm of the transept to contain the relics. During the last third of the 17th century, the previous cloister was destroyed and replaced with a new one. On July 20 and 21, 1731, a fire damaged the abbey. But it had enough resources: it ran six granges and ten hydraulic mills, and it had herds of over three thousand animals. Its restoration was begun. In 1808, Napoleon's army was in Castile. The community abandoned the abbey which was pillaged and sacked by the locals. Its goods were sold at auction on June 10, 1821. Since 1984, it has been the property of the *Junta de Castilla y León.*

Entrance gate to abbey

On Fallow Ground

Don Ponce de Minerva, *alférez* of Alfonso VII, was captured by Moors and retained prisoner. He escaped and tradition says that, on the road to Santiago de Compostela, he stopped at a pilgrim hospital at Carrizo, in the valley of the Orbigo. Doña Estefanía Ramírez, his wife, founder of this hospital, took personal care of the pilgrims. When she began to wash the feet of Don Ponce, a ritual practice in hospitals for pilgrims, husband and wife recognized each other. In thanksgiving, in 1167 they founded Santa María de Sandoval, from *Saltus Novalis*, the first daughter of La Espina, on the banks of the Porma River, west of Mansilla de las Mulas, on lands that had been ceded to Don Ponce by Alfonso VII in 1142. Don Ponce died in 1174. Two years later, Doña Estefanía made a large donation to the Cistercian Order, including her lands in Carrizo, to have an abbey of nuns established there. Until her death in 1183, although she was not the abbess, she ran Santa María de Carrizo, whose first abbess was her daughter María. The two founders of Sandoval and Carrizo were buried in the abbey church of Sandoval, where their remains lie in tombs with recumbent figures.

The abbey church

Les Vaux de Cernay

Abbey blazon

In 1118, monks from the Norman abbey of Savigny settled in the heart of the Yveline forest, in the valley of Cernay where Les Vaux brook runs, on lands given by Simon III of Neauphle le Château, a future Constable of France, and his wife, Eve. The recipient of many donations during the 12th and 13th centuries, Les Vaux de Cernay Abbey, placed under the protection of King Louis VII in 1142, developed rapidly. In 1137, it founded the abbey of Breuil Benoît in the Eure. Attached to the Cistercian Order in the Clairvaux affiliation at the same time as Savigny in 1147, Les Vaux de Cernay Abbey became a great centre of spiritual and intellectual life and one of the Order's most important houses. Partly destroyed in 1193, during the conflict between Philip Augustus and the Plantagenets, it was rebuilt starting in 1195. In 1208, its abbot, Guy, who had taken part in the Fourth Crusade, was charged by Pope Innocent III with preaching the crusade against the Albigensians along with the abbot of Citeaux. Guy convinced Simon de Montfort to take the cross in 1208 and in 1212 as a reward for his dedication received for his devotion the bishopric of Carcassonne, where he died in 1224. Under Abbot Thomas (1212-1229), the nearby female abbey of Saint Marie de Porrois, better known under the name of Port Royal, was attached to Citeaux under the supervision of Les Vaux de Cernay. His pious and humble life brought renown to the ninth abbot of les Vaux, Thibault of Marly (1236-1247). There were so many recruits during his abbacy that the

Saint Thibault's fountain

Royal Descendants

In despair at not having children with Queen Marguerite, King Louis IX (St) summoned Abbot Thibault of Marly from Les Vaux de Cernay. His humble existence entirely devoted to prayer and work had given a great reputation for sanctity to the son of the noble Bouchard 1st of Marly, related to Montmorency and to Mathilde de Châteaufort, granddaughter of King Louis VI. Abbot Thibault assured the king of his prayers and welcomed Queen Marguerite at Les Vaux de Cernay so that she could drink at the abbey's fertile spring. A short time later, the saint's prayers were answered. Queen Marguerite became pregnant and in 1240 gave birth to Blanche, the eldest of the royal couple's eleven children.

Abbey church aisle

monastery had to be enlarged. Legend has it that through his prayers he managed to make Queen Marguerite, the wife of Saint Louis, fertile. When Thibault was canonized in 1270, his relics were placed in Les Vaux de Cernay abbey church, where kings and humble pilgrims came to worship them. Partly ruined during the Hundred Years War, the abbey came under commendam in 1542, before suffering during the Wars of Religion. Restored after 1606, in 1615 it joined the Strict Observance. At the Revolution, the remains of St. Thibault were burned, except his head, kept in the church of Cernay la Ville. The abbey was sold, its furnishings scattered. Its successive owners used it as a quarry before the Rothschild family bought it in 1873. The ruins of the church and the monks' buildings were then consolidated and the other monastic buildings were restored. Today, the abbey has been converted into a high-quality hotel-restaurant.

After the visitor passes the hamlet of Les Vaux de Cernay and the abbey's two gates, he sees the beautiful ruins of the abbey church, dating from the second half of the 12th century, standing in the park. Its western façade is decorated with a large rose window, topping two oculi above the central doorway. Its layout comprises a nave with five bays with side aisles, a transept opening onto two chapels and a choir with a flat chevet. The tombstone of Saint Thibault stands in the south aisle. In the extension of the north transept, the 13th century monks' room has retained its ground floor with two naves, with intersecting rib vaulting, which was perhaps used as a *scriptorium.* The upper floor, where the dormitory used to be, has disappeared.

Carved in Wood

The monks' room in Les Vaux de Cernay has recently been furnished with remarkable wooden stalls, carved in the 19th century, brought from the Norman abbey of Saint Martin de Sées. They show domestic, clerical and theological virtues.

Stall detail, monks' room

Albigensian History

Pierre, the nephew of Abbot Guy of Les Vaux de Cernay, was the author of *Albigensian History*, one of three great medieval texts relating the history of the crusade against the Cathars in Languedoc. A monk in Les Vaux de Cernay Abbey, Pierre used to follow his uncle to distant parts. In 1202, during the Fourth Crusade, he accompanied him to Dalmatia, where Guy tried in vain to prevent the crusaders from taking Zara. In 1210, Pierre went with him to join Simon de Montfort in the south of France, and returned once again when Guy was elected bishop of Carcassonne. From that time until about 1218, Pierre stayed occasionally in Languedoc. Written in Latin, his *Historia Albigensis* aimed at justifying the crusade's military operations. But despite its bias, it remains an importance source of information for historians because Pierre was accurate in spite of his excesses. It was well documented because he had access to the crusade's archives, which he sometimes reproduced word for word, leading to suppositions that he may have been the official historiographer. His work is divided into three parts: the Cathar heresy, the Roman Catholic Church's preaching, and the crusade.

The first part of the *Historia*, finished in 1213, was dedicated to Pope Innocent III. It was completed by two volumes written during the course of events.

The monks' room

The abbey church

Façade of abbey church

Santes Creus

Capital in great cloister

In 1149, the Moncada Family donated its lands in Valldaura to the Cistercians of Grandselve Abbey, a daughter of Clairvaux. In 1158, monks settled permanently on the left bank of the Gaya River, in a place where crosses had been erected in memory of supernatural lights that had appeared there. Right from the early years of its foundation, the Catalonian-Aragonese kings had placed Santes Creus under their protection and some of them even chose to be buried there. The abbey participated in the progress of agriculture on its lands because it encouraged their population. The monastery also profited from privileges granted by the Holy See, and in 1296 the Catalonian-Aragonese kings gave its abbots the title of Grand Chaplain. In 1375, King Peter III the Ceremonious had the monastery fortified and it took on the appearance of a fortress.

For seven centuries, the monks of Santes Creus lived in peace and fidelity to the Rule. In the 19th century, community life was disturbed by Napoleon's armies, harbinger of the end. After the French invasion, in 1820 the constitution of the Cortès expelled the monks from their abbey, which was sold at auction along with its properties. Santes Creus was totally suppressed in 1835 and sacked by revolutionaries. The precious works in its library were taken to Tarragona. The monastic buildings were destined for a more bitter end. Abandoned, they were threatened with complete ruin, while anything that could be transported disappeared. Several exiled monks nonetheless decided to protect their abbey and settled in Santes Creus. The provincial commission for monuments came to their help and in 1921 Santes Creus Monastery was declared a national monument.

Built starting in 1174, Santes Creus Church has a Bernardine or Cistercian plan. It consists of a nave with side aisles, a transept serving four chapels and a small sanctuary with a flat chevet. Its façade contains a fine Romanesque doorway with three voussoirs, surmounted by a high third point window. The inside of the church has intersecting ribbed vaulting and the nave's ribs extend along the walls, stopping on multiple corbelled consoles three metres above the ground. The royal tombs of Peter the Great (1276-1285), of James II (1291-1327) and his wife Blanche of Anjou stand in the abbey church. Construction of the cloister, to the south of the church, began in 1303. With its ribbed vaulting and windows filled with tracery, it is one of the first Spanish Gothic cloisters. The south and west galleries in Flamboyant

Royal patio

Old Rivalry

Santes Creus and Poblet, founded nearly at the same time, often quarrelled over which of the two was the oldest. The provincial Council of Tarragona of 1620 claimed that it was Poblet; the council of 1630 said it was Santes Creus. Lively discussions of the question began again in 1735 and finally, in 1750, Pope Benedict XIV decided in favour of Santes Creus.

Royal tomb

Chapter house

Gothic style were built during the reign of James II and his wife, who brought the English master Raynard Fonoyll to make them. The capitals are richly decorated with motifs drawn from animals, plants, heraldry and mythology. In the east gallery, a semicircular doorway, framed by two openings, is that of the chapter house. Square in shape, the room is covered with nine vaults with intersecting ribs, supported in the centre by four columns with soberly sculpted capitals. The tombstones of six abbots and a bishop are set in the ground. Two tiers of stones on which the monks used to sit run the length of the walls. The dormitory, dating from 1173, covered with visible beams, takes up the second storey. In the cloister's south wing, facing the refectory and projecting into the garden, the lavatorium, consisting of a fine marble basin, stands inside a hexagonal building. Each of its sides has gemel openings, alternately topped with a lozenge or an oculus. The storeroom, containing the original barrels, is one of the oldest rooms in the monastery. Vaulted on intersecting ribs, it has beautiful carved capitals. Another cloister, called the *Old Cloister*, extends to the south-west of the regular buildings.

12th c. Christ

Lavatorium

The cloister

Cloister and abbey church

Poblet

In 1151, after the recapture of Catalonia, the Count of Barcelona Ramon Berenguer IV called on the monks of Fontfroide to found a new abbey on his lands. The monks settled near the sources of the Francolí River, between Tarragona and Lerida, in a place filled with stands of poplar trees. The name of the monastery was derived from the Latin name for this tree, *populetum.* Soon Poblet was receiving new recruits belonging to the cream of the local nobility, and in 1194, it founded its first daughter, Piedra, in the diocese of Tarazona. The son of the founder, Alfonso II, enriched the abbey's properties, granted it numerous privileges and chose to be buried there, starting a tradition that was to be perpetuated by his successors. At the beginning of the 13th century, the events of the Albigensian Crusade grievously affected life at the monastery. In 1209, Pope Innocent III confided the religious direction of the crusade to Arnaud Amaury, Poblet's former abbot, who had become abbot of Citeaux. As for Peter II of Aragon, the great victor at Las Navas de Tolosa in 1212, overlord of vast territories including the possessions of the Counts of Toulouse, Comminges and Foix, he finally chose the camp of his feudatories against the crusading troops of Simon de Montfort. He was killed at the Battle of Muret in September 1213. When the conflict ended, Poblet continued its expansion. Abbot Ponce de Copons (1316-1348) encouraged studying at the monastery and enriched its library, as well as undertaking construction work during this period of Gothic architecture. Before the terrible plague of 1348, the abbey had no less than two hundred monks. During the reign of Peter III the Ceremonious (1336-1387), Poblet was provided with a huge wall, 608 metres long, and it became one of the principal fortresses of the Kingdom of Catalonia and Aragon. As a strategic location, Poblet was not limited to its monastic buildings. Beyond the monastery, a second wall protected the other

Abbey church façade

Cloister capitals

St Bernard of Alzira

Hamet was the son of a Saracen emir. In 1156, Zaen, the king of Valencia, sent him to Catalonia as an ambassador. Getting lost during his return, he asked the monks of Poblet for hospitality. Won over by the local harmony and the men's fervour, he converted and took the name Bernard, then took the habit in Poblet where he became the cellarer. Bernard hoped to convert his family so with the abbot's agreement, he left for Valencia and was able to convince his aunt and his two sisters, but not his brother, Almanzor. He decided to return to Catalonia with his sisters, whom he baptized under the names of Grace and Mary. Caught by Almanzor and his henchmen, Bernard was the first to be executed. His brother had hoped to reason with his sisters, but in vain. They in turn were beheaded with a sabre. These three martyrs perished on August 23, 1180 and their bodies were abandoned without being buried. After the departure of the troops, a witness buried the bodies. Their remains were discovered in the next century by James the Conqueror. The shrine he built on the spot, near Alzira, was entrusted to Trinitarians, the order charged with freeing Christian prisoners of the Saracens.

Gothic gallery in cloister

SCRIPTA NON MANENT

At the end of the 12th century, the library in Poblet had nearly fifty volumes, five of which had been presented in 1180 by Stephen, its former abbot who had become the bishop of Huesca. The abbey also had a *scriptorium.* In 1343, the monk copyists in Poblet reproduced, on parchment, the *Libre dels Feyts,* a chronicle of the reign of James 1st the Conqueror, a work of reference about Catalonian historiography. Few of the manuscripts produced in Poblet's *scriptorium* have survived. Among them is a *Commentary on the Apocalypse* by Beatus of Liebana.

buildings outside the enclosure – besides the abbey church, chapels, the hospital, hostelry, and those containing the many tradesmen employed by the monastery. In 1480, through a papal bull, Poblet became independent of Fontfroide. During the 16th century, Abbot Juan Guimera (1564-1583) was charged with directing the construction work of the Urgel canal. His successor, Francisco Oliver de Boteller, welcomed the Abbot of Clairvaux, Edmund de La Croix, to Poblet. In 1616, the Cistercian monasteries of Aragon joined together in a congregation independent of Citeaux, in accordance with the wishes of King Philip III. In the course of the 17th and 18th centuries, Poblet suffered from the wars afflicting Spain. Civil wars, struggles against Portuguese independence, against Sardinia and Sicily, against France and England, against Austria, followed in succession, provoking the kingdom's bankruptcy. In 1793, Spain declared war on the Convention, then finally allied with France against England. After the resounding defeat at Trafalgar in 1805, Napoleon took advantage of the situation to name his brother, Joseph, King of Spain (1808). After this the war for independence broke out, at the end of which the Cortès gave the country a liberal constitution. This was followed by a terrible civil war opposing revolutionaries and royalists. The abbey of Poblet, suppressed a first time in 1823, was completely abandoned by its monks in 1835, before being sacked by revolutionaries. After the monarchy was re-established in 1875, restoration work began in Poblet. In 1935, the church was re-consecrated and in 1940, monks from the Italian Congregation of Saint Bernard arrived to populate the monastery.

The church faces east and is eighty-five metres long. Its construction began in 1166 and finished at the end of the 12th century. The nave with seven bays, with pointed barrel vaults, rises to a height of twenty-eight metres and communicates through large third point arcades to side aisles with ribbed vaulting. Each transept arm ends in a semicircular apsidal chapel. On either side of the crossing, two large depressed arches support the tombs of

Lavatorium

The kitchen

Alabaster screen

Storeroom

the kings of Catalonia-Aragon. A great sculpted, alabaster screen stands in the apse. Behind the apse of the sanctuary, dating from the 16th century, the ambulatory with ribbed vaulting serves five radiating chapels. The galleries of the *reading cloister*, built starting in 1208 to the north of the church, also have ribbed vaulting. The south gallery abutting the church, in Romanesque style, has gemel semicircular openings. In the two other Gothic galleries, the arcades are divided into bays with trefoil arches surmounted by rose windows. In the galleries, the stone benches on which monks used to sit and read still remain. The passage from the 13th century chapter house to the east gallery leads through a Romanesque doorway, framed with two openings. Four octagonal pillars, with delicately carved capitals, hold up the vaulting ribs. Three gemel bays, topped with arcades decorated with Romanesque voussoirs, provide light from the rising sun. Below stand the tombstones of eleven abbots, carved in relief. At the north-east corner of the cloister, the fifty-metre long monks' room is divided into two parts; today, the larger section contains the library, the other, the *scriptorium*. The dormitory takes up the entire upper floor of the eastern gallery. The northern gallery contains the refectory, the kitchen and the heating room. Protruding into the garden, the monks' lavatorium is set inside a hexagonal building with semicircular gemel arcades. The lay brothers' buildings extend beyond the north-west corner of the cloister.

The dormitory

The Pantheon of Catalonian-Aragonese Counts and Kings

In 1137, Petronilla, daughter of the king of Aragon, Ramiro II, married a Templar knight, the Count of Barcelona, Ramon Berenguer IV, who founded Poblet twelve years later. From that time on, the County of Barcelona was joined to the Kingdom of Aragon by a dynastic union that was never again called into question. Although Ramon Berenguer had wanted to be buried at Ripoll Abbey like his ancestors, his son, Alfonso the Chaste (1162-1196), granted numerous privileges and donations to Poblet, including the construction of the church in which he was buried, according to his wishes. His grandson, James 1st, nicknamed "the Conqueror", won fame in the conquest of Majorca in 1229 and Valencia in 1238. In 1258, by the Treaty of Corbeil, Saint Louis ceded Cerdagne and the Roussillon to him. He died in 1276 and was buried

Detail of Peter III's tomb

in Poblet. In 1387, Poblet abbey church received the tomb of Peter III the Ceremonious, who had had the royal pantheon built there. Peter III had dealt with the war started in 1336 by the king of Castile, Peter I, and during his reign Poblet Abbey was surrounded by a fortified enclosure. His sons, John 1st and Martin the Humanist, who reigned successively from 1387 to 1410, were both buried in Poblet. The death of Martin the Humanist marked the end of a dynasty that had left its imprint on the history of the Kingdom of Catalonia/Aragon. His nephew and successor, Ferdinand of Antequera belonged to the Castilian family of Trastámara. He took over the destinies of Aragon, Catalonia and Valencia in 1412, and faithful to tradition, found his final resting place in Poblet. The crown then went to Alfonso IV the Magnanimous (1416-1458), who conquered the Kingdom of Naples in 1443. He and his brother and successor John II (1458-1479) were the last two monarchs of the Catalonian/Aragonese kingdom to be buried in Poblet.

Royal pantheon, tombs of John II and his wife

Chapter house

Arcades in cloister galleries

Alcobaça

Located between Lisbon and Coimbra, in a narrow valley of the Leiria district where the Alcoa and Baça Rivers flow together, Alcobaça Abbey, a daughter of Clairvaux, was founded in 1153 by King Alfonso Henriques 1st. The first king of Portugal, Alfonso Henriques consecrated his country's independence by breaking all ties with Castile and by pushing the Moors ever further south. In 1147, he captured Santarem and in the same year, he conquered Lisbon after several months of siege, with the help of a fleet of crusaders. Establishing a Cistercian abbey of the Clairvaux line on newly captured territories at a time when the influence and prestige of Bernard of Clairvaux were at a high point within the Church ensured and consolidated the king's power. Not only busy with clearing and farming the lands that were granted to them, the white monks began to build their abbey in 1178. But Moors invaded Alcobaça in 1195 and massacred the community. As soon as possible, the monks returned and reconstruction work began under the abbacy of Ferdinand Méndez (1206-1215). As the beneficiary of numerous privileges and large donations from monarchs, Alcobaça soon became the most powerful abbey in Portugal. The monks owned many granges and took advantage of the sunny hillsides of their lands to cultivate olive trees and grapevines. They also set up forges at

The Love of Silence

Ever since the Desert Fathers, silence has been an essential component of monasticism. In order to communicate without disturbing the other monks, the Cistercians perfected a system of visual signs that form a real language. This system was adopted in Molesme, then adapted by Robert who transmitted it to Citeaux. Thus, in Clairvaux, two hundred and twenty-seven signs allowed the transmission of information about food, liturgical or ecclesiastical objects, buildings, etc.

A gallery in the cloister

Lavatorium

Aguas Bellas, Quinto and Ferraria. The abbey also exercised great intellectual influence, created a college in Lisbon and participated in running the University of Coimbra. In 1290, King Dom Dinis had the cloister built. The monks of Alcobaça played an important role not only in economics but also in the kingdom's politics. They took part in the Royal Council and sat in the Cortès. As the defenders of Portugal, they supported the struggles against the Castilians and the Moors, and they had a role in the founding of the Order of Avis, affiliated to Citeaux in the 12th century, as well as the Order of Christ in the 14th century. At the end of the 15th century, the equilibrium of the Benedictine Rule was lost when a situation of economic ease made its original ideals of simplicity and poverty forgotten. Furthermore, in 1475, commendam was instituted in Alcobaça and its abbot, named by the king, settled in as lord and absolute master of a great domain. He took the title of "Grantee of the Crown, Grand Almoner, King's Councillor, and Governor General" and the command of thirteen cities, three ports and two châteaus. The monastery underwent important transformations. As commendatory abbots, cardinals Dom Alfonso and Dom Henriques built another cloister and an abbey palace that was later changed into an inn. In 1567, with the approval of Pope Pius V, the Portuguese Cistercian monasteries decided to reform and regain their independence. They united in the Congregation of Saint Bernard of Portugal, and the abbot of Alcobaça, elected from then on for a period of three years, became the General Abbot, charged with visiting the kingdom's Cistercian and Benedictine monasteries. During the 18th century, Alcobaça was once again devout and rich. The monks decided to renew the altars and gave their church a Baroque façade. Then in 1775, Alcobaça endowed itself with one of the greatest libraries in the kingdom. However the abbey also suffered from several ordeals. The 1755 earthquake and the floods of 1772 damaged the buildings and caused much material loss. The second invasion of Napoleonic troops brought trouble to the heart of the community. In 1811, the soldiers of Count Erlon desecrated the tombs of Inès de Castro and King Dom Pedro while searching for treasure, and mutilated the carved figures and statues. At the abolition of religious orders in 1834, the monks had to leave their monastery. Today, Alcobaça church is a parish church and in 1985 the entire monastery was listed by Unesco as a Natural and Cultural World Heritage Site.

The façade of the abbey church, opening with a large Gothic doorway surmounted with two imposing towers, was rebuilt during the 18th century, the Baroque period. But the interior has retained the simplicity and majesty of the end of the 12th century. The grandeur and purity of lines reaching for the heights that announced the beginnings of Gothic architecture make it a masterpiece of Cistercian architecture. A hundred and six metres long, twenty metres high, this vast church was built according to the plan of Clairvaux abbey church, rebuilt after Bernard's death. It consists of a long nave with side chapels, with ribbed

THE ORDER OF CHRIST

After the suppression of the Order of the Temple in 1312, King Dom Dinis (1279-1319) decided to create a new order in his kingdom to be its legitimate successor. Hence the Order of Christ was born on March 15, 1319 through a bull of Pope John XXII. It received most of the goods that the Templars had possessed in Portugal. Starting in 1357, the fortress of Tomar (*below*) became the seat of the Order of Christ.

Tomar, Manueline window

Cloister and abbey church

Kitchen fireplace

vaulting, a wide transept with four chapels opening onto it, and a chevet with an ambulatory and radiating chapels. In each of the transept's arms, stand the tombs of Inès de Castro and King Dom Pedro, masterpieces of Portuguese Gothic funerary sculpture. The north aisle provides access to the *Cloister of Silence*, built from 1308 to 1311, during the reign of Dom Dinis. The galleries, with their intersecting rib vaulting, open onto the garden through arcades whose tympana have rose windows. Each arcade is divided into two or three bays, supported by gemel columns. The upper storey was added in the 16th century. In the east gallery, a Romanesque door, framed by gemel openings, opens onto the chapter house with its three naves with intersecting ribbed vaulting. In the north-east corner, a staircase leads to the monks' dormitory. The two rows of columns holding up the ribs of the vault are decorated with geometrical or plant motifs. In the north gallery, beyond the monks' room, the kitchen, rebuilt in the 18th century, is crossed by a channel of water, which is in fact a branch of the Alcoa River, and contains an immense fireplace. Facing the lavatorium, the 13th century refectory contains a flight of steps, emphasized by five Romanesque arcades in a row, that lead to a pulpit. In the west gallery is the Kings' Hall from the 18th century, where statues of the kings of Portugal as far as Dom José stand on consoles, halfway up the walls. They are the work of monks. There is also a set of ceramic tiles (*azulejos*) illustrating the history of the monastery's foundation.

A Temple of Gluttony

The fireplace in the kitchen of Alcobaça Abbey (*above*) could roast eight oxen. In 1794, the connoisseur William Beckford appreciated the dishes coming from this "temple of gluttony, the most distinguished in Europe".

Reader's pulpit

The Dead Queen

In 1336, Dom Pedro, the son of King Alfonso IV of Portugal, married Constance, Infanta of Castile.
But soon, the prince fell passionately in love with Inès de Castro, one of his wife's ladies-in-waiting. After the death of Constance in 1345, he secretly married Inès, with whom he had children. However, Alfonso IV was afraid that Inès's brothers, who belonged to a noble and influential family of Castile, would interfere in the kingdom's affairs and so, to preserve the rights of the legitimate heir, decided to have Inès assassinated at Santa Clara, a suburb of Coimbra. Mad with grief from bitterness and despair, Dom Pedro revolted against his father and, with his men, devastated the region between Douro and Minho. When he succeeded to the throne at the death of Alfonso IV, he obtained the extradition of Inès's murderers, who had taken refuge in Castile, and had them tortured and executed. Recognizing Inès as his legitimate wife, he ordered her body transferred to Alcobaça. Is it true that, as legend has it, he had her dead body seated at his side and crowned queen? In any case and according to his wishes, the king's tomb is placed before that of the queen in Alcobaça church, feet facing feet, so that on the Day of the Last Judgment they will be face to face, united forever. The tragic story of Inès inspired Velez de Guevara's play, *Reinar despuès de morir*, and Montherlant's, *La Reine Morte*. In the latter work, the heroine addresses Ferrante, the king of Portugal and father of Dom Pedro, in speaking of her lover, "The day I met him was like the day I was born. On that day, my heart was taken away from me and replaced with a human face."

Detail of king's tomb

Tomb of Inès de Castro

Entrance to the chapter house

Piedra

Homage Tower

At the end of the 12th century, Poblet Abbey wished to diffuse and found its first daughter abbey. Two locations were considered: one at Peralejos, five leagues north of Teruel on the banks of the Alfambra, and at Piedra, the ancient *Bilbilis*, five leagues south-west of Calatayud. Since 1186, Poblet had owned lands and a castle at Piedra, which had been granted by Alfonso II of Aragon (1162-1196). On May 10, 1194, thirteen monks, led by Gaufrido de Rocaberti, formerly a monk in Clairvaux and Bernard's companion, left Poblet. They took the direction of Teruel, crossing the magnificent and austere lands of this part of Aragon, reconnoitred the Peralejos site and continued on to Piedra, where they arrived on May 20th. The chronicles do not mention the monks' feelings at that moment. They were probably exhausted by the long walk over the plateau under an already hot spring sunshine when they arrived from the south at the top of a cliff overlooking a depression, an oasis of coolness invaded by luxuriant vegetation, resounding with the sound of the torrents of the Piedra River. They were most certainly captivated, like everyone else, by the site's beauty and they immediately decided to establish their abbey there. And indeed, the original abbey stood at the edge of the cliff, where today the Hermitage of the White Virgin stands with, at its foot, a rocky peak rising in the heart of the cirque, on the shore of a lake with clear water. Ever

Façade of former hospital

Cloister

since they have been called, respectively, *peña del Diablo*, the Devil's peak, and *lago del Espejo*, Mirror Lake. In 1218, the community moved to the other side of the basin, closer to the castle. Piedra was a constant beneficiary of generosity and protection by the Aragonese kings, particularly Alfonso II, Peter II (1196-1213) and James 1st the Conqueror (1213-1276), but also by their successors. It was also able to count on support from the papacy and Innocent III (1198-1216), with two bulls in 1201 and 1212, insisted on confirming its possessions. It must be said that in 1208 the pope had called for a crusade against the Albigensians and, in 1211, had invited the Christian kingdoms to unite in the struggle against the Almohads. The pope thus could refuse nothing to Arnaud Amaury, the former abbot of Poblet and then abbot of Citeaux, but also papal legate in charge of eradicating the Cathar heresy in Languedoc, nor to Peter II of Aragon, one of the great victors of the battle at Las Navas de Tolosa in 1212, ever since called "the Catholic". Piedra Abbey soon found itself at the head of a large patrimony. It ran a grange at Carenas and another at Peralejos. Among other possessions, it owned vineyards, shops and dyeing workshops in Calatayud, lands in Daroca, and salt mines. This wealth inspired envy, especially during the first half of the 14th century when harvests decreased because of climatic problems and the Black Death epidemic that spread from Messina in 1347. In 1335, villagers in Nuevalos, Monterde and Llumes attacked the monastery and its goods. Peter IV (1336-1387) had to intervene to protect them. Trouble persisted and the monarch had to impose order in 1344 and 1360. At the beginning of the 15th century, a former Hieronymite, Martin de Vargas, was a member of the Piedra community. Wishing to return to a stricter observance of the founding principles of the Cistercian Order, in 1427, strengthened by the support of Pope Martin V (1417-1431), Vargas left Piedra with eleven companions. They founded the abbey of Montesión near Toledo, and created the Cistercian Congregation of Castile. At the end of the 15th century, the abbot of Piedra wrote to the Catholic Kings to inform them that only the abbeys of Montesión, Valbuena and La Sierra had remained faithful to the ideas of Martin de Vargas, who had died imprisoned in 1446. In the 17th century, Piedra abbey church had been restored but the entire monastery was devastated in 1835. Today, it is completely renovated and part of it has been refitted into a very comfortable hotel. Coming from Nuevalos, access to the site is through the *puerta Colorada*, the coloured door, opening in the surrounding wall. At the north-west corner of the enclosure, overlooking the park, stands the Homage Tower from the 12th century. Within the walls, the façade of the former hospital is marked with pilasters. The abbey church, in ruin, has retained its chevet supported by solid abutments, and is overlooked in the south by a square steeple. Access to the hotel is through Saint Martin's Square. The glass doors on either side of the reception hall open onto the steps of a monumental staircase, covered by a vast nave with lierne vaulting from the 14th century. The Gothic arches of the cloister's galleries surround a garden where cypress trees grow. The chapter house, with ribbed vaulting, opens onto the south gallery.

THE REFORMER'S WORK

In 1425, Martin de Vargas, a former Hieronymite who had become a monk in Piedra, complained to Pope Martin V (1417-1431) of the slackening of the Rule in Castile's Cistercian abbeys. Through the bull *Pia supplicum vota*, he obtained the pope's authorization to found two observant abbeys, under the authority of the abbot of Poblet. In 1426, near Toledo, the reformer created the abbey Santa María de Montesión, and in 1427 took charge of the abbey at Valbuena. This was the birth of the Congregation of Castile. Abbacies became triennial in these abbeys. Citeaux's General Chapter condemned this observance, which spread thanks to the support of Álvaro de Luna, a favourite of King John II. In 1445, he had Martin de Vargas put in prison, where he died a year later. Pope Calixtus II (1455-1458) recognized the congregation in 1455, but its only adherents were Montesión, Valbuena and La Sierra. It was not until the end of the 15th century that the reform, supported by the Catholic Kings, recovered its strength. In 1531, the General Chapter sent Edmund de Saulieu, Abbot of Clairvaux, to curb the movement. But it was too late. In 1551, the Congregation of Castile endowed itself with constitutions and set its seat at the abbey of Palazuelos.

Waterfall called *La Cola de Caballo*

A GARDEN OF EDEN

The Piedra River crosses the rather arid Aragon plateau before falling into a depression – an enclosure of coolness and greenery – at the foot of the monastery to which it gave its name. It enters there through *Las Pradillas*, before falling through a series of waterfalls: the *Trinidad*, the *Caprichosa* which spills into Diane's Bath, and *Los Fresnos*, followed by the *Iris*. The river then catches its breath, and on its way feeds the Lake of Ducks. Then it drops fifty metres at the *Cola del Caballo*, the horse's tail. It calms down at the foot of the *Peña del Diablo*, which is a centre of fish breeding. It is then joined by one of its races, which is spilled by the waterfall called *Los Chorreadores* that, after losing its energy, rests in the *Lago del Espejo*, Mirror Lake. After this eventful passage, the river's waters can slow down in the *Tranquera* reservoir, before they meet the waters of the Jalón, between Calatayud and Alhama de Aragón. Visiting the park is enchanting. The sun plays hide-and-seek among the foliage that echoes with birdsong and sounds from the river. The well-drawn paths meander among waterfalls, lakes and caves. They sometimes run through tunnels carved out of the rock. And as though Nature had not been generous enough in this place, on April 20, 1859, local villagers discovered a cave called *Iris* behind the *Cola del Caballo*. It can be entered from the upper level of the waterfall by a staircase that runs along the waterfall, sometimes below ground. Below there is an unforgettable sight: behind the liquid curtain of the waterfall, a large room sets off an emerald green lake, into which crystal drops fall without stopping from the rocky vault.

The abbey

Valle Crucis

Valle Crucis was founded in 1201 by Madog ap Gruffudd Maelor, Prince of Powys. Cistercians from the abbey of Strata Marcella, granddaughter of Clairvaux through the intermediary of Whitland, came to settle in the valley of the Dee, thirty-five kilometres south-west of Chester. A fire during the first half of the 13th century slowed down construction that had begun with the monks' arrival. Then, the sporadic wars by King Edward 1st (1272-1307) against the last independent Prince of Wales, Llywelyn ap Gruffudd, did not spare the abbey's properties. Despite these troubles, and thanks to the liberal gifts from the prince and neighbouring lords, the community flourished, organized the farming of its lands and, by the beginning of the 14th century when peace had finally been established, Valle Crucis had become one of the most important Cistercian monasteries in Wales. Soon the community had to cope with the Black Death plague epidemic which broke out in 1349, followed by difficulties caused by a lack of labour. In 1415, it once again suffered from the English re-conquest, after the Welsh uprising under Owain Glyndwr. By the middle of the century, Valle Crucis began to prosper again. Its abbots, shrewd and wise scholars, were well respected and many poets sang the praises of the abbey, like Guto'r Glynn who spent the final years of his life there. However, the fervent austerity of the early years had disappeared. By the beginning of the 16th century, the abbots were living luxuriously, offering sumptuous banquets to their guests. In 1535, the imprisonment of the next-to-last abbot, Robert Salusbury, who had turned out to be the head of a band of thieves, precipitated the abbey's inevitable end. In that same year, King Henry VIII carried out an evaluation of the possessions belonging to English and Welsh monasteries. Valle Crucis survived until January, 1537. After its dissolution, the new owner, Sir Pickering, did not manage to avoid the ever more numerous thefts of stones. As a result, at the beginning of the 17th century, Valle Crucis fell into ruin, even though they were romantic ruins that inspired many artists, like J.M.W. Turner (1775-1851). During Turner's time, the buildings were used by a farm, the refectory had become a barn. Starting in 1872, the State restored the site, which has belonged to the Welsh Society for Historical Monuments since 1950.

Construction of Valle Crucis church, in the form of a Latin cross facing east, began around 1225-1240. Its 14th century façade contains a doorway with four voussoirs, topped by three tall decorated Gothic windows, in turn surmounted by a seven-foiled rose window. Originally the church consisted of a nave with side aisles, a wide transept with four chapels and a sanctuary with a flat chevet. In the south aisle, a doorway with a Gothic arch with three voussoirs and sculpted capitals opens onto the cloister whose east wing remains. Beyond the sacristy and the tracery-filled windows of the *armarium*, the chapter house with three naves has a rib-vaulted roof. Beyond the chapter house, a staircase leads to the monks' dormitory upstairs.

2

CITEAUX AND OTHER LINEAGES

After its difficult beginnings, under the abbacy of Stephen Harding Citeaux produced its first daughter, La Ferté, in 1113. It was followed by the foundations of Pontigny in 1114, Clairvaux and Morimond in 1115. Prolific in their turn, these first daughters were to form the Order's four mother branches, attached to the main trunk of Citeaux. All the abbeys founded subsequently, established all over Europe and the Near East, entered one of these five affiliations. Within the Order Citeaux's other direct daughters did not have the special status nor the pre-eminence of the first four. Some, however, did exert a lot of influence, like Bonnevaux founded in 1119, L'Aumône in 1121 or Obazine in 1147.

The library

A gallery in the cloister

Citeaux

Decorated letter, Citeaux manuscript

In March, 1098, Abbot Robert and several monks from Molesme settled in the forest of Citeaux, south of Dijon. Within their first year, the first church of their New Monastery was consecrated. In July, Alberic succeeded Robert, who had to return to Molesme. The beginnings were difficult and, very quickly, the New Monastery was transferred half a league south, close to the course of the Vouge River which the monks wanted to develop. Placed under the protection of the Holy See in 1100, the abbey was chosen in 1103 as a burial site by the Duke of Burgundy, Eudes 1st, starting a tradition that would continue until the end of his dynasty at the death of Philippe de Rouvres, in 1361. A new abbey church was consecrated in 1106 – the future Saint Edmund Chapel – where the first abbots were buried. In 1109, Stephen Harding took over the abbacy and welcomed new recruits, including Bernard of Fontaine in 1112, or 1113 according to other sources. As its numbers increased, the New Monastery produced its first four daughter abbeys between 1113 and 1115: La Ferté, Pontigny, Clairvaux and Morimond. And in 1119, the first General Chapter of the Cistercian Order was held at the mother abbey, which was soon to take the name of Citeaux. Between 1140 and 1150, work began on a new abbey church, consecrated in 1193. During the 13th century, great figures – such as the theologian Alan of Lille (†1203), whose tomb was discovered in 1960 – retired to Citeaux, an abbey protected by popes and kings and enjoying enormous prestige. In 1262, near the chevet of the abbey church, construction started on a building intended to contain the copyists carrels. It was raised after 1498 by a storey containing the library, completed in 1509. Citeaux, numbering five hundred people in 1300, was not spared by the Hundred Years War; it was plundered by marauders in 1350 and 1360. In 1400, several buildings were rebuilt. In 1477, at the death of Duke Charles the Hardy, Abbot Jean de Cirey rallied to the cause of Louis XI. He and his successors held the title of Prime Councillor (*primus consiliarius natus*) in Burgundy's parliament, and Philippe Pot, seneschal of Burgundy, was buried at the abbey in 1494. There were two hundred people living at Citeaux in 1501. The abbey possessed large properties, in particular the vineyard of Le Clos de Vougeot, where Abbot Jean Loisier built a château in 1551. But the successive looting during the Wars of Religion – in 1574, 1589, 1595 – destroyed the abbey's patrimony. In 1636, it was plundered once again by the troops of Gallas, after the attempt by Louis XIII to annex Franche Comté. In the course of the 17th century, Citeaux did not adhere

The convent buildings

The Definitory of Citeaux

Starting in 1265, and even perhaps from the end of the 12th century, the General Chapter of Citeaux was run by the definition, composed of twenty-five definitors. These were the abbot of Citeaux, the four first Fathers – i.e., the abbots of La Ferté, Pontigny, Clairvaux and Morimond –, along with twenty abbots named by the abbot of Citeaux and these first Fathers, each of whom chose four abbeys from among their affiliation.
The definitory's role was essential because the definitors prepared the questions and problems to be posed during the Order's General Chapter, studied them and then proposed solutions, or definitions. To welcome the college of the definitors, in 1683 Abbot Dom Jean Petit ordered the construction of a large building that was completed in 1699 and it took the name of definitory. Dom Petit also assigned to the building the purpose of sheltering the noviciate of Citeaux, which was common to several abbeys depending on it. On the ground floor of the definitory, a huge building measuring 80 metres by 16, there is a large vaulted hall along with a smaller room, probably the novices' chapel. Upstairs lay the dormitory, divided into cells.

LE CLOS DE VOUGEOT

"Having consideration for the constitution of those who are weak, we believe that a hemina of wine suffices for each for the day."
Rule of Saint Benedict (40.3)

According to the Cistercian Rule, a monastery is supposed to be self-sufficient. Among the foods that are basic necessities is wine; for meals, the monks had the right to a hemina (about half a pint) of wine daily, but it was also used during holy offices, as wine for mass. But the swampy lands surrounding Citeaux were not very favourable for vineyards. Stephen Harding's monks discovered well-exposed hillsides to the west of their New Monastery, upriver of the Vouge River. Although their community was very poor, after 1109, some generous benefactors, including the lords of Vergy, permitted the abbey to acquire eight *journaux* of fallow lands, barely three hectares. Starting in 1116, the monks built a grange in the heart of this piece of land which new donations rapidly increased in size. They worked the land and their vines gave wine of excellent quality, which they produced in vats and kept in the grange's cellars. A bull by Pope Alexander III (1159-1181) mentioned for first time the "*cellarium* of Vooget", whose surface reached its current size at the beginning of the 13th century. The Vougeot wine-cellar, which the monks enclosed with a protective wall, became Le Clos de Vougeot in 1212. The priory of Gilly was located between Citeaux and Le Clos de Vougeot. It depended on the Parisian Abbey of Saint Germain des Prés. Relations between Citeaux Abbey and the priory were good until the day the Cistercians decided to run a path across the priory's lands to make communication between the abbey and Le Clos easier. Gilly's monks prevented their plans so successfully that Citeaux finally acquired Gilly's lands in September, 1300. But the quarrel lasted until 1499. In the middle of the 15th century, insects ravaged the grapevines of Le Clos de Vougeot, and several years went by before vines could be planted once again. In 1551, the forty-eighth abbot of Citeaux, Jean Loisier, had the buildings of Le Clos de Vougeot refitted and built a Renaissance-style château. Until the Revolution, the quality of the wine produced at Le Clos increased steadily. Then, on February 13, 1790, Citeaux Abbey and its possessions, including Le Clos de Vougeot were declared state property. In January, 1791, the lands and goods of Le Clos were sold at auction; they included over one hundred and thirty *journaux* of land, the château and its outbuildings which contained four presses, thirty-seven vats and numerous casks. A single buyer paid 770,553 pounds

The château

ɔr the lot. But since the purchaser ɔrgot to pay the sum owed, it was Le :los' cellarer, Dom Goblet, who ran ɪe enterprise for the Nation. Since ɪen, Le Clos and its château have hanged hands several times. The fty-hectare vineyard is today divided mong eighty farmers. Vougeot's ines have several quality labels AOC), including four *premier cru* and ne *grand cru*. As for the château of

The large cellar

e Clos, one of its owners, Léonce ocquet, was ruined trying to restore and was buried in front of the doors 1913. Since 1944, the château as become the headquarters of ɪe Confrérie of the Chevaliers du astevin, created in 1935 by two men om Burgundy who wished to promote urgundy wines. The association is ɹn by a grand council and its name omes from the "tâtevin", a metal dish used by winemakers and wine-merchants to taste wine. Its motto is *Jamais en vain, toujours en vin* (never in vain, always in wine), and it is proud of its purple and gold coat of arms. There are about ten thousand members world wide, and commanderies exist in many countries, among them – Japan, Canada, China, Morocco, Ivory Coast and the U.S.A., where thirty-five states have a sub-commandery. The buildings of the château du Clos are set around a large courtyard in the centre of which stands the *Porteur de Bénaton*, a sculpture by Henri Bouchard. On the south side, the 12th century cellar is the seat of ceremonies for the Confrérie of the Chevaliers du Tastevin. A covered staircase leads upstairs to what was formerly the dormitory of the lay

One of the presses

brothers who worked the vineyards. To the west, the four galleries of the vat house, dating from the 12th century, surround a central patio. A large press with a capstan stands in each of the square's four corners. The north gallery contains eight oak wine-presses in which the lay brothers pressed the grapes with their feet at the end of a day of harvesting. The main building stands in the east side of the courtyard. To the right of its entrance, a porch leads to a well adjoining the 16th century kitchen. The well has a mechanism that brought water up from a depth of twenty-eight metres without too much effort. Through the château's door, a staircase with two flights leads upstairs to the dining room, its entrance marked with the motto of Abbot Loisier, *Dita servata fide* "wealth conserved by loyalty", and a large reception room where the enthronement ceremonies of the Confrérie des Chevaliers du Tastevin are usually held.

The abbey church chevet

Pontigny

Stalls in the abbey church

The second daughter-abbey of Citeaux, after La Ferté, Pontigny was founded in 1114, on land offered to Stephen Harding by the priest Ansius, in the valley of the Serein R. Hugues of Mâcon, one of Bernard's companions who entered Citeaux in 1112-1113, became its first abbot. Soon the abbey's property increased in size because of donations and recruits flooded in. In 1119, Pontigny founded Bouras Abbey, in the diocese of Auxerre. Thirteen other foundations followed throughout Europe as far as Hungary, and they too were prolific. In 1136, Hugues was named Bishop of Auxerre and, subsequently, nine other abbots from Pontigny were raised to the rank of bishop, archbishop or cardinal. Construction of a church and a larger monastery was undertaken in 1140, thanks to the beneficial actions of Thibaud the Great, Count of Champagne. Starting in 1164, Pontigny became a sanctuary for three successive archbishops of Canterbury – Thomas à Becket, Stephen Langton and Edmund Rich – all in conflict with the English crown. At his death in 1240, Edmund Rich was buried at the abbey, in accordance with his wishes. After his canonization six years later, his relics, objects of worship for many pilgrims, were solemnly transferred into the abbey's shrine on June 9, 1247, in the presence of Louis IX and Blanche of Castile. The king's grandmother, Alix of Champagne, the wife of Louis VII and mother of Philip Augustus, had been buried there in 1206. In 1350, during the Hundred Years War, Pontigny was pillaged by English troops and its property devastated. In the course of the 15th century, it was faced with serious material problems. This was followed, in 1543, by the difficult days of the commendam. In 1568, the violence of the Wars of Religion reached the area of Auxerre and the abbey was sacked. Only the remains of Saint Edmund, hidden safely away by the monks, escaped havoc. When free abbey elections were re-established in the 17th century, the abbey's resources had greatly diminished. Pontigny Abbey's last abbot tried to restore authentic monastic life but the Revolution did not allow him enough time to complete his work. In 1789, the church, as a popular pilgrimage site, was spared. Left in a state of abandon, the regular buildings were used as a quarry for the village's construction. After the 1801 Concordat, the church became a parish church and the priest's work was carried out by a former monk. The abbey was purchased in 1842 by Abbot Jean-Baptiste Muard who founded a *Society of Auxiliary Priests* there, and afterwards, in 1849, the religious congregation of the *Fathers of Saint Edmund*. The monks were expelled by the Law of 1901 and an academic, Paul Desjardins, bought the

The Virgin of Mercy

Saint Edmund

On June 9, 1247, the body of St Edmund was placed in a stone mausoleum (*below*) above the high altar in Pontigny Abbey Church, in the presence of Louis IX and Blanche of Castile. Since the king was about to leave to defend the Holy Land, the monks wished to present him with a piece of the saint's body. But Louis answered that he would never bear that the "body that God left intact" be mutilated.

Tomb of St Edmund

Abbey church façade

abbey in 1905. In summertime, over a period of ten days, he organized the *decades de Pontigny*, gathering together artists, writers and intellectuals from various countries. At his death in 1940, the Fathers of St Edmund recovered their property. In 1947, they opened a Franco-American college, St. Edmund's College. In 1954, Pope Pius XII established the seat of the *Mission de France* within the abbey's enclosure. When the mission was transferred to Val de Marne outside Paris in 1967, LADAPT, League to Adapt the Physically Diminished to Work, was established in Pontigny.
With its imposing size, one hundred and twenty-five metres long and fifty-two metres wide at the level of the transept, Pontigny Abbey Church is the largest Cistercian church preserved in France. The entrance porch presents the visitor with its Romanesque façade, dating from the first stage of construction between 1140 and 1160. Inside, the long nave with its two storeys with ribbed vaulting, communicates with its side aisles by large arcades. The capitals are austerely sculpted with leaves. The huge transept is the oldest part of the church; with groined arches, it has several chapels with flat ends. In the centre of the south arm, the 16th century Virgin protects the praying bishop, priest, monk and layman with her coat. Originally, the church ended with a small shrine with a flat chevet. Construction of the present chevet, with an ambulatory and radiating chapels, began in 1185 and ended in 1208. Above the red marble high altar stands the reliquary of Saint Edmund. Located to the north of the abbey church, the cloister retains only its south gallery with groined arches. The cellar and lay brothers' dormitory are all that remain of the monastery.

Chaalis

Located at the edge of the forests of Ermenonville and Chantilly, the abbey of Notre Dame de Chaalis (*opposite*) was founded in 1136 by King Louis VI le Gros, who offered it to Pontigny. Chaalis rapidly prospered upon receiving large donations. Saint Louis often stayed there and, as in Royaumont, liked to share the monks' simple, humble life. In the 16th century, the abbey was given in commendam. In 1154, Hippolyte d'Este, Cardinal of Ferrara and the king's cousin, was put in charge of the abbey where he created an Italian-style park.
In the 18th century, the regular buildings in poor condition were destroyed and rebuilt. The abbey fell to Mme de Vatry in 1850 and she made herself a castle out of it. Today it belongs to the Institut de France and contains the collections of the Jacquemart-André Museum and the Jean-Jacques Rousseau collection.

The abbey of Chaalis

FROM CANTERBURY TO PONTIGNY

Starting in 1164, Pontigny was the refuge of three famous archbishops of Canterbury: Thomas à Becket, Stephen Langton and Edmund Rich. Thomas à Becket (1118-1170) was chancellor of the Kingdom of England before becoming Archbishop of Canterbury in 1161. He thereby entered into conflict with King Henry II Plantagenet, his former friend, who wanted the church to submit to his authority. The quarrel deepened and Becket, forced into exile, settled in Pontigny at the end of 1164. However, in 1166, Henry II threatened to expel the Cistercian monks established in England if Pontigny continued to shelter the archbishop. Becket left the abbey and spent four years in Sens. In 1170, constrained by threats from Pope Alexander III, Henry II, pretending reconciliation, called Becket back to England. In December of the same year, four of the king's knights entered Canterbury Cathedral and murdered the archbishop. Unanimously condemned, the king was compelled to do penance while crowds gathered around the tomb of Thomas à Becket, canonized in 1173 and worshipped as a saint and hero. The drama inspired artists and writers, among them T.S. Eliot (1888-1965), author of the play, *Murder in the Cathedral* (1935). From 1208 to 1213, Pontigny welcomed Stephen Langton, a famous exegete, theologian and liturgical poet who was named cardinal in 1206, and while in Rome that same year, Archbishop of Canterbury. However, King John Landless entered into conflict with Pope Innocent III about the nomination and proscribed Stephen Langton, who spent most of his six years of exile in Pontigny. But in 1213, the excommunicated John Landless submitted to pontifical will.

Charles VII's Dream, Canterbury

His kingdom became a fief of the Holy See and Stephen Langton was allowed to return to his country and his cathedral. During the remaining fifteen years of his life, the archbishop worked to reconcile English royalty with the papacy and participated in the elaboration of the *Magna Carta* (1215), which was to play a decisive role in the evolution of English political life and which constituted one of the texts leading to the *Declaration of the Rights of Man*. Born in about 1170, Edmund Rich taught theology at Oxford before being named Archbishop of Canterbury in 1234. His determination to reduce the clergy's benefits and preserve the independence of the Church in the face of royal power soon brought protest from the monks in his chapter and the animosity of Henry III. In 1240, wishing to obtain advice from the Holy See, he went to the continent, stopping in Pontigny for a visit. However, falling ill, he could not continue his journey. Deciding to return to England, he died on the way, at Soisy near Provins, on November 16, 1240. According to his wishes, his body was buried at Pontigny. Canonized in 1246, Saint Edmund was venerated in England and the Auxerrois. His body was the object of a pilgrimage inaugurated by Saint Louis in 1247.

The Miracle of St Thomas, Canterbury

The cloister

Cadouin

In 1115, several hermits, disciples of Géraud of Sales, joined together at Cadouin, in the hollow of a valley of Bessède Forest in the Perigord. The hermitage was affiliated to the Cistercian Order in 1119, placing itself under the authority of the abbot of Pontigny. The monks began to build their abbey church, consecrated in 1154, in which they placed the precious relic of the Holy Shroud that had been offered to them in 1117 by crusaders returning from Antioch. A famous pilgrimage site, visited by Eleanor of Aquitaine, Richard the Lionheart, Jeanne of Valois – daughter of Louis XI, Cadouin flourished and developed. But during the Hundred Years War, the cloister was devastated and the monks placed the shroud in Toulouse for safety. After the victory of Castillon in 1453, the shroud was returned to Cadouin, where a new Gothic-style cloister had been built during the abbacy of Pierre de Gaing. The commendam system and then the troubles of the Wars of Religion both affected life at the community, which resisted nonetheless, and in 1643 joined the Strict Observance. However, at the Revolution the buildings were looted and the archives burned. The monastery was purchased by the village mayor and its church became the parish church in 1797, saving it from destruction. Restored during the 19th and 20th centuries under the direction of the Society for Historical Monuments, today the abbey belongs to the local council and the Dordogne department. As for the Holy Shroud, an evaluation carried out on the precious material in 1933 showed that it dated from the 11th century! Embroidered in the very weft of the cloth, a Kufic inscription mentioning an emir called Musta Ali renders thanks to Allah. Pilgrimages stopped immediately but the beautiful Fatimid cloth is still exhibited in the abbey's chapter house.

Consecrated in 1154, Cadouin church was built according to the plan of numerous other Aquitaine churches. Its façade, decorated with a tall row of blind arcades, has a doorway with a semicircular arch and four voussoirs. The church consists of a nave with side aisles, a small transept serving two semicircular chapels and a sanctuary ending with a semicircular apse. The nave and side aisles have pointed barrel vaults and the transept crossing is covered with a small dome on pendentives. Opening in the wall of the central apse, five semicircular windows light up the altar. The steeple, entirely covered by a pyramidal double roof, rises above the transept crossing. The cloister was rebuilt at the end of the 15th century on the ruins of the original cloister, destroyed during the Hundred Years War. Built in Flamboyant Gothic style, it is covered in ribbed vaulting with hanging keystones. The sculpted capitals in the galleries illustrate the great biblical parables. Built into one of the cloister walls, the abbot's seat is framed with two high-relief friezes presenting the road to Calvary and a procession of monks. The back of the chair shows the abbey's blazon. The cloister has retained the chapter house containing the famous shroud and, in the lay brothers' wing the visitor can still see the long, pointed barrel-vaulted room that used to be the abbey's storeroom.

The abbot's seat

Géraud of Sales

A canon at Saint Avit Sénieur in his youth, Géraud of Sales became an itinerant hermit in the Perigord. From 1113 to 1114, he wandered throughout Aquitaine, gathering many followers. He recommended the Fontevriste model to women; for men he created hermitages, which he visited regularly. At his death in 1120, conscious of the progress of coenobitism but still faithful to his eremitic vocation, he advised his disciples to adopt the Rule of Saint Benedict, "in imitation of the Cistercians".

Cloister gallery

The abbey

The cornice of the chevet

Sylvanès

In 1132, Lord Pons de Léras, the lord-repented bandit, along with several companions founded the little hermitage of Saint Mary of Mas Théron, not far from Sylvanès in an isolated, forested valley of the Rouergue, where the Cabot River flows. Donations enlarged the hermitage's property and an ever-increasing number of disciples rapidly formed a real community. Pons thus considered affiliating with Citeaux and, in 1136, he offered his monastery to the abbot of Mazan, in the Vivarais valley, one of the daughters of Bonnevaux. A former monk of Mazan, Adhemar, became the first abbot of Mas Théron which, in 1138, took the name of Sylvanès. Pons, who wished to remain a monk, died in 1140 in the humility of manual labour and continual prayer. Throughout the 12th century, Sylvanès enjoyed an extremely favourable period. John Comnenius, Emperor of Constantinople, Roger II, King of Sicily and Thibaud, Count of Champagne, all made generous gifts to the abbey, that Innocent II placed under his protection. The monks worked the fields, the vineyards and pastures of their huge domain, which contained waters from mineral springs, ever since called the *monks' spring*. In 1146, Sylvanès founded the nuns' abbey at Nonenque. However, since the mineral waters attracted many visitors, the community decided to move away from the crowds, two thousand metres upriver along the Cabot, where a larger abbey was built. Starting in 1477, the abbey was placed in commendam, to the detriment of monastic life. Then in 1591, Huguenots threatened Sylvanès, finally spared thanks to François de Lauzières who managed to repel them in time. By 1768, the abbey contained only six monks and the Commission of Regulars, established by Louis XVI, considered suppressing it. Finally, it was the Revolution that scattered the little community. In 1791, the abbey church became a parish church and the monastic buildings were put up for sale and most of them were demolished. Today, the church, chapter house, the large monks' hall and four bays of the cloister's east gallery still show the former splendour of Sylvanès. The abbey organizes many concerts, especially within the framework of the Summer Music Festival, and holds various artistic workshops.

Begun about 1157, the church, in the shape of a Latin cross, consists of a nave covered with pointed barrel vaulting, without side aisles. The lateral walls have arcaded openings that provide light, and the capitals are sculpted with motifs of plants or cephalomorphic figures. The groined arches of the transept crossing, without ribs, look like ribbed vaulting. Two chapels surround the sanctuary with its flat chevet. The church façade contains two Romanesque doors surmounted by a window with Gothic tracery. The monastic buildings are located to the south of the church, along the Cabot. In the east gallery, the sacristy's tympanum represents the Trinity: the three arcatures symbolize heaven, the residence of the Father; the lamb represents the Son, and the dove, the Holy Spirit. The chapter opens onto the cloister through a door framed by two gemel openings, their capitals decorated with leaves.

Gothic window

Acts of Contrition

Pons, Lord of Léras, owned a castle at Pas de l'Escalette, near Lodève. Fearing neither God nor man, he looted and betrayed as he liked until, realizing the wretchedness of his acts, he gave his goods to the poor and returned what he had stolen. With six companions, he came barefoot to the bishop of Lodève and did public penance. He then made a pilgrimage to Saint Guilhem le Désert and Santiago de Compostela. Dedicating his life to God, in 1132 he founded Mas Théron hermitage on the lands of Lord Arnaud de Pont.

Cloister capital

The lavatorium

Le Thoronet

Founded in 1136 by Ramon Berenguer IV, Count of Barcelona and Marquis of Provence, who called on monks from Mazan Abbey, a daughter of Bonnevaux, Thoronet Abbey is the eldest of the "Provençal sisters". Silvacane was founded in 1147, and Sénanque in 1148. The monks settled near Tourtour, in the diocese of Fréjus, in the depths of a valley watered by the Florielle River. The new foundation took the name of Florège, from the name of the river. Etienne of Baux and his son, Hugues, were among the first benefactors of the abbey, to which they granted the Marignane saltworks. About ten years later, the site's inhospitality led the monks to move about twenty kilometres away, to Le Thoronet, near Lorgues, where more fertile lands were offered by Ramon Berenguer. Construction of the current building was then undertaken. The abbey received many donations from the kings of Aragon and the lords of Castellane, and was soon the owner of a vast domain. It then diffused to the island of Porquerolles, the largest of the Hyères islands, but the new foundation was destroyed by Moors in 1160. In 1199, Thoronet's abbot tried to repopulate a former abbey, but was opposed by the General Chapter which considered that Thoronet should first of all face up to its overly great expenses. The abbey thus remained without a daughter. In 1328, the monks rebelled against their abbot, provoking the intervention of the bishop of Fréjus at the request of Pope John XXII. Then the commendam system, established in Thoronet in 1435, brought about the ruin of its worldly possessions. In 1614, during the Wars of Religion, the abbey fell into Protestant hands and its monks had to flee. When peace was re-established, the few monks at Thoronet were living in such miserable conditions that, in 1787, the abbey was annexed to the bishopric of Digne. The Revolution expelled the seven remaining monks and the local administration inherited the abbey with its agricultural lands. Saved from destruction by Prosper Mérimée, it was bought by the State in 1854. Entirely restored by the Historical Monument Society, Thoronet Abbey is one of the masterpieces of Cistercian architecture.

The church façade with its plain dry-bonded hard stones, with no portal door, pierced solely with two Romanesque openings, topped with a large oculus, bare of decoration, is a foretaste of the extreme austerity of the interior. Built between 1160 and 1180, the church of Thoronet, small in size, follows the traditional plan of the first Cistercian churches. Facing east, in the shape of a Latin cross, it has a large nave with three bays, covered with pointed barrel vaults, communicating with the aisles through large arcades, a vast transept onto which open four semicircular chapels, and a small sanctuary ending in a semicircular apse. Outside, a square stone steeple, each of its sides pierced by a semicircular opening, rises above the transept crossing. The cloister, located to the north of the church, has a trapezoid shape because of the slope of the ground. Only the south gallery is set at the same level as the church, the others are lower down. The galleries are covered with pointed barrel vaulting.

Abbey church chevet

Mazan Abbey

Mazan Abbey (*below*) was founded in 1119 in the Vivarais, in the diocese of Viviers, by monks coming from Bonnevaux Abbey, the seventh daughter-abbey of Citeaux. Mazan itself diffused to Florielle and Le Thoronet in 1136, to Bonneval in 1147, and to Sénanque in 1148. Sylvanès was affiliated with it in 1136.

Mazan

The chapter house

It opens onto the garden through Romanesque arcades set in the thickness of the walls. Its galleries are covered with pointed barrel vaults. The cloister opens onto the garden through semicircular arcades opening in the thick walls. Each arcade is divided into two gemel openings, supported by a column and topped by a tympanum with an oculus in it. Like in the church, there is no superfluous decoration to distract the visitor in a place dedicated to contemplation. In the east gallery, beyond the *armarium* and the sacristy, a doorway framed by two openings, divided into three semicircular arcades, provides access to the chapter house. It has six bays, vaulted on crossed ogives, supported in the centre by two columns with carved capitals. One of them is decorated with leaves, flowers and a hand holding the abbey cross. The other is sculpted with pinecones and Christ's cross. After the passage, a staircase leads to the dormitory that fills the upper storey. This large room, with pointed barrel vaulting, lit by narrow Romanesque windows, gives onto the terrace overlooking the cloister. The kitchen, refectory and the heating room have disappeared from the north gallery. Protruding into the garden opposite the refectory entrance, the monks' lavatorium stands under a hexagonal chapel, vaulted on intersecting ribs and with openings made of semicircular arcades. The cloister's west wing contains the abbey's storeroom. The lay brothers' buildings, separated from the regular premises, extend further west, parallel to the storeroom. The large room on the ground floor used to be the refectory and the dormitory lay upstairs.

THE WILD STONES

In his novel *The Wild Stones*, the architect Fernand Pouillon, whose work was profoundly inspired by Cistercian art, imagined a diary kept by the master architect who built Thoronet Abbey in the 12th century.

The dormitory

FIN'AMOR AND THE LOVE OF GOD

The son of a Genoese merchant established in Marseille during the second half of the 12th century, Foulque received an advanced education and took over the family business. Wealthy, married and the father of two sons, he was also welcome in high society because of his poetic gifts. Between 1179 and 1195, he composed fourteen love *cansos*, one *tenso*, a *cobla*, a *plahn*, then, tired of the niceties of *fin'amor*, he wrote two crusading songs in which, placing his art in God's service, he encourage the powerful to go and fight the Saracens in the Holy Land and in Spain. The talented and admired poet, cited by Petrarch in *The Triumph of Love*, and whom Dante placed in Paradise among the souls who love heaven and Venus, gave up the world and poetry in 1195 to take the monk's habit in Thoronet. He was chosen as the community's abbot in 1199. Seven years later, he was elected Bishop of Toulouse. With Dominic, Foulque then actively supported Innocent III's policies against the Cathar heretics. In particular, in his new bishopric he organized the White Confrerie. He led its five thousand men to the ramparts of Lavaur in May 1211, to lend a helping hand to Simon de Montfort's crusaders. On April 12, 1229, he was present on the parvis of Notre Dame in Paris, at the side of Louis IX, for the ceremony reconciling Count Raymond VII of Toulouse with the Church. He died in 1231 and was buried in the Cistercian abbey of Grandselve.

The cloister

The abbey church nave

The abbey church nave

The abbey church

STABILITY

The threat was always present for the white monks at Tibhirine, daughter of Aiguebelle, but they changed nothing in their way of life and prayer, even refusing all protection. On March 27, 1996, the seven monks were confined and then beheaded on May 21. A Cistercian abbey is still living in the heart of the Algerian Atlas Mountains.

AIGUEBELLE

North gallery of the cloister

Located in the Drôme, not far from Montélimar, Aiguebelle Abbey was founded in 1137 by Gontard Loup, the lord of Rochefort en Valdaine, who offered it to the monks of Morimond. Aiguebelle spread in turn, first of all to Frayssinet in 1160 although this daughter became a grange, then to Haute Auvergne where Val Honnête Abbey was established in 1173. The latter founded Bouchet Abbey, also known as Vauluisant, in 1198. In the middle of the 13th century, its property spread as far as the Vivarais, where Combemaure grange ran a farm of nearly three thousand hectares. In the 15th century, there were fewer recruits, labour was becoming scarce and some of the domains were sold. Aiguebelle came under commendam in 1490. The Wars of Religion arrived next. In 1562, the cloister was devastated, the church's vaulting was destroyed and the abbey set on fire. In 1790, the abbey and its properties were put up for sale. However, in 1816, Dom Augustin de Lestrange purchased Aiguebelle and established a group of Cistercians in it, thus reviving the flame of Citeaux. The ever greater number of recruits allowed the foundation of Staoueli Monastery, in 1843 in the diocese of Algiers, the first daughter of a long lineage. In 1849, Aiguebelle spread to Notre Dame des Neiges, in Viviers diocese; in 1852, it founded Sainte Marie du Désert, in the diocese of Toulouse; and in 1863, Notre Dame des Dombes, in Belley diocese. In 1873, monks from Aiguebelle repopulated Acey Abbey in the Jura, then that of Bonnecombe in the diocese of Rodez in 1876. Soon Aiguebelle's daughters began to diffuse in their turn, spreading the affiliation to Spain. In 1934, Aiguebelle became the mother-abbey of Notre Dame de l'Atlas, at Tibhirine in the diocese of Algiers. In 1951, it founded Koutaba Monastery in Cameroon, thus increasing the fertile family of the Cistercian Order of the Strict Observance.

Aiguebelle Abbey has been restored respecting the original buildings. The church, mainly with ribbed vaulting, has retained its nave, its side aisles and its transept from the end of the 12th century. The four semicircular chapels of the transept and the apse of the sanctuary date from the 19th century. Of the cloister, only the Romanesque gallery adjoining the church remains intact. It looks towards the garden through triple semicircular openings, supported by thin gemel columns with decorated capitals. The east gallery contains the chapter house, covered with groined arches resting on two square pillars. The south gallery contains the refectory. Separated from the cloister by a small courtyard, the lay brothers' building consists of the storeroom, a refectory and the dormitory upstairs.

Lay brothers' passage

Entrance to the chapter house

The spring that feeds the lavatorium

L'Escale Dieu

Capital in chapter house

Founded in 1137, the abbey of L'Escale Dieu was the fourteenth daughter of Morimond. At first, the white monks settled in Campan Valley, near the Gripp cascades, but the harsh climate forced them to move and, in 1140, they settled in the Arros Valley, at the foot of the Pic du Midi de Bigorre. Thanks to the monks' labour and the generous gifts of local lords, L'Escale Dieu developed quickly and was soon able to diffuse in turn. Helped and protected by the Countess Petronilla and her husbands, the abbey was influential in the 13th century and its abbots participated in the Estates General of Bigorre. During the 14th century, the abbey founded new villages on its lands, but the castle of Mauvezin built less than a league away, on the heights of the plateau of Lannemezan, attracted many aggressive knights to the vicinity of the monastery. In 1360, following the Treaty of Brétigny that put a temporary end to the Hundred Years War, Edward III renounced claims to the French crown and, in compensation, received Calais, a part of Picardy, and all the south-west. Mauvezin hence passed under English domination. The Black Prince, son of Edward III, was named governor of Aquitaine and imposed heavy taxes on his new possessions. The people of Bigorre revolted, called on the king, and hence the troops of Du Guesclin and the Duke of Anjou stayed at L'Escale Dieu. In the 16th century, Protestants sacked the abbey. When peace returned, religious life declined. The General Chapter decided to send the undisciplined monks to other abbeys and asked the monks of Boulbonne, La Bénisson Dieu and Eaunes to replace them. But the culprits took possession of the abbey and imprisoned the new arrivals. By the time the governor of Guyenne arrived to re-establish order, they had already fled. The monastic buildings, destroyed by the various wars, were rebuilt during the 17th and 18th centuries. During the Revolution, the abbey was put up for sale in 1793. It was used as a stone quarry during the 19th century. The cloister, the refectory and the lay brothers' wing all disappeared.

L'Escale Dieu abbey church was built towards 1143 and consecrated in 1160. In the shape of a Latin cross, it consists of a nave with side aisles and a transept with four rectangular chapels. Its façade and chevet have disappeared. Adjacent to the church, three semicircular arcades are the remains of the former *armarium*. In the east wing of the cloister courtyard, a Romanesque doorway, framed by two gemel openings, leads to the chapter house. In the centre, four marble columns, topped with capitals sculpted with leaves, support the ogives of the vault.

Mauvezin Castle

Petronilla of Bigorre

Petronilla of Bigorre, the "countess with five husbands", showered gifts on L'Escale Dieu Abbey. In 1251, she retired to the abbey, bequeathing to the monks her gold vases, her jewels and precious furniture. She died at L'Escale Dieu and was buried there, according to her wishes.

Abbey church steeple

Abbey church nave

Léoncel

In 1137, monks from Bonnevaux settled in an isolated valley of the Vercors, east of Valence, at an altitude of more than 900 metres. Their abbey, located on the bank of the source of the Lionne River, received the name *Lionnae cella,* which became Léoncel. Placed under pontifical protection in 1142, the recipient of numerous donations, Léoncel developed and flourished despite the bandits roaming in the area. Its third abbot, Hugues de Châteauneuf, elected in 1163, is the most famous of its abbots. In 1165, he obtained a bull protecting and confirming the abbey's domains from Pope Alexander III. Elected abbot of Bonnevaux in 1169, he interceded in 1177 with Emperor Frederick Barbarossa to encourage him to recognize Alexander III's legitimacy and put an end to the schism within the Church. In 1194, the small community of La Part Dieu, established at the foot of the mountains of Léoncel, affiliated itself with Citeaux by joining Léoncel. In the course of the 13th century, the monks enlarged their properties and built a mill at La Part Dieu. But Léoncel's isolated lands and granges were ideal targets for bandits and plunderers, so that in 1247, Pope Innocent IV urged the archbishop of Vienne to ensure the monks' defence. The 14th century was the beginning of a dire period for the abbey and its region: they were, first of all, victims of the conflict opposing the bishops of Valence and the counts of the Valentinois, then came the famine of 1346, soon followed by the plague epidemic called the Black Death. With the Hundred Years War, devastation by the Grandes Companies followed the truce of 1356. In 1389, Raymond of Turenne, fighting with the counts of Valentinois, destroyed and plundered Léoncel's domains before setting the abbey on fire. The monks found refuge in Romans where they remained for many years. During the Wars of Religion, in 1567, Léoncel was plundered once again. In 1591, Henry IV had the abbey closed because the abbot had joined the League. The monks did not recover their goods until after the king had converted to Catholicism. The impoverished abbey contained only five monks when it was placed in commendam in 1681. It was put up for sale at the Revolution. Only the church was spared. In its simplicity, the church of Léoncel, with its form of a Latin cross facing east, conforms to the Cistercian ideal. Its nave with five bays, vaulted on intersecting ribs, communicates with the aisles through slightly pointed arcades. Two semicircular chapels, framing the choir, open onto the transept. The crossing, lit by a large oculus, is covered by a dome on squinches. The sanctuary ends by an apse with three semicircular openings that light up the altar. However, the thirty-three metre high steeple, rising at the transept crossing, does not follow the Rule. Cistercian churches were supposed to be satisfied with a simple belfry to contain the two statutory bells. Perhaps the violence in Léoncel's high valley allowed it some special authorization by the General Chapter to explain why its abbey church was endowed with such a large stone tower.

The lavatorium seen from the cloister

Maulbronn

Arcade of a cloister gallery

Maulbronn is located between the towns of Bretten, in the lands of Baden, and Mühlacker, in Wurtemburg. In 1138, monks from the Alsatian abbey of Neubourg, great-granddaughter of Morimond through the intermediary of Lucelle, came to settle in Eckenweiher Forest, on lands granted to them by the knight Walter von Lomersheim before he took the monk's habit. Less than ten years later, the monks moved onto lands in the Salzach valley offered by the bishop of Spire, Gunther, Count of Henneberg, to a wild and isolated site where water, stone and wood were abundant. On March 29, 1148, Pope Eugene III placed the monastery under his protection while the monks undertook construction of the church. For three hundred and ninety years, Cistercian monks lived within the walls of Maulbronn, a rich and powerful abbey. But in 1537, the Reformation provoked the departure of the monks and Maulbronn, which provided itself with a castle, became the residence of the dukes of Wurtemberg. The abbey church was allotted to the Protestant parish in 1547. In 1556, Duke Christopher installed a seminary in the monastery, intended to prepare future pastors. Famous people, such as the astronomer Johannes Kepler, the future diplomat and friend of Goethe, Karl Friedrich Reinhard, the poet Hölderlin, the writer Hermann Hesse, were seminarians there.

The Alchemist of Maulbronn

The great alchemist Johannes Faust was called to Maulbronn in 1516 by Abbot Entenfuss to make gold. He worked in the abbey's kitchen and lived in the tower set in the south-east corner of the monastery walls.

The monastery's founders presenting a model of the church to the Virgin

The *Paradise* porch dates from 1220 and, although Romanesque dominates, the window tracery is a sign of the coming of Gothic architecture. The porch welcomed visitors who were not allowed to enter the church, reserved for monks and lay brothers. Entrance into the church was through a Romanesque portal door that has retained its original hinges. Built between 1147 and 1178, in the form of a Latin cross and facing east, the abbey church has a long nave with side aisles, a transept lined with six chapels, and a square-shaped sanctuary. The nave and aisles, originally covered with simple roof-beams, were vaulted in 1424 when the ten rectangular chapels of the south aisle were installed. The rood screen separated the monks' choir in the east from the lay brothers' choir in the west. Behind the lay brothers' altar stands a 15th century crucifix, and a niche in the south baldaquin contains a wooden Madonna from the 14th century. The Cistercian Rule authorized only these

The lavatorium

THE MASTER AND PARADISE

The church porch, the cloister's south wing, and the refectory are the work of an architect trained in France on the sites of the great cathedrals, where he learned Gothic techniques. Two opposing crescent moons, carved in stone, are the signature of this anonymous master, called the "Master of the Paradise of Maulbronn".

The abbey

two figurative representations. The windows with Gothic tracery in the sanctuary were added in around 1340. The monks' stalls, dating from 1450, are carved with biblical scenes. Access to the cloister is through the north aisle. The sandstone galleries open onto the garden through large openings with tracery, in the Rayonnant Gothic style. In the east wing, a double arcade and three windows mark the openings of the chapter house, with its octagonal plan. The north gallery leads to the heating room, whose warm air came from the floor underneath through holes made in the floor, and the brightly-lit refectory, built in 1225, covered with sexpartite vaulting. Opposite, the monks' lavatorium stands inside a Gothic chapel, opening with tracery windows, and raised with half-timbering in 1511. The lay brothers' buildings stood in the west gallery.

Lay brothers' passage

The chapter house

Veruela

The abbey of Veruela was founded in 1145 on lands granted by the king of Navarre García V (1134-1150), north of Tarazona and protected from the north-west by the Sierra del Moncayo. Veruela was a daughter of Niencebas Abbey, recently incorporated into the Cistercian Order as a daughter of L'Escale Dieu before transferring to Fitero. The region of Tarazona was disputed by the king of Navarre and the count of Barcelona, Ramon Berenguer IV (1131-1162), the husband of Petronilla, Queen of Aragon (1137-1162). In 1149, when peace was re-established after its recapture by Aragon, Ramon Berenguer confirmed the act of donation by his former adversary in 1145. The lands were rich, watered by the Huecha River, and over time the monks of Veruela worked hard to exploit them. They cultivated wheat, barley, vineyards, olive trees, planted apple and pear trees, gathered walnuts and hazelnuts and produced highly-appreciated oils that they could trade for other goods. They ran a fulling-mill that provided them with fine woollen cloth. They owned many granges, as far away as Huesca, and their herds moved to summer pastures in the Pyrenees piedmont. Their direct exploitation of the land relied on their lay brothers but also on servile Muslim labourers. These resources provided the means to build and arrange their abbey, where they settled in 1171. To that end, in 1184 Alfonso II of Aragon (1162-1196) granted them a stone quarry at Aljara, near Trasmoz, a league away from the monastery. The five apsidal chapels in the abbey church's chevet were built from 1168 to 1182; San Miguel Chapel opening in the south arm of the transept was completed in 1178. In 1248, the altar in the chancel was consecrated. A statue of Our Lady of Veruela, dating from the end of the 15th century, stands on it today. One year later, San Lorenzo altar was consecrated, in the first west aisle of the nave. In 1260, James 1st (1213-1276) had his eldest son, Don Alfonso, buried in the abbey church's choir, where the carved funerary plaque with its Aragon coat of arms is still visible. But in 1323, construction of the church had still not finished since, in that same year, Don Martín López de Rueda bequeathed three thousand sols to complete the vaulting of the nave. Peter 1st of Castile (1350-1369) and Peter IV of Aragon (1336-1387) were fighting each other. In 1357, Veruela was occupied by the Castilians who destroyed the cloister and the heating room. During the abbacy of Don Sancho Marcilla (1362-1383), a new cloister was built thanks to donations by the Luna family, several members of which were buried in the church at the end of the 13th century and during the 14th. But the abbey's economic situation began to deteriorate. Harvests were affected by drought in 1359 and 1361 and it became difficult to recruit lay brothers. Veruela was forced to abandon direct exploitation in favour of leasing its lands. In 1472, the abbey was placed into commendam. Its first commendatory abbot was Juan de Aragon (1472-1475), one of the illegitimate sons of John II of Aragon (1458-1479) and archbishop of Zaragoza. During the abbacies of Don Hernando of Aragon (1535-1539),

Abbey church chevet

Granddaughter of L'Escale Dieu

On one of the pillars in the abbey church choir, a plaque has a text carved in stone, reminding that Veruela lay in the lineage of *Scale Dei*, L'Escale Dieu, or Escaladieu. This latter abbey, set on the north side of the Pyrenees, was a daughter of Morimond.

***Scale Dei* inscription**

A lavatorium gargoyle

grandson of Ferdinand the Catholic, and Don Lope Marco (1539-1560), work was undertaken. From 1541 to 1553, the perimeter walls were rebuilt starting from the Homage Tower, itself built from 1268 to 1292. The new ramparts formed a perimeter of one thousand meters, defining an area of five hectares. Between 1548 and 1551, the vaulting of the dormitory and refectory were redone. The cloister received three of its upper galleries. The fourth, west, gallery was made under the abbacy of Don Francisco Hurtado de Mendoza (1595-1602). St Bernard's Chapel, in the extension of the transept's north arm, was built between 1547 and 1550. It contains the alabaster tomb of Don Lope Marco, created by Pedro de Moreto in 1552-1553. A large reredos was ordered for the choir apse. Abbot Don Carlos Cerdán Gurrea (1560-1586) had an abbey palace built outside the enclosure. It closes the large square in the south. Under the authority of Abbot Juan Ximénez Tabar (1613-1617), Veruela entered the Cistercian Congregation of Aragon, started in 1616. Before becoming the first Vicar General of the congregation in 1617, this abbot launched construction work on a new monastery, east of the old one. Its buildings contained sixty-five individual cells for the monks and a new sacristy. During the first third of the 19th century, Veruela underwent the same problems as many other Spanish monasteries, with the War of Independence (1808-1813), the *Exclaustración* in 1820 and the *Desamortización* of 1835. From then on, there were no more monks at the abbey but the buildings remained intact. However, they were damaged and plundered before the auction sale in 1844. The great

Another Reredos

In 1556, Don Lope Marco ordered a reredos for St Bernard's Chapel from the sculptor Arnaud of Brussels. At the beginning of the 20th century, it was transferred to the church of the neighbouring village of Vera de Moncayo, where it still stands behind the high altar.

Gothic gallery in cloister

The a

reredos and many books in the library disappeared. The Becquer brothers stayed in Veruela, which had become a romantic ruin, during the winter of 1863 to 1864. From 1877 to 1973, Veruela was occupied by Jesuits, although they had to leave during the years 1932 to 1939. In 1919, Veruela was designated a national monument. Since 1998 it has been the property of the *Diputación de Zaragoza*, which has undertaken restoration work and organizes an annual music festival, "*Veruela Musica Viva*".
The church doorway dates from the end of the 12th century. Inside, the nave and side aisles have six bays. In the transept's north arm lies the chapel of Saint Thomas of Canterbury, and the chapel of San Miguel lies in the south arm. The choir, formed by an aisle and a semicircular apse, is surrounded by an ambulatory that serves five radiating chapels, forming on the outside a well-structured chevet, finely bonded in pure Romanesque style. The cloister lies to the north. The four lower galleries, from the end of the 14th century, are very homogeneous in style. The monks entered the refectory through the south gallery. Before entering they washed at the hexagonal-shaped lavatorium standing just opposite in the cloister garden. In the chapter house, opening onto the east gallery, there are fourteen funerary slabs and the tombs of Don Lope Jiménez de Agón, from the 13th century, and Don Sancho Marcilla, from the 14th. At the corner of the east and south galleries, a door provides access to the 13th century monks' hall. And the *cilla*, storeroom and cellar, dating from the 13th and 14th centuries, adjoins the west wing.

Capital in the chapter house

A Place of Inspiration

After 1844, Veruela became an excursion destination for travellers interested in old stone ruins, looking for solitude and a change of scenery. The poet Gustavo Adolfo Becquer and his brother, the painter Valeriano Becquer, stayed there with their families from December, 1863 to July, 1864. Gustavo Adolfo was already aware of the region's natural beauty because his wife came from the village of Noviercas, south-west of the Sierra del Moncayo. He wrote nine letters, gathered under the title *Desde mi celda*, From My Cell, and published in the Madrid daily *El Contemporáneo* from May to October, 1864. These letters are a descriptive chronicle of his stay on these lands that this new "solitary walker", heralding Machado, covered. In the cemetery of Trasmoz, he confronted the silent presence of death. Valeriano, who made drawings and watercolours in which his brother's figure sometimes appeared, returned to Veruela in August, 1865. Some of his works appeared in the collection *Expedición de Veruela*. The Becquers brought back from "this land still pure and resistant to civilizing innovations" subjects for other works of an anthropological character.

The abbey church

Obazine

At the beginning of the 12th century, Stephen and Peter, priests in the diocese of Limoges, distributed their goods to the poor and retired to the solitudes of Obazine Forest, a wild and nearly inaccessible area between Brive and Tulle, on the left bank of the Corrèze River. With the few disciples who came to share their ascetic life, they created a monastery. Stephen soon wished to adopt a Rule for his community and, in 1142, the monastery was joined to the nearby abbey of Dalon, founded by Géraud of Sales, a disciple of Robert of Arbrissel. Then in 1147, Obazine, in full expansion, was affiliated with the Cistercian Order, under the direct dependence of Citeaux. Despite new foundations – La Valette in 1142, Bonnaigue and La Garde Dieu in 1150, La Frenade in 1151 – the community became ever more numerous and the abbey's well could no longer provide for its needs. The monks therefore undertook tremendous works to capture the waters of the Coyroux River, from its gorges half a league away. In 1310, the abbot of Obazine, Raymond de Pléaux, was charged with writing the statutes for Grandmont Abbey, along with Arnaud Nouvel, Abbot of Fontfroide. But the destruction of the Hundred Years War reduced the abbey to extreme poverty. When Obazine passed into commendam in the 15th century, the General Chapter had to remind its abbots to respect the Order's statutes on numerous occasions. When the Wars of Religion arrived,

A misericord

Reclinent super misericordias

It was tiring for aging monks to stand for long. They therefore used a little seat called a misericord (*above*), or mercy, placed under the seat of the stall, used once the stall was closed. "Let them lean on the misericords!", wrote Stephen Harding.

The Order of Grandmont

On his return from Calabria, Stephen, son of the Viscount of Thiers, established a hermitage at Muret, near Ambazac, in the diocese of Limoges. He led a life of prayer and meditation there for forty-six years. He ate nothing but rye gruel, wore armour against his bare skin and slept in a ditch dug in the ground. At his death in 1124, his disciples moved to the wooded hills of Grandmont. In about 1150, one of them, Stephen of Liciac, wrote a rule inspired by the founder's maxims. The Order spread throughout France and England. The cells of the Grandmontains, built according to the same plan in the middle of woods, gathered a community of ten to fifteen monks led by a prior around an oblong church. In order that the friars' worship not be disturbed, material tasks were carried out by lay brothers. In 1185 and 1214, the latter revolted and the papacy intervened to remedy the Rule's inadequacies. In 1310, the abbots of Fontfroide and Obazine were charged with writing new statutes for Grandmont, approved by Pope Clement V.
In 1317, Pope John XXII raised Grandmont to an abbey and gathered the monks into thirty priories.
The Order lasted until the end of the 18th century. Grandmont Abbey was destroyed in 1817.

Saint Michel de Grandmont

Stained-glass window

In his *Commentary on the Mystery of Mary*, Bernard wrote, "As the splendour of the sun passes through glass without breaking it and penetrates its solidity with impalpable subtleness, without making holes when it enters and without breaking on its way out, so does the Word of God, light of the Father, penetrate the abode of the Virgin and leave intact from her breast."

Obazine collapsed under the plundering and exactions. Little by little, religious fervour seemed to revive in the ruins and, in 1667, the abbey was even chosen by the General Chapter to house the central noviciate of the Common Observance. However, by the end of the 17th century, there were only four monks left in Obazine. At the Revolution, the abbey and its properties were sold and its church became a parish church.

Obazine church was built starting in 1156, after joining the Cistercians, and was completed, along with the rest of the buildings, in 1190. Entirely covered with pointed barrel vaulting, it had a nave of nine bays with side aisles but, in 1757, the last six were demolished before they collapsed. The long transept served six chapels with flat chevets. In the transept's south arm, the tomb of Stephen, founder and first abbot of Obazine, was remarkably sculpted by an anonymous artist of the 13th century. At the crossing there is a dome on pendentives, identical to the one at Cadouin. The sanctuary ends with a five-sided apse, containing three semicircular windows. The church in Obazine is the only one in France to have kept three of its original stained glass windows, characteristic of Cistercian art. Like the other architectural elements, the stained glass windows were to be simple and plain, "white and without images", according to the expression of the General Chapter in 1134. Obazine cloister has disappeared, but the east wing has retained the chapter house, with two naves with groined arches, as well as the monks' hall. The kitchen with its fireplace lies in the north wing.

The tomb of St Stephen

Mastering Hydraulics

Because a Cistercian abbey was a self-contained economic microcosm, where the monks working with their hands produced all they needed to support themselves, the abbey could not be satisfied with a simple spring, although they were always established near a source of water. The white monks used hydraulic techniques to supply their monasteries with the running water needed for their various craft activities and to allow them to raise fish, irrigate their lands, drive their millwheels and the tilt hammers of their forges. Hence, in Obazine, the monks' canal captured water in the torrent of the Coyroux River, seventeen hundred metres from the abbey, in the highest part of the gorge. Peacefully running along the side of the hill, the water tumbled down behind the abbey like a mountain stream, passed under the monastery and sprang out to fill a vast three metre deep fishpond. Once again canalized in the west, it followed its course to drive the wheels of a mill, before calmly joining the Corrèze River, a kilometre away. Masters of hydraulics, the Cistercians were called on for work on a regional scale. By 1180, monasteries at Moreilles, Bois Grolland, La Grâce Dieu, Charron and Saint Léonard des Chaumes organized draining and drying works in the marshes of Poitou. In order to do this, the Cistercians perfected a draining technique that was quite similar to that used by the Dutch in the 19th century. Monks from Vieuville took part in making polders in the bay of Mont Saint Michel and Cistercians from the abbey of Buzay improved swamp lands to provide pastures for their famous horses. Fontenay captured water from the Fontenay brook to feed the canal that supplied power for their mill and their forge. At Orval, at the beginning of the 16th century, the monks even built a dam to develop an iron industry on the site. But on March 26, 1691, the dikes burst and almost carried away the walls of the abbey.

The Monks' Canal at Obazine

Poitevin Marshes

Abbey church nave

Silvacane

In the 11th century, a group of hermits settled in the valley of the Durance River, in a place called Gontard, depending on St Victor's Abbey in Marseilles. Set on the edge of marshes, the new foundation took the name of Silvacane, or "forest of reeds". The monks drained the swamps, raised a small chapel dedicated to Saint Victor and cleared paths around their monastery. In 1145, after the passage of Bernard of Clairvaux through the region when he tried to contradict the heresies of Pierre de Bruys, the monks of Silvacane decided to affiliate with the Cistercian Order. Two years later, in 1147, Cistercians from Morimond arrived to incorporate Silvacane into the Order. Raymond of Baux, Lord of Berre, offered the monks lands that he owned around the abbey. New recruits arrived and in 1188 Silvacane spread to La Valsainte, not far from Apt. Its properties grew ever greater with the help of various lords, and the monks endowed themselves with a great church and a new monastery. At the beginning of the 13th century, Silvacane came into conflict with the monks at the Benedictine monastery of Montmajour. The latter invaded the cloister and expelled the Cistercians, who could not return to Silvacane until 1289. In 1358, a group of bandits led by Rican Corvi, Lord of Aubignan, plundered the monastery and its granges. The hard frosts of 1364 damaged vine stocks and olive trees, ruining harvests. These successive hardships marked the beginning of the end. By the beginning of the 15th century, there was no longer an abbot at the head of Silvacane, so that, in 1455, it was incorporated into the cathedral chapter of Aix, despite opposition by the abbot of Citeaux. Its church became a parish church. During the Wars of Religion, Catholics and Protestants invaded the abbey in turns, inflicting much damage. Then, in 1590, Silvacane became the lair of robbers and disbanded soldiers who went out only on raids and to spread terror throughout the area. Castellane d'Ampus, head of the Leagues in Aix, finally managed to chase them away. In the 17th century, religion was re-established in Silvacane but, following the creation of a new church, the abbey church was progressively abandoned. At the Revolution, the abbey was put up for sale as State property. The church was used as a pigeon house, the refectory as a hayloft, and the chapter house as a stable. The State finally purchased Silvacane and began to restore it.

Construction of Silvacane church lasted from 1175 to 1230, using light-coloured well-bonded stone. The Romanesque doorway in the façade is topped with a tympanum on which, in the 15th century, canons from Aix cathedral had their chapter's coat of arms carved, showing the Easter lamb and a plaque sculpted with a small cross. The extremely austere church interior consists of a nave with side aisles, a vast transept, each of its arms containing two chapels with flat chevets and a sanctuary as wide as the nave, also with a flat chevet. The nave with three bays is covered with pointed barrel vaulting with double-roller transverse ribs.

Bracket in the refectory

Pointed Barrel Vaulting

Cistercian ideals were expressed in simple architecture, stripped of any useless decoration. Building used high-quality bonding and construction of the nave often used the pointed barrel vault technique, preserving, as in Silvacane (*opposite*), great purity of line and equilibrium within the structure, which did not however exclude the monumental.

South aisle

The abbey

Frieze detail in cloister

Over the transept crossing, covered with ribbed vaulting, a square steeple rises above the church, its sides pierced with double openings. The sanctuary is lit up by three semicircular windows, surmounted with an eight-lobed rose window. The church's capitals are carved with very finely drawn leaves. The door in the third aisle of the north transept leads to the cloister. Built later than the church, between 1250 and 1300, it lies 1.6 metres lower down. The galleries, covered with semicircular barrel vaulting on transverse ribs, open onto the garden through mighty arcades with thick walls. Like in Sénanque or Thoronet, a terrace runs above the galleries. The cloister's vaults rest on bases sculpted with plant motifs – grape, oak or fig leaves, as well as animals – an owl, a bird pecking at a fig. In the east gallery of

The East gallery in the cloister

the cloister, beyond the sacristy, a semicircular door, framed with two gemel openings, leads into the chapter house. The vault's ribs rest on two central columns. One of them is composed of four thin columns; the other is decorated with twisted fluting. The capitals are soberly carved with leaves. On the right outside the door, a staircase leads to the dormitory, formerly shared by all the monks. The large monks' hall, with its cross-ribbed vaulting, was also used as a heating room. A large fireplace stands in the north-east corner. The north gallery runs along the refectory. Rebuilt in the 15th century, during the Gothic period, by Abbot Antoine de Boniface, the refectory is vaulted on intersecting ribs and lit up by three tall lancet windows. Built into the thickness of the wall, a staircase leads to the reader's pulpit. The lay brothers' buildings that used to extend to the west have entirely disappeared.

The chapter house

The dormitory

The cloister

Sénanque

Sénanque Abbey was built in a narrow, isolated and wooded valley of the Sénancole, in the north of the Luberon, on the edge of the Vaucluse plateau. Twelve monks from Mazan Abbey, a daughter of Bonnevaux, were called by the bishop of Cavaillon to settle here in 1148, on lands offered by the lords of Simiane, the overlords of Gordes. Peter was its first abbot and in 1152 a daughter, Chambons, was founded in the Vivarais, not far from the mother-abbey. All through the 13th century, recruits arrived at Sénanque, whose domain increased considerably thanks to lordly generosity. The abbey's many possessions extended in the south of the Dauphiné to the Albion plateau, in the Luberon as far as Arles and Marseilles. Recruitment became more difficult during the 15th century, but soon a new abbot, John Casaletti (1475-1509), a doctor from the University of Avignon, took the abbey's future in hand. Once the abbey was subject to Strict Observance of the Rule, recruitment started again. John Casaletti founded the college of St Bernard of Sénanque in Avignon for the young monks. His successor, François d'Estaing (1509-1529), lavished care on plague victims during the epidemic that reached Carpentras in 1507. This "father of the poor" was the first of Sénanque's commendatory abbots, all of whom carried out their duties properly. In 1544, the abbey suffered from the violence of the times. Bands of Waldensians, led by the renegade

Gordes

A Scent of Lavender

In our imagination, the chevet of Sénanque's abbey church is forever associated with fields of lavender, above which it rises in the July heat. However, the lavender fields were planted here only a few decades ago.

The abbey church chevet

Squinch at the transept crossing

Like Mother, Like Daughter

The transept crossing in Sénanque is covered by a dome on squinches (*above*), similar to that at its mother-abbey, Mazan. This technique, characteristic of Romanesque churches in the Vivarais and Velay, is also used in Le Puy Cathedral.

priest of Ménerbes, appalled by the repressive measures taken against them, invaded Sénanque, sacked, plundered and burnt it. Two of its monks were allegedly hanged and the community was scattered. Subsequent abbots attempted to restore the damaged buildings and tried, in vain, to rebuild their community. But Sénanque never contained more than a few monks. In 1780, the last representative of the community died. One year later, the abbey's administration was entrusted to the prior of Le Thoronet, Dom Dreux. Put up for sale at the Revolution, the monastic buildings were purchased and maintained by a former officer of the king, Alex de Léouze. However, the flame of Citeaux had not been extinguished. In 1854, Sénanque passed into the hands of Abbot Barnouin, who established his community there. The monks immediately got to work and undertook the needed restoration. Following the advice of the abbot of Aiguebelle, the Sénanque community soon became affiliated with the Cistercian Order. In 1858, it repopulated the abbey of Fontfroide and, in 1869, that of Lérins. In 1872, the community became the Congregation of the Immaculate Conception of Sénanque, affiliated with the Order of the Common Observance of Citeaux. Father Barnouin then established his residence of the Abbot-President of the Congregation at Lérins. Expelled in 1880 and again in 1903, the monks of Sénanque, after a brief return from 1928 to 1965, gathered in Lérins. Then in 1988, six monks from Saint Honoratus Monastery established themselves in Sénanque, bringing it back to life once again.

The heating room

IMMACULATE CONCEPTION

In 1872 the community of Sénanque became the Congregation of the Immaculate Conception. It is not surprising that the Cistercians chose one of the names for the Queen of Heaven for their congregation, thus fitting in with current events since the dogma of Immaculate Conception had been promulgated by Pope Pius IX in the bull *Ineffabilis Deus* in 1854, the year the community of Father Barnouin was established in Sénanque. This dogma claimed that the Virgin had been "preserved and immunized" from original sin at her birth. Recognition of this grace created numerous debates. Theologians did not manage to reconcile it with the Principle of Universal Redemption. Augustine, followed by Bernard, emphasized the contradiction resolved by John Duns Scott in the 12th century by attributing advance redemption for the Mother of Christ. On November 27, 1830, while addressing a young novice, Jeanne Labouré, Our Lady defined herself as "conceived without sin". And on March 25, 1858 in Lourdes, in her sixteenth appearance, she confirmed her message by declaring to Bernadette, "*Que soy era Immaculada Councepciou*".

Virgin with Child

THE WALDENSIANS

In about 1175, Pierre Valdo, or Valdès, a rich merchant from Lyons, renounced his worldly goods after reading the Gospels, which he had translated into Provençal. He left his wife, leaving her his lands, put his daughters into Fontevrault

Oppède le Vieux

Abbey and distributed the rest of his goods to the poor. Surrounded by a few disciples, he started to lead a wandering life, preaching a return to evangelical purity and cursing the wealth of the clergy. As the Lutherans were to do later, he wanted the Bible to be translated into vulgate language so that it would be accessible to the greatest number. He soon questioned the Church's hierarchy, the sacraments other than Baptism and Holy Communion, and attacked the cult of saints. His doctrine was condemned by the Lateran Council in 1179 and, in 1184 Valdès and his disciples were excommunicated, at the same time as the Cathars, by the Council of Verona. At the beginning of the 13th century, some Waldensians were reconciled with the Church of Rome. Some, like Durand of Huesca, even wrote treatises refuting the Cathar theses, such as *Liber antiheresis* or the *Contra manicheos*. The others were the object of persecution and eighty of them were burnt at the stake in Strasbourg in 1211. The *poor people of Lyons* found refuge in the Luberon and in the heart of the Alps as far as the Piedmont slopes. But their troubles were far from over. In 1390, near Freissinières, one hundred and twenty, including forty children, were burned. In 1487, Albert of Catania called for a crusade against the Waldensians. A last, small group gathered in Dormillouse, called "the poor man's Montségur" by Samivel, before being exterminated in the Phazy caves, also near Freissinières. Claiming to be under the authority of the Gospels, the remaining Waldensians rallied to the Protestant Reformation in 1532, at the synod of Chanforans, in the Italian valley of Angrogna. Despite the many bloody repressions of

Ménerbes

which they were the object in the past, there are to this day Waldensians in Italy and France. The Waldensian Evangelical Church, made up of autonomous communities each led by a pastor, today regroups most Italian Protestants.

The south transept and the tomb of the Lord of Venasque

Construction of the church in Sénanque began in 1160 and ended at the beginning of the 13th century. The narrow space in the valley and the necessity of establishing the monastic buildings near the stream led the architects to place their church facing north and not east. The very plain church façade does not have a portal door, but simply two small doors leading to the aisles. The church, small in size, was used only by the monks and lay brothers. The plan is that of a simple Latin cross, ending with a semicircular sanctuary. The nave is vaulted with a pointed barrel vault and communicates with the side aisles through large, slightly pointed, arcades. The four chapels, ending with a semidome vault and opening onto the wide transept, have retained their stone altars from the 12th century. A dome on

The Tarasque

squinches rises above the transept crossing. Its architecture is meticulous; each squinch, decorated with six lobes, rests on a curved slab, held up by a small, fluted pilaster, supported by a console. The sanctuary, with its broken barrel vault, ends with an apse. The chevet wall is pierced with three semicircular windows that light up the altar. Located to the west of the church, the cloister is barrel vaulted. The vault's transverse ribs drop onto carefully sculpted consoles. Each gallery opens onto the garden through a series of semicircular arcades, supported by double pillars and columns. The capitals are finely decorated with plant motifs, cables, palmettes or interlacing. In the north gallery, three steps lead to the chapter house which opens onto the cloister through a Romanesque door, framed with double windows. Inside, two columns with ornamented capitals hold up the vault's ribs. Some of the keystones are carved with leaves. Beyond the passage, a staircase leads to the monks' dormitory, a large room with a pointed barrel vault. Next lies the heating room, the only warm room in the monastery and which, in Sénanque, was also the *scriptorium*. It has three Romanesque windows with wide embrasures, allowing a lot of light to enter. A powerful column with a sculpted capital, its pedestal decorated with four turtles, supports the groined arches. The room has retained its ancient hearth, with its truncated cone hood and, outside, two chimneys stand on the roof. The monks' refectory opens onto the west gallery of the cloister. Burned by the Waldensians in 1544, it was rebuilt in the 17th century. Today, it is used as a chapel by the community. The monks' lavatorium used to stand opposite the refectory door, protruding from the south-west corner of the courtyard, although only the toothing in the wall remains today. The lay brothers' wing, burned in 1544 like the refectory, was rebuilt at the end of the 17th century by Abbot Armand de Béthune, who installed his abbey lodgings there as well as housing for visitors.

THE TARASQUE

One of the ribs of the vault in the north gallery in the Sénanque cloister rests on a console sculpted with the Tarasque (*opposite*). This amphibious monster, a legendary dragon hidden in the waters of the Rhone River, crawled out of its lair to capture young men and women.

Nave detail

An arcade in the cloister's west gallery

La Oliva

The abbey church chevet

La Oliva Abbey is located north of Las Bardenas Reales, in the valley of the Aragon River, west of the village of Carcastillo. The site, near Santacara, the ancient *Cara*, was already occupied in Roman times, as attested by epigraphs carved on stones discovered in 1828 and 1996. In the middle of the 12th century, it was located on the border between the kingdoms of Navarre and Aragon who fought over it. In 1145, the lands of La Oliva were ceded by the king of Navarre, García V (1134-1150), to the abbey of Niencebas. Two years later, the donation was confirmed to the advantage of the same abbey, which had just been incorporated into the Cistercian Order before moving to Fitero, and to Veruela, its daughter-abbey founded in 1145. In 1149, Ramón Berenguer IV (1131-1162), Count of Barcelona, acting for his wife Petronilla (1137-1162), Queen of Aragon, confirmed the act after conquering the region. That same year, when peace was re-established, García V recovered his lands and confirmed his donation of 1145. Fitero spread to La Oliva in 1150 and Bertrand was the first abbot of the new foundation. In 1161, La Oliva and Fitero were affiliated directly with L'Escale Dieu, Fitero's mother-abbey, and henceforth visited by the abbot of this daughter of Morimond, located on the northern piedmont of the Pyrenees. La Oliva, with the support of the kings of Navarre and close to their palace at Olite, extended its possessions in Navarre and Aragon. When Leyre was incorporated into the Cistercian Order in 1307, it was as a daughter of La

Fitero, Terrible Daughter

In 1158, when Raymond, Abbot of Fitero, took charge of defending Calatrava, he neglected to inform L'Escale Dieu. Considered extremely unruly, in 1191 Fitero received visitors sent by the Order's General Chapter to re-establish lapsed discipline.

The abbey church

San Jesucristo Chapel

Oliva. Its abbots became members of the Cortes of Navarre; others became royal councillors, like Lope de Gallur (1332-1362) to Carlos II (1349-1387) during the 14th century. In the late 15th century, Abbot Pedro de Eraso (1468-1502) was regent of the kingdom in the absence of its sovereigns. In the 18th century, Abbot Francisco Morales was elected General of the Cistercian Congregation of the Crown of Aragon (and Navarre), to which La Oliva had belonged since 1634. In 1809, Napoleon's soldiers expelled the monks who returned in 1814, only to be chased out once again in 1821 by the Liberals. Returning in 1823, the monks had to leave the abbey during the *Desamortización* of 1835. In 1927, monks of the Cistercian Order of the Strict Observance, coming from Getafe, brought life back to La Oliva Monastery, which had become a national monument in 1880, and recovered its ranking as an abbey in 1948.

A first church, the Chapel of San Jesucristo, was built as soon as the abbey was founded. Very well bonded, with its eight buttresses and its shale roof, it was located to the north-east of the great abbey church. It is probable that the same craftsmen took part in building the two shrines, since the chevet of the abbey church is a copy, on a larger scale, of that of the chapel. Work on the abbey church began in 1164. It was dedicated under the abbacy of Aznarius de Falces, during the reign of Sancho VII the Strong (1194-1234), on July 13, 1195. The western façade, dating from

When Caesar...

It was on March 19, 1812 that the Cortes promulgated the Spanish Constitution of Cadiz. Ferdinand VII, the king of Spain (1808; 1814-1833) had been living in comfortable exile in France since his abdication in favour of Napoleon in 1808. The new laws, inspired by work on the French Constituent Assembly of 1791, included several anticlerical measures. This Constitution was abolished by Ferdinand VII on May 4, 1814, on his return from exile, but he was forced to re-establish it on March 9, 1820, inaugurating the three-year Liberal Triennum. For three years, measures of *Exclaustración* against monks and *Desamortización* of ecclesiastical belongings were put into practice, as planned by the Cortes of Cadiz. The second measure consisted of converting the Church's property into state property and putting it up for sale. On October 1, 1823, Ferdinand VII put an end to the process by declaring the constitutional government's actions null and void. But in 1835, Juan Alvárez y Méndez, known as Mendizábal, became Minister of the Interior. He started the *Desamortización* procedure again and led it to its conclusion. Within two years, most of the Spanish monks and nuns had to leave their monasteries.

The cloister

Cornice on the abbey church façade (detail)

the end of the 13th and early 14th centuries, is very original with its square steeple over the porch vaulting. In the porch's embrasure, stands the portal door whose twelve voussoirs, of slightly pointed arches, drop on both left and right onto fine columns topped with monoliths decorated with leaf designs, providing a visual impression of several juxtaposed capitals. On the upper part of the tympanum, a bas-relief of the *Agnus Dei* is framed by bas-reliefs of a Nativity and a Christ Pantocrator surrounded by a tetramorph. The faces of abbots are carved on the capitals framing the door, the one of the left holding the cross of Calatrava. Above the archivolt, a cornice is formed by twenty-seven modillions representing musicians, alternating with scenes showing various themes: a crucified Christ, the wheel of fortune, an Annunciation. The nave, flanked with side aisles, has six bays. The slightly protruding transept separates it from the choir with its circular apse, framed on either side by two chapels with flat chevets that open onto the arms of the transept. In the choir, a Gothic statue of Santa María la Real de La Oliva has stood at the top of a column behind the altar since 1932. The vault above the transept crossing is surmounted by a ciborium. The capitals are generally decorated with plant motifs, although some in the first aisle are carved with sirens and grotesque faces. On the back of the façade, on the north side, a Romanesque sepulchre, whose sculptures are somewhat damaged, was probably intended for Sancho VII, who was eventually buried at Roncesvalles. The cloister flanks the church on its north side. It was built during the 14th and 15th centuries in Gothic style. The west gallery was built during the abbacy of Lope de Gallur. It is the oldest and a semicircular door and four windows open onto the chapter house. The north gallery, the most recent, dates from the abbacy of Pedro de Eraso. Carved decorations cover the capitals and the brackets, taking their themes from grapes and wine. One capital has a man's mouth, celebrating spring, with vine branches and leaves sprouting from it; another, a dog nibbles a bunch of grapes From the earliest times, the monks of La Oliva worked their vineyards and still today they produce an excellent Navarrese wine.

Abbey church chevet

Flaran

A daughter of L'Escale Dieu and granddaughter of Morimond, the abbey of Flaran was founded in 1151 in the diocese of Auch. The monks settled on the banks of the Baïse River, on a little island that they arranged by diverting the confluence of the Auloue in order to increase water supplies for their monastery and to work the millwheel. Soon many recruits arrived, and the property increased in size as neighbouring lords made donations. The monks built the current abbey which developed rapidly. In the middle of the 13th century, to cope with a lack of manpower, the abbot of Flaran agreed with the Count of Armagnac to found the bastide of Valence, at the top of the hill located on the other side of the Baïse. From the beginning of the 14th century and throughout the entire Hundred Years War, Gascony was the theatre of violent conflict between the English and the French as they fought over territory. Starting in 1315, sometimes under English domination, sometimes under French, Flaran was subject to plundering and devastation. To protect themselves, on the south side the monks built a rampart with a fortified gate. In 1481, the county of Gascony was definitively annexed to France and peace was re-established. The first commendatory abbot arrived in Flaran in 1484. His successor undertook restoration work but in 1569, during the Wars of Religion, Montgomery's Protestant troops destroyed the abbey and set fire to the church. The four monks who managed to escape the massacre took refuge in Valence sur Baïse. Starting in 1573, Abbot Jean de Boyer began to restore the monastery and rebuilt its patrimony. However, after the 17th century the commendatory abbots no longer lived in Flaran which, abandoned to its fate, contained no more than five or six monks. Several abbots nonetheless made essential repairs and in 1759 a small palace, later called the abbot's lodging and intended to house visiting commendatory abbots, was built on the site of the former lay brothers' building. At the Revolution, the remaining three monks had to leave and the abbey was put up for sale. The new owners lived in the abbey lodgings and the other buildings were used as farm outbuildings. In 1913, the Gers Archaeological Society barely managed to avoid having the cloister's stones sold to a Parisian antiques dealer with good contacts in New York. In compensation, the dealer received the church's north doorway and the fountain from the reception room of the abbey dwelling house. The doorway was returned to the church in 1937, despite reluctance by the owner at the time who, in 1936, had not hesitated before demolishing the stucco work in the choir and was trying to sell the varnished ceramic tiles from a medieval pavement. In 1970, a fire damaged the abbey dwelling and the cloister's west wing. The Gers Department, after becoming the owner in 1972, began to work with the Historical Monuments Association to restore the entire abbey.

Construction of Flaran church began about 1170 and was completed in 1210. The church's western façade opens with a central

Romanesque tower, Gothic and Plateresque cloisters

Huerta

Abbey church façade

In 1151, the abbey of Berdoues, a daughter of Morimond in the diocese of Auch, spread to Cántabos, on the banks of the Nágima River, a tributary of the Jalón. By 1152, the new community was running a grange at Huerta, where it decided to settle in 1162. The third abbot of Santa María de Huerta was Don Martín de Finojosa, a member of a noble Castilian family that was in favour at the court of Alfonso VIII (1158-1214). The abbey received privileges and donations. In 1164, Pope Alexander III (1159-1181) confirmed its possessions and exempted the abbey from paying the tithe. By 1179, the first stone was laid for the construction of the abbey church. Huerta was provided with a *scriptorium* and, before the end of the 12th century, it had produced a *Vita Sanctorum*, large in size and illuminated, and a *Graduale Cisterciense*. Don Martín participated in the institution of the Congregation of Las Huelgas Reales in 1187. He was named bishop of Sigüenza in 1186 but retired to Huerta in 1192. While travelling on September 16, 1213, he died in the odour of sanctity in Sotoca, in the Alcarria, not far from the valley of the Tagus River. He was buried in Huerta. The archbishop of Toledo, Don Rodrigo Jiménez de Rada (1208-1247), who had been present at Las Navas de Tolosa in 1212, then supported the abbey and helped it to continue the construction programme that had been started by Don Martín. He bequeathed the abbey his library which, unfortunately, was sold in the 18th century. His remains lie in the abbey church. Huerta suffered not only from problems common in Europe during the first half of the 14th century, poor harvests and the plague epidemic, but also the war fought from 1357 to 1361 by Peter 1st of Castile (1350-1369) and Peter IV of Aragon (1336-1387). Because it was in contact with both kingdoms, it suffered the consequences. In the 15th century, the abbot's authority was occasionally contested – one because he was not worth of his post; others because their election by a divided community was controversial. The Dukes of Medinaceli, taking advantage of the disorder, tried to interfere in the monastery. In such a context, instauration of commendam seemed like a lesser evil. There were four commendatory abbots in succession. The last two, Benedictine monks, Don García of Leon and his nephew, Don Álvaro López of Leon, worked to integrate their abbey into the Cistercian Congregation of Castile at the end of the 15th century. The 16th and 17th centuries were the golden age of Huerta, even though the Dukes of Medinaceli still coveted its temporal power. Within the framework of the Congregation, discipline was restored by the first reform abbot, Don Tomás de Campuzano. Like the other members of the Congregation, Huerta affirmed its independence with respect to the Order's General Chapter and in 1533, its abbot energetically opposed a visit by the abbot of Clairvaux, Edmund de Saulieu. There was intense spiritual life at the abbey and it became a great intellectual centre. During the second half of the 16th century, Friar Luis de Estrada was charged by the Congregation's General Chapter with writing a commentary on the Rule of Saint Benedict in Latin and in the vernacular. As for Ángel Manrique, a monk trained

Distinguished Relics

In the centre of the *Herreriano* cloister of Santa María de Huerta, stand the statues of San Martín de Finojosa and Don Rodrigo Jiménez de Rada, side by side. The remains of these two persons, who left a lasting influence on the first century of the abbey's existence, are kept in two chests made of black marble from Calatorao, decorated with chiselled bronze, standing on either side of the reredos in the great chapel, behind gates of gilded bronze. The two identical chests were ordered in 1656 by the Duke of Medinaceli and are, for that reason, carved with the ducal coat of arms. The precious relics of the abbot and the archbishop were transferred in 1660. Not much remained of the abbot, even his head had been stolen. On the other hand, the mummified body of the archbishop had remained nearly intact, as did his clothing, including the mitre and the pallium – distinctions of metropolitans – and the chasuble. These exceptional pieces, restored in 1968, are carefully kept at the abbey but not exhibited to the public. At the south-west corner of the abbey church, under the monks' choir, the original tomb of the former archbishop of Toledo still stands.

South gallery of Gothic cloister

TWO RENAISSANCE STYLES

The Plateresque style takes its name from, *platero*, the Castilian word for silversmith. It was most popular in the middle of the 16th century and in sculpture and architecture is characterized by its exuberant and abundant decoration. Its main practitioners were Diego de Siloe in Burgos, Rodrigo Gil de Hontañón in Toledo, and Alcalá de Henares and Juan de Badajoz in Leon. During the second half of the 16th century, monumentality, sobriety and classicism were the characteristics of the *Herreriano* style of Juan de Herrera (1530-1597), *Maestro de la Obras Reales* of Philip II (1556-1598) and architect of the Escorial.

Medallion in Plateresque cloister

in Huerta and author of the four volumes of the *Cistercian Annals*, he became general abbot of the Congregation and then head prior of Calatrava and bishop of Badajoz. Huerta was a nursery for prelates and professors who taught in Alcalá, Salamanca and Valladolid. But the 18th and 19th centuries were difficult ones. During the Spanish War of Succession (1701-1714) between the Bourbons and the Austrians, soldiers from the Austrian garrison at Monteagudo pillaged Huerta and threatened to burn it down. In 1730, the community was divided and twenty monks went into exile in Rome. Bad weather also contributed and the abbey was flooded three times between 1761 and 1772. The setting up of the reredos of the high altar in 1766 certainly brought some joy to the monks of Huerta who had to welcome brothers expelled from their houses in France during the Revolution a few years later. In 1809, Napoleon's troops arrived in the area. Huerta's belongings were disposed of and the monks expelled. Two of them remained and were joined two years later by four others. In 1820, under the Liberal Triennium, the government expelled the monks, but they returned in 1823. Santa María de Huerta began to flourish once again since, by 1828, there were seventy monks. But with the *Desamortización*, which was the end for the Congregation of Castile, all the monks were evicted on October 15, 1835. There was no monastic life in Huerta for nearly a century. The buildings were spared thanks to the vigilance of Don Gregorio Pérez Alonso, the former prior who, in 1849, had become the parish priest of Santa María de Huerta. Thanks were also due to his parishioners and to the declaration of 1882, making Huerta into a national monument. Monks brought life back to Huerta in 1930, when it was simply a priory. They belonged to the Cistercian Order of the Strict Observance, formed under the authority of Pope Leon XIII in 1892. The Spanish Civil War (1936-1939) did not encourage the community's development. It was not until 1965 that Huerta was made into an abbey. The first abbot of the new era was Dom Ignacio Astorga.

Santa María de Huerta, a living abbey, presents the visitor with an architectural and artistic heritage covering several centuries. The Gothic cloister dates from the 13th century. In the abbey church, the chevet, with its central apse flanked on either side by two apsidal chapels and the transept were completed at the beginning of the 13th century. The five bays of the nave were built later. The paintings in the choir are the work of Bartolome Matarana in 1580. The large reredos, completed by Felix Malo in 1766, contains the remains of Don Martín and Don Rodrigo. To the west of the nave, a railing set up in 1776 closes off the space covered by the monks' choir, sculpted out of walnut wood in 1557. On the upper floor of the Gothic cloister, the Plateresque cloister, built starting in 1531, has coffered ceilings although only the wooden ones in the north gallery are original; the remaining plaster ceilings are the result of restoration work. The Royal staircase dating from 1600 leads upstairs from the north-east corner of the Gothic cloister. The 13th century monks' refectory opens onto the north gallery of the Gothic cloister, adjoining the 13th century kitchen and the lay brothers' refectory, which runs along the north gallery of the *Herreriano* cloister built from 1582 to 1630.

Monks' refectory

The cloister

Valbuena

Estefanía de Armengol, the daughter of the Count of Urgel and granddaughter of Count Ansurez, Lord of Valladolid, founded a Benedictine monastery in 1143 on the right bank of the Duero, two leagues west of Peñafiel. In 1151, it was incorporated into the Cistercian Order. Monks from Berdoues, a daughter of Morimond, came to settle at Santa María de Valbuena. One of them, Ebrard, became the head of the new community. The abbey benefited from the support of the kings of Castile who granted it rights and privileges. In 1163, during the abbacy of William, Alfonso VIII (1158-1214) affiliated to Valbuena the monastery of San Andrés de Valveni, later moved to Palazuelo, and in 1175 granted it lands at Bonaval where it founded an abbey. In 1218, Ferdinand III (1217-1252) guaranteed it freedom of pasture for its herds and in 1229 exempted it from the *portazgo*, a tax on the movement of goods. Valbuena prospered in this rich Duero valley, where its monks grew wheat and worked vineyards. It also spread to Rioseco and Matallana. It also had the trust of the Order's General Chapter which in 1397 and 1398 charged its abbot with recovering contributions unpaid by several Castilian abbeys. In 1430, conflict arose between Abbot Ferdinand de Benavente and his monks. To re-establish calm within the community, the king of Castile John II (1406-1454) and the bishop of Palencia, Gutierro, entrusted the destiny of Valbuena to Martin de Vargas who introduced his reform and affiliated the abbey with Poblet. An eminent member of the Congregation of Castile until 1555, the abbey took the name of Saint Bernard of Valbuena and its "passage to the Observance" was confirmed in 1432 by Pope Eugene IV (1431-1447). The Cistercian General Chapter did not approve of the situation and broke its affiliate links with Valbuena and Rioseco in 1444, and with Matallana and Palazuelos in 1454. During the 17th and 18th centuries, the abbey slowly declined. The Liberal Triennium(1820-1823) and the 1835 *Desamortización* of Mendizábal put a term to any monastic life at the abbey. It was named a national monument in 1931 and became the property of the National Institute of Colonization in 1950.

The abbey church was built from the end of the 12th century to the end of the 13th. To the east, the Romanesque choir has a semicircular apse. It contains a Baroque reredos from the 18th century dedicated to the Virgin. Four chapels that are also Romanesque surround it and open onto the transept. The two on either side of it have semicircular apses, the others have flat chevets. The nave, with two aisles and four bays, is Gothic. The walls of St Peter's Chapel, built in the second half of the 13th century, are decorated with Gothic frescoes showing a badly altered Nativity, life at court and the struggle against the Moors. The cloister is located south of the abbey church. The lower galleries date from the 13th century, the upper Plateresque galleries from the early 16th. The former serve the *scriptorium*, from the end of the 12th century, and the 13th century refectory. The chapter house was replaced by a sacristy in the 18th century.

Fresco in St Peter's Chapel

In the Lord's Vineyards

Manual labour was part of Cistercian monks' life and, since the creation of the *Novum Monasterium* in 1098, they had often worked the land. Their granges were real agricultural operations. If the land was favourable, they planted grapevines and produced wine that they sold but that they also used in holy offices or drank in their refectories within the very reasonable limit of one hemina (~ half a pint) per day. In this respect, the monks at Valbuena took good advantage of the alluvial terraces of the Ribera del Duero and still today the region produces vines like the Vega Sicilia, among the most famous of Spanish wines. The Navarrese abbey of La Oliva still obtains a large part of its revenue from grapes and wine. The *terroir* of Saint Julien de Septime, the oldest of Fontfroide's granges in the Languedoc, produces an A.O.C. Corbières wine of high quality. In Burgundy, Pontigny lies just north of the famous vineyards of Chablis and Le Clos de Vougeot was a grange belonging to Citeaux. Le Clos de Vougeot is a *grand cru* of Burgundy and the former grange has become the seat of the famous Confrérie of the Chevaliers du Tastevin.

The lavatorium

Valmagne

Valmagne Abbey is located in the midst of the Languedoc vineyards, near the Etang de Thau, about thirty kilometres south-west of Montpellier. It was founded in 1139 by monks from Ardorel, a Benedictine abbey attached to Fontevrault, on the lands of *Vallis Magna*, presented to the monks by Raymond Trencavel, the son of the founder of Ardorel. First of all placed under the authority of Cadouin Abbey in Perigord, Valmagne was definitely attached to the Cistercian Order in 1159 as a daughter of Bonnevaux. Soon, numerous donations increased the size of the abbey's domain and it was granted multiple privileges by neighbouring lords. Starting in 1208, Valmagne supported the papacy in its struggle against the Cathar heretics and its abbot, Bernard de la Costa, was even present at the side of Simon of Montfort at the battle of Muret in 1213. In 1252, Abbot Bertrand of Auriac founded Valmagne College in Montpellier intended for new recruits. In 1257, because of a lack of space, the monks undertook the construction of a larger church and cloister. But in the 14th century, a series of calamities befell the abbey and its region – a famine affected Languedoc towards 1340, followed by the Black Death in 1348, added to the ravages of the Hundred Years War. Impoverished, Valmagne had to sell part of its lands in order to survive. Being placed in commendam in 1477, shortly before the horrors of the Wars of Religion, once again disturbed life at the community. By 1571, masses were no longer said at Valmagne. Its abbot had joined the Reformation and in 1575 he even took part in sacking the abbey and in the massacre of the monks and Catholics who had taken refuge there. Abandoned by its monks, Valmagne fell into the hands of brigands and barely escaped the destruction ordered by Damville, Languedoc's governor, who wanted to cleanse the region. In 1578, Pierre VIII de Guers was named abbot of Valmagne and in the beginning of the 17th century, thanks to the de Guers and de Vairac families, restoration work was undertaken. During the second half of the 17th century, commendatory abbots of Italian origin, among them Cardinal Pierre de Bonzi, a Florentine nobleman, transformed Valmagne into a magnificent bishops' manor where they lived luxuriously. On the eve of the Revolution, the heavily indebted community numbered only a few monks. In 1791, Valmagne was sold to a private owner who ran its vast wine-producing domain and placed the large barrels for aging the wine inside the church. At his death in 1838, the Count of Turenne purchased the abbey with the bishop's authorization. His descendants are still the owners and work to restore and maintain it.

Valmagne church was built starting in 1257 in the Gothic style of the large cathedrals in northern France. It is fronted by a narthex whose capitals, contrary to the Rule, show human figures, like a monk torn between Good and Evil. In the shape of a Latin cross, the church has a long nave with side aisles, a vast

Abbey church nave

The Trencavel Destiny

During the 10th and 11th centuries, the Trencavels possessed the viscounties of Albi, Nîmes, Béziers, Agde and Carcassonne. Raymond, the donor of the Valmagne lands, was assassinated in 1167 in the Madeleine Abbey in Béziers. His son Roger married the daughter of Raymond V of Toulouse. The well-known Cathar sympathies of his successor, Raymond-Roger, provided the northern barons crusading in response to a call by Pope Innocent III with a pretext for seizing, in 1209, Béziers and the city of Carcassonne, to which the young viscount had retired. Taken prisoner, Raymond-Roger died in a Carcassonne jail on November 10, 1209, some said of dysentery, others said murder. The son of the latter lived in exile at the court of the king of Aragon. In 1240, with the support of many *faidit* lords, including Olivier de Termes, he tried to recapture the lands of his fathers but failed before the walls of Carcassonne. He had to return to exile.

transept with two square chapels and a shrine with an ambulatory and radiating chapels. The chapel in the chevet contains a fine statue of the Virgin from the 17th century. The keystones are finely carved; the one in the apse shows the coronation of the Virgin, the one in the bay of the choir presents St Bernard and St Benedict. The church windows were blocked up after the Wars of Religion, but six of them have just been reopened. Located to the south of the church, the cloister, dating from the 14th century, is covered with ribbed vaulting. The east gallery, which is the Romanesque section of the abbey church, contains the *armarium*, the sacristy and the chapter house. The doors of the *armarium* and the sacristy have saw-toothed semicircular arches. The chapter house, covered by ribbed vaulting, opens onto the cloister through wide Romanesque openings, supported by groups of narrow columns whose capitals are sculpted with leaves. The cloister's north gallery contains the refectory. Opposite its entrance, protruding into the garden, the monks' lavatorium stands inside an octagonal chapel made from elements of the first cloister.

Vase in chapter house

The cloister

Cardinal de Bonzi

Pierre de Bonzi, born into Florentine nobility, was first of all named Bishop of Béziers by King Louis XI, who used the prelate's negotiating talents for extraordinary ambassadorial missions to Venice, Poland and Spain. Having become the almoner to Queen Maria Theresa, he was promoted to Archbishop of Toulouse where, in 1672, he received a cardinal's hat. In 1673, the king named him to the See of Narbonne and entrusted him with governing the States of Languedoc. Pierre de Bonzi administered Valmagne Abbey from 1680 to 1697. His refitting of the abbey was inspired by the festivities held in Le Nôtre's gardens at Versailles and he turned it into a palace. He raised the cloister by one storey, removed the dormitory to make guest rooms and provided the abbey with magnificent French-style gardens decorated with sculpted vases (*above*) which today stand on the ledges of the openings in the chapter house.

ROBERT OF ARBRISSEL

The son of a priest, Robert was born in Arbrissel, near Rennes, in about 1045. As a student in Paris, in 1089 he was called by the bishop of Rennes to help reform the Church in his diocese and he became an archdeacon. Then Robert took up his studies again in Angers to be a master in theology. He next decided to retire to the forest of Craon, on the border between Brittany and Anjou where many anchorites were living, to live as an itinerant hermit. His preaching talent attracted many disciples, for whom he founded a male monastery at La Roë in Mayenne subject to the Rule of Saint Augustine. Since Pope Urban II gave Robert the right to preach anywhere, he continued his wandering life and was soon followed by a crowd of men and women. About 1100, he

Eleanor of Aquitaine

established them at Fontevrault, in the Maine-Loire area in the diocese of Poitiers. It was immediately successful and the founder's charisma attracted donations. Robert organized a vast monastic community with five distinct buildings: Grand Moûtier, dedicated to Our Lady, for virgins and widows; Saint Benedict for the infirm and the ill; Saint Lazarus for lepers; Magdalene for repented female sinners; and St John of the Habit for men. Each community, placed under the authority of the abbess of Fontevrault, had its own church, refectory, dormitory and cloister. The men followed St Augustine's Rule and the nuns followed the Rule of St Benedict. After Arbrissel's death in 1116, the Order, which had adopted a centralized organization similar to that at Cluny even while it allowed its priories a fair amount of autonomy, received favours from Foulque of Anjou, then from Henry Plantagenet and Eleanor of Aquitaine. It rapidly spread throughout France, England and Spain and, until its disappearance in 1790, it remained under the authority of the abbess of Fontevrault who was always high born, and occasionally of royal blood.

Fontevrault

The cloister

Loc Dieu

In 1123, a group of monks who had left Dordogne to look for a favourable site on which to establish their new monastery stopped in Rouergue. They came from Dalon Abbey, founded in 1117 by Géraud of Sales. The location they choose lay at the foot of a wooded height called Puech d'Elves, on top of which stood a large dolmen. Gloomy legends said that the place chosen by the monks was beset by demonic powers. Furthermore, it was also used by bands of robbers from the region, and it was known by the name of *Locus diaboli* (the place of the devil). Laying the foundations of their abbey, the monks undertook large-scale clearing and draining of the land so that it would become *Locus Dei*, and the abbey of *Loc Dieu* (the place of God), the Lord's abbey, was born. They requested affiliation with the Order of Citeaux and joined in 1162, at the same time as most of Géraud of Sales's other foundations, through the intermediary of Pontigny. However, financial difficulties, worsened by pro-Cathar armed bands who, in 1175, burned the abbey's granges and threatened the monks' lives, blocked construction of the abbey church. The community called on Bonneval Abbey which paid its debts, while Pontigny, the mother-abbey, sent a Burgundy master builder to complete work on the church, finally consecrated in 1189. The number of monks and properties increased considerably; in 1311, Philip the Fair granted it royal protection. But the Hundred Years War arrived and the abbey was invaded, plundered and, finally, burned by the English in 1411. The church was spared and during reconstruction of the regular buildings, between 1430 and 1470, fortifications were also built. The Revolution expelled the three last monks and Loc Dieu Abbey, sold as state property, was used as a barn and a stable. It was falling into ruin when a family from Villefranche de Rouergue bought it and began restoration work.

Abbey church nave

The Summer of 1940

In 1940 after the Armistice, Paris was occupied by German troops. Several paintings from the Louvre, including the *Mona Lisa* and *The Wedding at Canaan*, were brought to Loc Dieu in June, after a stopover at Chambord. But at the end of the summer, in the heart of Rouergue the humidity level was too high for these paintings and on October 7 they were taken to the Ingres Museum in Montauban.

The abbey

Tombstone in chapter house

The Mudejar style tower and cloister

Rueda

In 1152, two knights of Aragonese nobility, Gerardo de la Marca-Anda and his son-in-law Pedro Fernández de Huesca, went to the Gascon abbey of Gimont, a daughter of Morimond. They asked the abbot to establish a daughter-abbey in Aragon. Their undertaking was supported by the Count of Barcelona, Ramon Berenguer IV (1131-1162) and his wife, Petronilla, Queen of Aragon (1137-1142). In 1154, monks from Gimont founded Our Lady of Salz, in the Gallego River valley, north of Zaragoza. They set up a grange and then established a daughter-abbey, Our Lady of Juncería, whose existence was attested in 1166 when Guillermo Pérez became its abbot. Two years later, faced with various difficulties, the Salz community had to abandon its abbey and return to Gimont. In 1177, during the visit by Humbert, Abbot of Gimont, to Juncería, Alfonso II (1162-1196) confirmed the latter in his authority and rights over the Aragonese establishment. The king of Aragon was a great benefactor of the abbey and in 1175 granted it properties at Gotor, in the valley of the Aranda, a tributary of the Jalón, north of Calatayud. And in 1181, he granted the lands and castle of Escatrón, in the valley of the Ebro. But he requested that the community of Juncería be transferred there so that it would find more favourable conditions for its Cistercian ideals and its material development in this deserted place. Work began on the left bank of the river, in a place called Rueda, facing the castle overlooking the opposite bank. The name Rueda was possibly of Moorish origin. In any case, at the end of the 12th century, the Saracens were not far away and in 1194, the monks had to negotiate safe conducts with them to guarantee their safety. In 1196, the completed Saint Peter's Chapel received the relic of the Holy Thorn, a gift to Juncería from the archbishop of Zaragoza, Pedro de Torroja. That same year, Peter II (1196-1213) succeeded Alfonso II. A major figure in the *Reconquista* and an ally of the Count of Toulouse, in conflict with the king of France and the papacy, he could not help Rueda where the Juncería community settled starting in 1202. In 1226, Abbot Martin of Nogarol (1220-1226), until then abbot of Nuestra Señora de Rueda and just elected abbot of Gimont, laid the first stone of the abbey church whose high altar was consecrated in 1238. Because of a lack of resources, the work dragged on but the situation improved when James 1st (1213-1276) took Rueda under his protection in 1251. During the 16th century, the abbey, placed under commendam, declined. Abbot Miguel Rubio (1558-1580) started restoration work. The abbey joined the Cistercian Congregation of Aragon, instituted in 1616. The first third of the 19th century was to be fatal with the trilogy of the War of Independence, the Liberal Triennium and the *Desamortización*. Listed as a historical monument in 1922, the abbey was restored. It is the property of the *Diputación* of Zaragoza.

A cloister capital

Discovering Rueda

The royal door fitted into the abbot's palace in the early 17th century forms the entrance to the monastery. The doorway opens onto San Pedro square, closed in the north by the hospital dating from the end of the 16th century; in the south by a gallery from the second half of the 16th century, and in the east by medieval buildings. The church, without a transept, is a simple rectangle with three naves and five bays. In the east, an axial chapel forms the choir, flanked by two little chapels. All three have flat chevets. Three chapels were added on the north side: the 13th century Santo Cristo Chapel in the centre was, perhaps, the start of a transept. St Bernard's Chapel on the left dates from the 17th century; St Barbara's on the right, from the 18th. In the early of the 17th century, a reredos presenting six episodes from the life of the Virgin was placed in the axial chapel. During the *Desamortización*, it was transferred to the church of Escatrón, where it is still visible. In the cloister to the south of the church, the east gallery serving the chapter house, parlour and *scriptorium* dates from the mid-13th century, as does the south gallery onto which the refectory, opposite the lavatorium, opens. The north gallery was built in the last quarter of the 13th century, and the west gallery in the mid-14th century. The height of the steeple is surprising and the original church did not have one. Built in the 14th century, its base is made of stone, but the upper section, in Mudejar style, is brick.

The abbey church

The heating room

Capital in the sacristy

L'ÉPAU

Berengaria, the widow of Richard the Lionheart, founded L'Épau Abbey in a wooded spot on the banks of the Huisne River, not far from Le Mans, in 1229. Monks from Citeaux Abbey came to settle there. The bishop of Le Mans, Monseigneur de Laval, consecrated the church in 1234 before it was even completed. In 1365, during the Hundred Years War, the inhabitants of Le Mans feared that the English might invest the abbey and entrench themselves in it so they set fire to the buildings. The ensuing difficult restoration lasted nearly a century. The abbey remained in activity until the Revolution which scattered the six last monks from the monastery. Put up for sale, L'Épau was used as a farm until 1958 when the Sarthe Department took possession of it. With the help of the Historical Monument Association, much restoration work was undertaken, thanks to which the abbey has recovered its original splendour.

Although it was never completed, with its surprisingly pure lines L'Épau abbey church has the grandeur and ambition of the great cathedrals. The western façade has a doorway with a Gothic arch, surmounted by a large mullioned window. The forty-seven metre long nave has never been completed. It consists of three vaulted bays on intersecting ribs. The north aisle was never built. In each of the arms of the vast transept, large pointed arcades serve as openings for three square-shaped chapels. The sanctuary, with its flat chevet typ-

An abbey church façade

The sacristy

The scriptorium

Detail inside the church

The south aisle

ical of Bernardine architecture, is illuminated by a large window from the 14th century, formed by eight lancets surmounted by a rose window. The south transept provides access to the sacristy, vaulted on intersecting ribs. In the centre, two columns, their capitals decorated with leaves, support the ribs of the vaulting. Paintings from the 14th century subsist on the walls. Located to the south of the church, the cloister was never rebuilt after its destruction by a fire in the 14th century. The chapter house was built in the east wing towards 1250 and opens onto the courtyard through a fine Gothic doorway framed by two gemel openings. It contains nine square bays, vaulted on intersecting ribs, supported by four columns whose capitals are decorated with plant motifs. The keystone of the central bay presents the mystical lamb. The recumbent figure of Queen Berengaria, the founder of the abbey and who was buried in this room, shows her simply dressed, holding her prayer book. The monks' dormitory takes up the upper floor of the east wing. The vaulting overhead is wooden wainscoting and is lit up by a series of small Romanesque windows. At the far northern end, the abbot's room was also the monastery's strong-room. The monks' room, at the south-east corner of the cloister, was used as the community's *scriptorium*. Vaulted on intersecting ribs, it communicated with the heating room, or *calefactorium*, where the ink was liquefied. Beyond the heating room, there subsist the arcatures that used to cover the monks' lavatorium, as well as the arch of the great refectory door.

Berengaria of Navarre

The daughter of Sancho of Navarre and Sancha of Castile, Berengaria was born in 1170 in the Pyrenees. In 1191 she was chosen by Eleanor of Aquitaine to be the wife of Richard the Lionheart, her third and favourite son, who had just inherited the English crown but who, at the age of forty-three, was still single and without an heir. In the spring of 1191, Berengaria and her future mother-in-law landed in Messina, where she was to meet Richard who was about to leave for the Third Crusade. The new king of England, whose homosexuality was known, was nonetheless impressed by the young woman and he married her that same year at the cathedral of Limassol in Cyprus. Berengaria accompanied her husband to the Holy Land and was at his side during the capture of Acre and his victory over Saladin at the Battle of Arsuf. She returned to Rome in September, 1192. During his voyage home in December, Richard was taken prisoner by Duke Leopold of Austria. Eleanor managed to gather the enormous ransom of 150,000 silver marks demanded for the liberation of her son, who was allowed to return to England in 1194. Berengaria, rather abandoned in a castle in Aquitaine, learned of the death of her husband in 1199, after he was mortally wounded at the siege of Châlus. In 1204, after the death of Eleanor, Berengaria received Falaise and Domfort which she ceded to Philip Augustus in exchange for the dower of Le Mans, where she lived until her death in 1230, a year after founding the abbey of L'Épau.

Recumbent figure of Queen Berengaria in the chapter house

The abbey

Royaumont

In 1229, at the age of fourteen, the future king Louis IX (Saint) founded Royaumont Abbey near his castle at Asnières sur Oise. It was done to fulfill the wishes of his father, Louis VIII, who at his death in 1226 wanted part of his goods reserved for the construction of an abbey dedicated to the Virgin. St Louis offered the abbey to the Cistercian Order and Royaumont became a direct daughter of Citeaux. The king had the church built on the model of the abbey church at Longpont, a daughter of Clairvaux, and attended its consecration in 1236. During his life, Saint Louis retired on many occasions to the abbey, whose name retains the idea of royalty. One of the king's brothers, Philippe Dagobert, and three of his children were buried there. Thanks to the monarch's generosity and the community's labour, Royaumont flourished rapidly. The monks knew how to develop the hydraulic potential of the two tributaries of the Oise, the Thève and the Ysieux, flowing through the property. At the king's death in 1270, Royaumont received a third of the royal library. But Saint Louis's example was not followed by his successors and by the 14th century the monks had to beg the royal authorities to stop lodging their people and horses in the abbey's enclosure. The Hundred Years War and its accompanying violence arrived next. To avoid plundering and destruction, the community paid ransom several times, especially in 1353 to Charles the Bad. Royaumont was greatly weakened by the war; its lands had been sacked and its numbers decreased. The abbey was placed in commendam in 1549. The commendatory abbots led dissolute, worldly lives, described by Mathurin Régnier in one of his *Satires*. It was nevertheless at Royaumont that, in 1635, Richelieu organized a meeting to try to reconcile the respective supporters of the Common and Strict Observances. From 1651 to 1728, the Lorraine Family was placed at the head of the abbey, where several members of the family were buried. On the eve of the Revolution, life in Royaumont had nothing Cistercian about it. Its last commendatory abbot had a luxurious abbot's palace built on the model of the Petit Trianon in Versailles. In 1791, Royaumont Abbey was sold at auction and became a cotton mill. The purchaser unscrupulously had the church demolished and used the stones to build the factory. In 1864, the Sisters of the Holy Family of Bordeaux established their noviciate at Royaumont. They were expelled in 1904 when the State seized Church property and Jules Gouïn carefully restored the abbey. During the First World War, it was used as a military hospital. In 1923, Henri Gouïn purchased Royaumont. A music lover, he took good advantage of the building's exceptional acoustics and in 1936 the first concerts took place in the former monks' refectory. Since 1950, Royaumont has been welcoming researchers, intellectuals and artists from many countries.

Only the foundations providing an idea of the outline subsist of the beautiful and vast 13th century church. It was 105 metres long, had a nave with nine bays with side aisles, a vast transept and a

The Virgin of Royaumont

large sanctuary with an ambulatory with seven radiating chapels. At the south-east corner of the north transept arm, the turret containing the spiral staircase that led to the roof trussing still rises at a height of forty metres. It permits the visitor to imagine the beauty and delicacy of the church's architecture. In the former sacristy, refitted as a chapel, some vestiges of the church have been collected, including a fine keystone with plant motifs. Located south of the abbey church, the chapter house has been turned into a library. Beyond the passage leading outside, the monks' building, above which lay the dormitory, was rebuilt in the 19th century. The latrine building, consisting of two large rooms located on either side of the canal, used to communicate with the dormitory. It has undergone numerous transformations: in the 17th century, it was used as the prior's dwelling, before being transformed into an orangery in the 18th century. The south gallery contains the large and bright refectory. In its centre, five columns support the diagonal ribs of its vaulting. Concerts are held there and a reconstituted Romanesque organ has been placed in the pulpit. The refectory communicates with the kitchen through a wicket in the wall at which the monks came to get their food. The kitchens contain the Royaumont Virgin, a statue dating from the 14th century. In the cloister's west gallery, a small passage provides access to the lay brothers' buildings, transformed into guesthouses during the 17th century and currently inhabited by the owners.

The cloister

The turret

Louis the Ninth, King of France and Saint

"Just as the writer who has made his book illuminates it with gold and azure, the said king illuminated his kingdom with beautiful abbeys."
Joinville, *History of Saint Louis*

On Sunday, October 24, 1227, a year after the death of his father Louis VIII, the young king Louis IX attended the consecration of the abbey church of Longpont in the company of his mother, Blanche of Castile, to whom in 1226 the dying Louis VIII had entrusted the guardianship of his young son before the Cistercian bishops Gautier of Chartres and Foulque of Toulouse. Aged twelve, Louis IX was a gentle and serious child and, from a very early age, he had shown a sincere and deep piety which William of Chartres had resumed with a play on words. "*Mores enim ejus, actus et gestus, non solum regales, sed etiam regulares errant*" (his actions and his manners were not only those of a king, but those of a monk). In the course of the ceremony that consecrated the huge church, the nave of which was at least five hundred metres long and ended in a beautiful chevet with an ambulatory and radiating chapels, the child-king wa[s] struck by the beauty and majesty of the place. He conceived the plan of raising a similar shrine in the honour of Mary, in accordance with the wishes of his deceased father who, in his will, had ordered that the crown jewels be sold to pay for an abbey for the Order of Saint Victor, to the glory of Mary. However Saint Louis called on the Cistercians to populate the abbey he founded the following year, not far from his residence at Asnières sur Oise, and which he named *Regalis Mons*, Royal Mount or Royaumont. Construction work on the abbey began in 1229, shortly after the arrival of a group of monks from Citeaux. During his many visits to the abbey, the young king wanted to take part in the building with his own hands. After hearing the holy offices, he used to go and work with the monks and the lay brothers, helping them carry stones, lime and mortar in the silence imposed by the Rule. In 1235, the twenty-one year-old king had just come of age when he attended the consecration of Royaumont's abbey church accompanied by the sixteen-year old Marguerite of Provence, whom he had married a year earlier. The consecrating priest was the Cistercian John, Archbishop of Mytilène, who had attended the coronation of the young king in Reims in November 1226, after the death of Louis VIII. Whenever he stayed at the castle of Asnières sur Oise, Saint Louis often went to visit Royaumont Abbey where he even had a small room fitted up for himself at the end of the monks' dormitory, near the stairway leading to the church, in order to be able to

Nave of the abbey church at Longpont

ttend the night vigils. The king used to
ɔ to confession and receive discipline
very Friday, wherever he was. At
oyaumont, he did his penance in the
acristy. According to William of Saint
athus, author of a *Life of Saint Louis*,
ne saintly king liked to serve the
nonks in their refectory, carry their
owls, and pour their drinks with the
ame humility he showed in his youth
uring the construction of the
nonastery. He also liked to attend the
eremony of the washing of the feet,
ne *mandatum*. In accordance with the
rescriptions of the Rule of Saint
enedict, every Saturday in the cloister
allery adjacent to the church, before
ne spiritual reading, or *collatio*, and
Compline, the two monks charged with
erving in the kitchen – the one finishing
s week and the one starting his – had
) wash the feet of their brothers. This
as in imitation of Christ who, giving a
st example of charity and humility
efore the Passion, washed his disci-
es' feet saying, "I leave you a new
ommandment, to love one another
ne way I loved you". Saint Louis also
ished to wash the feet of the monks,
ut the abbot exempted him from
oing so. He never missed visiting the
firmary where there was a leprous
onk; he cut the meat the ill were
lowed by the Rule and put the pieces
the leper's mouth. At first, the
istercians allowed burial within the
onastery's enclosure only to members of the Order. However, each monk had the privilege of having two of his relatives or friends and his wife buried in the abbey's cemetery. In 1157, the General Chapter allowed the founder of an abbey to be buried in the cloister, the church being reserved for kings, queens and bishops. Saint Louis chose to be buried at the royal abbey of Saint Denis, in the company of his ancestors. However, his family was buried at Royaumont: his brother, Dagobert, who died in 1235 at the age of thirteen; his eldest daughter, Blanche, who died in 1243, only three years old; John, his third son, only a few months old, in 1248; and finally, Louis, his eldest son, destined for the throne, who died at the beginning of 1260 at the age of sixteen.

Royaumont refectory

Tiles in pavement in Royaumont refectory

Abbey church chevet

Leyre

On the southern foothills of the Sierra of Errando, known as Leyre, overlooking the valley of the Aragon River, a Benedictine community was established in the middle of the 9th century. In 848, it was visited by Eulogus, a Mozarab Christian martyr who, three years later, from his prison in Cordoba wrote to Willesindo, Bishop of Pamplona, to praise the monastery of Leyre and its abbot Fortunio. In 880, the relics of Nunilo and Alodia were transferred from Osca – Huesca – to Leyre. The devout cult of these saints in the region and the wealth of its scriptorium gave great influence to Leyre, which was reinforced by the support and donations of the kings of Navarre, who made it into their pantheon. At the beginning of the 9th century, relations between al Andalus and the Navarrese became tense. King Sancho Garcés I (905-926), allied to the king of Leon, Ordoño II (914-924), captured the fortresses of Calahorra, Nájera and Viguera from the Moors. In 924, Abderramán retaliated and defeated the Navarrese troops near Hoz de Lumbier, one league west of Leyre, before sacking and burning Pamplona deserted by its inhabitants. From 990 to 992, it was Almanzor who carried out raids in Navarre. Leyre was either badly damaged or destroyed. The reigns of Sancho Garcés III (1000-1035) and his son García III (1035-1054) marked a new period for San Salvador de Leyre where the abbot, named by the king of Navarre, held his charge concurrently with that of the bishopric of Pamplona. In 1025, Leyre was the location of the preliminary meeting before the Cluniac reform was undertaken in San Juan de la Peña . Construction of a new abbey church also began. A first consecration of the church took place on October 27, 1057, in the presence of the King of Navarre, Sancho Garcés IV, "*El de Peñalén*" (1054-1076), of Juan, Bishop of Pamplona and Abbot of Leyre, the King of Aragon Ramiro I, the abbot of San Juan de la Peña and numerous prelates. At the time, only the chevet, the crypt and the steeple were completed. After the murder of King Sancho in Peñalén in 1076, the Navarrese nobility gave the kingdom of Navarre into the hands of Sancho Ramírez, King of Aragon. Leyre lost its pre-eminence in favour of San Juan de la Peña and, by 1078, the abbot of Leyre was no longer entitled to the bishopric of Pamplona. But work continued at the monastery and a new consecration of the sanctuary was celebrated on October 24, 1098. Among the guests were the King of Aragon and Navarre, Peter 1st (1094-1104); Raymond, Abbot of San Salvador de Leyre (1083-1121); Peter of Andouque, Bishop of Pamplona; Diego Peláez, Bishop of Santiago de Compostela, and the abbots of Saint Pons of Thomières, Saint Victor of Marseilles, and San Pedro of Roda. The abbey church's nave with its wooden roof and the west doorway were nearly finished, just like the cloister located to the north of the church. Under the abbacy of Raymond, during the new impetus given to the Church by the Gregorian Reform, the Benedictine Rule was restored in Leyre. And from then on, the abbot was elected by the monks. The abbey enjoyed a period of prosperity, maintained under the abbacy of García (1122-1139), during which Navarre recovered its indepen-

San Virila's tunnel

A Nightingale Sang

The existence of Abbot Virila who died at Leyre in 950 is attested. And there is a fine legend glorifying him that deserves to be told. The good abbot liked to walk in the woods surrounding his monastery. He read, meditated, wondered about feelings of eternity. One day he sat beside a spring. The melodic sound of a singing nightingale was added to the noise of the running stream. Virila fell asleep. When he awoke, nature had changed, the trees had grown. He had a hard time finding his way. And what a surprise awaited him at the abbey! It had all changed. His little church was as big as Pamplona cathedral. He knocked at the door. But he did not recognize the porter friar. The latter wondered who the hoary old man could be. "I am Virila, the brother abbot!" They went to the *scriptorium*. In the archives, they found the chronicle of the abbot who had been lost in the woods three centuries earlier. The community was celebrating the remarkable miracle in the abbey church when a nightingale with an abbot's ring in its beak flew in and placed it on Virila's finger. Visitors today can go to the spring of San Virila. If they pay attention, they can hear the warbling of the kind nightingale and share several moments of eternity with it.

Detail of ivory reliquary

MAY MY FAITH LAST

In Adahuesca, near Alquézar, two little girls, Nunilo and Alodia, were born in the 9th century. Their Muslim father died and their Christian mother brought them up in her own faith. At her death, the two young girls were placed in charge of their father's half-brother who vainly tried to convert them to Islam. He denounced his nieces to the judge Calaf de Alquézar. Imprisoned, separated and tortured, they did not renounce their faith and the prefect of Huesca, deputy of Abderramán II (822-852), Emir of Cordoba, condemned them to death. Before having their throats cut, they lifted their hair to make the task easier for the executioner. Since a light shone above their tombs, the Muslim powers had their bodies thrown into a well, but the light moved too. Eneca, wife of the king of Pamplona, Iñigo Arista (820-851), recovered the two martyrs' remains and confided them to Leyre where the holy relics immediately became the objects of worship. At the beginning of the 11th century, they were placed in an ivory reliquary made in a Cordoba workshop in 1050. Today the object is kept at the Museum of Navarre and Pamplona. On September 5, 1672, Leyre ceded part of the relics – the tibias and the ribs – to the village where Nunilo and Alodia were born.

dence from the crown of Aragon after the death of Alfonso 1st in 1134. At the time, Leyre owned the rights over fifty-eight villages and seventy-one churches or monasteries. But times were becoming more difficult. The community had never accepted losing the episcopal seat of Pamplona in 1078 and accepted its supervision even less. It engaged trial after trial to free itself and lost them all. The abbey was even reproached for producing forgeries. In August 1188, Pope Clement III (1187-1191) closed the matter and subjected the monastery to the bishop of Pamplona. At the dawn of the 13th century, the situation of San Salvador de Leyre was not outstanding. To remedy this spiritual and economic crisis, Abbot Domingo de Mendavia (1230-1239) wanted to incorporate the abbey into the Cistercian Order. But the Benedictines were opposed to the idea. Throughout the years, white monks and black monks struggled for control of the abbey. Finally, in 1307, the Cistercians won; Leyre became a daughter of La Oliva. Dark clouds lay on the horizon of the 14th and 15th centuries: the Black Death of 1348; poor harvests; battles of the warring Carlos II (1349-1387) with Aragon, Castile and France; confrontations over the succession of Blanca 1st of Navarre (1425-1442) between her son Carlos, Prince of Viana, and her husband John II of Aragon, supported by Leyre. The Navarrese population decreased as did the number of monks at Leyre, whose abbot Miguel de Gallipienzo (1433-1459) could only take note of the sorry conditions. New work was undertaken during the reign of Catherine of Foix (1483-1516) and continued until the middle of the 16th century. The abbey church's nave received its vaulting and a new chap-

The crypt

San Juan de la Peña

The story of the foundation of San Juan de la Peña Monastery has something legendary about it. At the beginning of the 8th century, the mountainous region of the Pyrenees piedmont, located between the valleys of the Aragon and Gallego Rivers, was not completely controlled by al Andalus. Christian populations had even settled in a fortified position, the Pano. Towards 732, Abderramán I (731-788), Emir of Cordoba, sent his army to remove them. The population was massacred, although there were two young men among the survivors – Voto and Felix. Several years later, Voto went hunting deer in the mountains. He pursued his prey on horseback but the stag fell over a precipice that Voto was unable to avoid. As he fell, he prayed for the intercession of Saint John the Baptist and, miraculously, the horse landed gently on the ground. A path opened before the horseman. It led him to a shabby little church built under the overhang of a cliff. Near the altar, there lay a man who had just died. As his will and testament, he had engraved a text on a stone. He was the hermit who had built this tiny shrine. Voto asked Felix to join him and the two brothers led lives of anchorites, fed with bread every day by an angel. At their deaths, other hermits came to take their place and legend gave way to history. At the beginning of the 10th century, a large eremitic community was established at the foot of the Sierra de la Peña, under the dark and humid rocky overhang. While the region was being reconquered from the Muslims in about 920, the community soon decided to set up a coenobitic organization. When Abderramán III (912-961) devastated Navarre in 924, people came to seek refuge in the small monastery that included several hovels as well as its church dedicated to Saints Julian and Basil. During the reign of the king of Navarre, Sancho Garcés III el Mayor (1000-1035), after a meeting held in Leyre in 1025, Aragonese monks, who had taken refuge in Cluny at the end of the 10th century to escape Almanzor's henchmen, arrived at the monastery. They introduced the Cluniac reform into what became San Juan de la Peña. Ramiro 1st (1035-1063) was the first of the kings of Aragon. His capital, Jaca, was not far from San Juan de la Peña, which benefited from his support and that of his successors. In 1063, Ramiro 1st attended the Council of Jaca which decided to abandon the Mozarab rite in the liturgy and to use the Catholic one. But the new rite was introduced to San Juan de la Peña only on March 22, 1071, because, given its history, the monastery was very much attached to its Mozarab heritage. Sancho Ramírez (1063-1094) launched the construction of a new church that was consecrated by the bishop of Jaca on December 4, 1094, in the presence of the new king of Aragon, Peter 1st (1094-1104), who made San Juan de la Peña the pantheon of his dynasty. The cloister was built in the 12th century. But Ramon Berenguer IV, Count of Barcelona (1131-1162), married Petronilla, Queen of Aragon (1137-1162). Their son Alfonso II (1162-1196) thus joined Aragon and Catalonia under this authority and the kingdom of Aragon extended as far as the Mediterranean. San Juan de la Peña, lost in its mountains, was somewhat abandoned for the Cistercian abbey of Poblet, which was, in turn, transformed into the pantheon of the kings of Aragon.

Capital in cloister showing the Last Supper (detail)

Tympanum of the *Porta Speciosa*

ter house was set up. Catherine, the granddaughter of Gaston Fébus of Foix, was married to John III of Albret. The royal couple had two of their children buried in Leyre – Andrés Febo and Martín. Pedro de Usechi (1562-1568), the prior of the Carmelite convent in Pamplona and commendatory abbot of Leyre, named by Philip II, started construction work on a new monastery south of the abbey church. In 1613, in the course of the work that ended in 1648, a wall of the presbytery was demolished to make the church communicate with the new sacristy and two sarcophagi were brought to light. Hidden away in the 16th century, they contained the remains of Navarrese kings and nobles. In 1634, during the abbacy of Antonio de Peralta y Mauleón (1614-1652), Leyre joined the Cistercian Congregation of the Crown of Aragon and Navarre. From then on, abbots were elected for four-year periods. Leyre recovered its strength and prestige. But the 18th and 19th centuries were a time of successive misfortunes. During the War of Succession (1701-1714), Leyre's support of the Bourbons against the Austrians harmed its interests. In 1739, flooding by the Aragon River destroyed harvests and carried away a dam and a mill. Under the abbacy of Gregorio Álvarez (1792-1797), during the French Revolution, Navarre was invaded by French troops and Leyre lost its possessions north of the Pyrenees Mountains, like the priory of Saint Engrâce in the Upper Soule. The War of Independence (1808-1814) and the Liberal Triennium (1820-1823) disturbed monastic life at Leyre, which received a fatal blow in 1836 from the *Desamoritización*. In 1868, Leyre was listed as a national monument. Five years earlier, the remains of the kings of Navarre had been taken away for safety to the church of San Esteban de Yesa. On July 8, 1915 they were brought back to Leyre in a wooden chest. At the beginning of the 20th century, the abbey church and its crypt were once again used for religious services. In 1935, excavations in the church discovered the foundations of the 9th century church. Restoration of the monastery was started in 1945. On November 10, 1954, Benedictines of the Congregation of Solesmes coming from Santo Domingo de Silos settled in Leyre. Restoration was completed in 1979 and on July 25, Leyre was raised to the rank of an abbey. San Salvador de Leyre had revived.

SOLESMES

Dom Guéranger was ordained as a priest in 1827. On July 11, 1833, he settled at the priory of Solesmes, near Le Mans, with three companions and the intention of establishing a Benedictine community. In 1837, the Holy See raised Saint Pierre de Solesmes to the rank of an abbey. The new abbot gave pre-eminence to holy offices and attached great importance to intellectual work. The Solesmes library developed and its publications became authoritative. Pope Pius IX (1846-1878) entrusted Dom Guéranger with the preparatory work for the promulgation of the dogma of the Immaculate Conception in 1854. Solesmes began to spread. It restored life to Saint Martin of Ligugé in 1853 and, in 1866, founded a first house for nuns, Saint Cecile. Dom Guéranger died in 1875 so was not to live through the sad expulsion of his monks, who returned in 1895. But the Law of 1901 took the community on the road of exile and it settled in Quarr, a former Cistercian abbey on the Isle of Wight. It returned to Solesmes in 1922. Today, twenty-one male and eight female monasteries constitute the Congregation of Solesmes. In Spain, its monks are present at Leyre, Silos, Madrid and Valle de los Caídos.

The Arangoiti, the highest point of the Leyre sierra with its altitude of 1356 metres, offers a magnificence view over the site of the monastery and the Yesa reservoir. A narrow road leads to it from Biguezal, near the Hoz de Arbayun. The visitor comes upon the monastery by its 11th century Romanesque chevet. The crypt, also dating from the 11th century, forms a square with three apses alongside it on the east. The columns which structure it into four naves are short and of unequal heights. They support imposing capitals on which the projecting arches under the high barrel vaulting rest. The three apses and the first two bays of the upper church are Romanesque and they reproduce the plan of the crypt situated underneath. The statue of Our Lady of Leyre sits imposingly in the centre of the side chapel. The western side of the church, with Romanesque walls and Gothic vaulting, has a single nave. On the north side, the chest containing the remains of the kings of Navarre is placed in a niche protected by a railing. On the wall of the neighbouring bay, the Leyre Christ dates from the beginning of the 16th century. On the other side of the nave, the Chapel of the Holy Sacrament contains the reredos of Saints Nunilo and Alodia. The density of the sculpted decoration on the west doorway, from the 12th century, has given it its name of *Porta Speciosa.* On the tympanum, from left to right, stand Saint Peter, the Virgin, Jesus Christ, Saint John and St James the Greater. The capitals topping the columns of the piedroits and the one used as a pier were carved by Master Esteban, one of the sculptors of the cathedral in Compostela.

Our Lady of Leyre

View of the monastery and Yesa Lake

LES SAINTES RELIGIEUSES DE L'ORDRE DE CITEAU.

3

Abbeys of Nuns

By the end of the 12th century, and especially during the 13th century, Cistercian abbeys for nuns multiplied all over Europe. Some were born from the will of the powerful, such as Las Huelgas Reales of Burgos, founded in 1187 by King Alfonso VIII of Castile and his wife, or Notre Dame la Royale of Maubuisson, founded in 1236 by Blanche of Castile. Others, like Fontaine Guérard, already existed but wished to follow the holy rule of Citeaux and were incorporated into the Order. Although some were to have tragic destinies, like Port Royal, the great seat of Jansenism in the 17th century, others lasted through the centuries and today still live the original fervour at Las Huelgas, Cañas, Vallbona or Gradefes.

Port Royal des Champs before its destruction

The nuns gathered in the Solitude at Port Royal des Champs

Port Royal

In 1204, with the support of the bishop of Paris, Mahaut of Garlande founded an abbey for nuns at Porrois, south-west of the capital in the valley of the Rhodon. Our Lady of Porrois Abbey, later known as Port Royal, was incorporated into the Cistercian Order between 1216 and 1225, under the supervision of the nearby abbey of Les Vaux de Cernay. Enjoying the generosity of the lords of Montfort, Lévis and Marly, and that of kings like Saint Louis, Port Royal began to develop. But it suffered during the Hundred Years War and again during the Wars of Religion. Once under the commendam system, it gave in to the laxity common at the end of the 16th century. Restoration was the work of a young abbess, Jacqueline Arnauld (†1661), known as Angélique at her conversion. A descendant of Parisian *grande bourgeoisie*, she was the daughter of the king's lawyer, Antoine Arnauld, who had her enter the abbey in 1599, when she was eight years old, as the abbess's coadjutress with succession rights. Becoming the community's mother at the age of eleven, Angélique did not feel any religious vocation; novels were her favourite reading, and her life carried on monotonously, interrupted only by visits from her family. But through her random reading and two sermons on the Beatitudes heard in 1608 and 1609, she developed a deep faith. Resolving to re-establish poverty, abstinence, silence and prayer at regular hours, Angélique began her reform with "the day of the wicket", on September 25, 1609. When her family came to visit, she agreed to talk to them only through the wicket in the abbey door, which remained closed, and received her father only in the parlour, thus restoring enclosure as prescribed in the Benedictine Rule. Within a short time, the name of Port Royal became famous. Vocations increased, beginning with the abbess's sisters: Agnès, Anne and Marie-Claire took the veil in 1611, Madeleine in 1623. Their widowed mother joined them in 1641. Among many others, Racine's aunt, Agnès before 1651; Marie, her grandmother in 1651; Jacqueline, the sister of Pascal, in 1652; and Catherine, the daughter of the painter Philippe de Champaigne, in 1657 were all nuns at Port Royal. From 1618 to 1623, Angélique restored discipline in Maubuisson after the extremely permissive abbacy of Angélique d'Estrée. In 1625, she transferred her community to Paris, to a mansion in the Faubourg Saint Jacques, because of the dampness at the original abbey, called from then on Port Royal des Champs (of the fields). In 1627, conflict with the abbot of Citeaux, Dom de Nivelle, made Angélique decide to withdraw her community from the Cistercian Order's jurisdiction and place it under that of the Bishop of Langres, Sébastien Zamet, the reformer of Tart Abbey. (Until his death in 1622, François de Sales had been her director of conscience.) She thought of uniting that abbey with her own, then of forming a community of the Holy Sacrament, when Bishop Zamet introduced Jean Duvergier de Hauranne, Abbot of Saint Cyran, to Port Royal in 1634. This disciple of Jansenius and Bérulle became the spiritual adviser for the nuns, whose destiny became linked to the Jansenist movement. Starting in 1637, some elite personalities con-

Jacqueline Arnauld

The Name of Port Royal

Having gone hunting, King Philip Augustus (1180-1223) got lost in the deep forest of Yveline. With great difficulty, his men managed to find him in a small valley where there was a chapel dedicated to St. Laurence. To thank God, the king wanted to build a monastery in this place that had been a port of salvation for him. And the new foundation was named Port Royal, according to the legend explaining the abbey's name and origin. There is a more prosaic explanation – a deformation of a translation. The nuns' abbey founded by Mahaut of Garlande in 1204 in a valley called Porrois, where there was indeed a small oratory dedicated to St Laurence, took the name Our Lady of Porrois. But the bull of foundation written in Latin translated Porrois by *Portus Regius* which, retranslated into French, gave Port Royal.

Port Royal Gentlemen

Claude Lancelot (1615-1695)

Having participated in the founding of the Little Schools, Lancelot was the author of a series of books on Latin, Greek or Italian grammar, instituting important reforms in teaching languages. Rules and comments were no longer written, as had been the case beforehand, in the language being learned, but in the pupil's mother tongue. In 1657, he published his *Garden of Greek Roots* and collaborated on a *General and Reasoned Grammar* (1660). A tutor to the Duke of Chevreuse in 1656, then to the Princes of Conti, from 1672 to 1679 he retired to Saint Cyran Abbey, before being exiled to Quimperlé. His *Mémoires touchant à la vie de M. de Saint Cyran* appeared only in 1738.

Antoine Arnauld (1612-1694)

Called the Great Arnauld, he was the youngest brother of Mother Angélique. Converted by Saint Cyran in 1638, a priest and doctor at the Sorbonne in 1641, he attacked the Jesuits and defended Jansenism in his treatise *Of Frequent Communion* (1643). The movement's spokesman after death Saint-Cyran's, his two *Apologia for Mr. Jansenius* earned him the Holy See's condemnation in 1647. Excluded from the Sorbonne in 1656, after the publication of his *Second Letter to a Duke and Peer* in which he expounded his distinction between law and fact, he retired to the Port Royal Granges, pursuing the controversy with Nicole and Pascal. He collaborated on the *Grammar* and *Logic* and, in 1667, published his *New Elements of Geometry*. Semi-clandestine from 1660 to 1668, on his return to favour in 1669 he attacked Calvinism. He was forced into exile to Mons in1679, then to Brussels, where he died in 1694.

Pierre Nicole (1625-1695)

Attracted at an early age to Port Royal, where his aunt was a nun, Nicole taught at the Little Schools while pursuing his theological studies. A defender of Jansenism along with Arnauld and Pascal, he contributed to the elaboration of the *Provinciales*, which he translated into Latin. A famous teacher, he collaborated on the *Logic of Port Royal* (1661) and, starting in 1670, the first volumes of his *Essays on Morals* appeared.

Antoine Arnauld

verted by the abbot, often related to the nuns, retired to the abandoned solitude of Port Royal des Champs. The three Lemaître Brothers, the theologians Pierre Nicole and Antoine Arnauld, and the grammarian Lancelot were among the first *Solitaires*, with Pascal a regular visitor after 1654. Eminent teachers, at the same time theologians, writers, scientists and philosophers, the "Gentlemen from Port Royal" dedicated themselves to studying and writing, a bit of manual labour and especially to teaching children in the Little Schools, where Jean Racine was a pupil. In 1648, given the increasing number of nuns in Paris, Angélique reopened the Champs abbey and work was undertaken there. As the Solitaires were also more numerous, they moved to the Grange house, near which new buildings were put up in 1652 for the Little Schools. But hostility towards Port Royal hardened, uniting the clergy, particularly the Jesuits who had the monopoly of education, and the monarchy, which did not look favourably on a conception of faith in which the religion of the faithful did not pass through the mediation of the Church, seen as a fundamental structure for controlling the kingdom's subjects, but was instead a matter placed within the rigour of individual commitment. Saint Cyran was imprisoned in 1638. He nonetheless maintained close ties with Port Royal and in 1643, the year he was freed, Antoine Arnauld published a treatise synthesizing his doctrine – *Of Frequent Communion*. This treatise, whose title alluded to practices that the Jesuits considered latitudinarian since, according to Saint Cyran, communion and absolution should not be too frequent but prepared for with long penance, stirred up even more controversy. Saint Cyran, who died a short time later, had also been accused of inspiring the *Augustinus*, a posthumous (1640) work by his friend Jansenius, which systematized Saint Augustine's ideas about grace, in opposition to the Jesuits' Molinistic theses. In 1653, Rome judged five propositions supposedly drawn from the *Augustinus* heretical. The Solitaires, who protested brilliantly – Pascal published his *Provinciales* – were scattered and the Little Schools were closed in 1660. Although they had been spared so far, on April 23, 1660, the nuns were forced to sign a Formulary condemning the five propositions. On the same day, recruitment to the abbey was suspended and the young girls' boarding school that it contained was closed. The nuns were divided. In 1665, the "signers" gathered at the monastery in Paris, which came under Jesuit control in 1669. The rebels were deprived of the holy sacraments and were locked up at the abbey of Les Champs. But the election of Pope Clement IX in 1667 restored peace for some time. For ten years, from 1169 to 1679, a new era opened at Port Royal des Champs, with the return of the Solitaires – who published Pascal's *Pensées* – and the increase in regular visitors, among whom were members of the highest nobility, such as the Duke de Luynes, the Duke of Roanne, as well as the "*belles amies*" like the Princess de Guémené, the Duchesse of Longueville who built her mansion not far from the cloister, or Mademoiselle de Vertus. But this influence was to be the very cause of the convent's ruin. Persecution started again in 1679, and the Solitaires had to choose between exile and the Bastille prison. In 1705, the nuns from Les Champs were once again ordered to sign the Formulary. They demanded explanations, they appealed to Rome. This was enough for Louis XIV, who obtained a papal brief from Clement XI suppressing Port Royal des Champs Abbey, whose goods were given to the Parisian abbey. The buildings were invaded by Lieutenant d'Argenson and the twenty-four nuns living in the abbey were dis-

The 1662 ex-voto by Philippe de Champaigne

Port Royal Gentlemen

Robert Arnauld d'Andilly (1589-1674)

The elder brother of the Great Arnauld, Robert joined up with Saint Cyran fairly early. Out of his fifteen children, he sent six of his daughters to Port Royal, where he himself retired in 1644, at the death of his wife. His political relations – during his early society days, he composed a madrigal for the *Garland of Julie* (1634) and was nearly the Dauphin's tutor – helped to make Jansenism fashionable. A translator of the *Confessions* of Saint Augustine, the *Meditations* of Teresa of Avila, and the *History of the Jews* by Flavius Josèphe, he went into exile in 1664 at his son's in Pomponne, where he died in 1674.

Blaise Pascal (1623-1662)

The scholar of geometry, physics and philosophy entered into contact with Port Royal in 1647. But until his father's death and his sister's entrance into Port Royal, he led a worldly existence and dedicated himself only to science. The night of November 23, 1654, during which he had the "mystical experience of God sensitive to the heart", determined the close ties he established with the Solitaires. In 1656, he took the defence of Arnauld with his *Provinciales* in which he displayed his talent as a polemicist. These 18 letters presenting a character being initiated in debating at the Sorbonne were written and published secretly in 1656-1657, under the pseudonym of Louis de Montalte. Refusing any compromise, Pascal retired from polemics in 1661 to dedicate himself to his *Apology of the Christian Religion*, fragments of which the Solitaires published in 1670 under the title of *Pensées*.

L.I. Lemaître de Sacy (1613-1684)

The nephew of Mother Angélique, Louis Isaac Lemaître de Sacy was the younger brother of Antoine Lemaître, the brilliant lawyer who was the first to retire to Port Royal in 1637. An exegete, poet and writer, ordained to the priesthood in 1649, he became the nuns' spiritual director in 1664. Imprisoned from 1666 to 1668, his name remains linked to his translation of the Bible, whose first books appeared in 1672.

D'Argenson giving the Port Royal nuns the order to disperse

persed on October 29, 1709. Starting in 1711, "proceedings were started to raze the house, the church and all the buildings, as is done for the houses of assassins of kings, so that at the end not a stone shall be left standing", wrote Saint-Simon. So that the place would not become a pilgrimage site, it was ploughed and planted. The deceased buried in the convent's cemetery were exhumed. The remains of those who still had a family, like Jean Racine or the Arnaulds, were buried with dignity elsewhere; the others were just thrown "with the indecency that can be imagined", wrote the author of the *Mémoires*, into a common grave at Saint Lambert cemetery.

Blaise Pascal

The property of the Paris convent until the French Revolution, the "historical desert" of Port Royal, sold as state property at the Revolution, today belongs to the Society of Friends of Port Royal. On the site of the abbey, a grassy enclosure with a cross in its centre shows where the cloister used to be. A neo-classic oratory, with stained glass windows inspired by the paintings of Philippe de Champaigne, was built in 1891 on the site of the abbey church's transept. Overlooking the valley, the Granges domain where the Solitaires retired in 1648, consists of a farm, where these Gentlemen lived and where Pascal wrote his first *Provinciale,* and the building of the Little Schools. The latter contains the National Museum of the Granges of Port Royal, dedicated to the abbey's history and the Jansenist movement. Among other things, there are paintings by Philippe de Champaigne and original editions of the *Grammar* and *Logic* of Port Royal.

The Great Centre of Jansenism

After a 16th century marked by the end of Church unity, hereafter divided into several denominations, at first Jansenism appeared in the 17th century as a theological doctrine in rupture with the pious humanism preached by the Jesuits in the wake of the Council of Trent. In the course of several sessions from 1545 to 1563, the Council attempted to define Roman Catholic orthodoxy. This theological humanism, aiming to master human will for spiritual perfection, was particularly expressed in *The Concord of Free Will and Grace*, published by the Jesuit Molina in 1588. God grants each man, in all circumstances, a suitable grace – sufficient grace – allowing him to do good and to save himself, by respecting the Ten Commandments, the laws of the Church, doing good works… However, everyone remains free to use this divine aid or not. Jansenism took its name from the Dutch theologian Cornelius Otto Jansen, or Jansenius (1585-1638). Between 1600 and 1604, Jansenius studied at the University of Louvain, where he met a Frenchman from Bayonne, Jean Duvergier de Hauranne. The two men continued their studies in Paris. Returning to Louvain in 1616, he occupied the Chair of Professor of Holy Scripture at the university. With the advice of his friend, who had become abbot of Saint Cyran, in 1623 he began to write a general survey of the strictly interpreted thoughts of St Augustine (354-430). The work, the *Augustinus*, was nearly completed in 1636 when its author became Bishop of Ypres so it appeared only in 1640, two years after his death. Because of original sin, man is inevitably turned to doing evil through the delights of the flesh. Only divine grace – efficient grace – can make him feel the spiritual delight that will encourage him to do good. But this saving grace, without which will is capable only of evil, is not given to everyone. God, moving in mysterious ways, only grants it to certain predestined men. The Abbot of Saint Cyran spread Jansenius's thoughts in France. However, for Saint Cyran, more interested in practice than in theory, the reference to St Augustine was mainly used to glorify the power of God, reminding the believer of his humble condition. According to him, the experience of divine love, and of grace, can only come about if the believer renounces his own will through the most demanding personal asceticism, "strips the old man", and makes himself a blank. This was the basis for the Renewal to which the nuns at Port Royal converted after he became their spiritual advisor in 1634. To better receive the love of God, the believer must lead a life of penitence, receiving neither absolution nor communion. At the end of the ordeal, he should live in solitude in order to make his experience fruitful. A demanding and austere religious practice, Jansenism was particularly well received within the bourgeoisie of trade and the law, and it soon appeared subversive in the eyes of established power. In the footsteps of his friend Bérulle (1575-1629), the founder of the Oratory, Saint Cyran joined the Devout Party hostile to the foreign policy of Richelieu, who had chosen an alliance with Protestant countries against the Hapsburgs of Austria and Spain. In 1635, the pamphlet Jansenius published against the cardinal's policies brought Richelieu's wrath down on the abbot. And after the formation of the first community of Solitaires of Port Royal in 1637, Saint Cyran was accused of diverting the intellectual elite from public life. Imprisoned in Vincennes in 1638, he was freed only after the death of Richelieu in 1643, and he died shortly afterwards. Under Mazarin, who continued his predecessor's policies, the struggle against Jansenism became a constant in the politics of the French monarchy. Under pressure from the cardinal, in 1653 the pope published the bull *Cum Occasione* which condemned five propositions supposedly drawn from the *Augustinus*. The Great Arnauld replied by the famous distinction between law and fact; he established that the five propositions were at best summaries of Jansenius's thought, but were in no case directly taken from the *Augustinus*. Hence, although he approved the law according to which they were condemned, he denied the fact, that is, that they appeared in the *Augustinus*. Arnauld was excluded from the Sorbonne in 1656, and a short time later the doctors who had taken his side were also excluded. At the death of Mazarin in 1661, Louis XIV took up the struggle. But the Peace of the Church proclaimed by Clement IX in 1669 offered some respite to the Solitaires. However the king suspected the circle of aristocratic friendships that had formed around Port Royal – of which the most influential person was none other than his own cousin, the Duchess of Longueville, former heroine of the Fronde – of conspiring against his absolutism. And at the death of the duchess in 1679, there was nothing else to prevent his will from being carried out; after the dispersal of the nuns in 1709, Port Royal was destroyed starting in 1711.

Ambulatory in the abbey church

Gradefes

Abbey church door

In 1151, Alfonso VII (1126-1157) rewarded Don García Pérez for his bravery in the struggle against the Almohads by granting him the lands of Gradefes, a town located on the right bank of the Esla River, east of Leon, not very far from San Miguel de la Escalada. Don García was originally from Cea, north of Sahagún, where he lived with his wife, Doña Teresa. Four years after the death of Don García, in 1168, Doña Teresa founded Santa María de Gradefes, a Cistercian abbey to which nuns from Tulebras came to settle. She was its first abbess. Under her abbacy, construction of the abbey church was started in 1177, as attested on a carving on a stone placed in the north wall of the abbey church, near the tomb and recumbent figure of Don Nicolás Pérez, chaplain of the house, who died in 1327. Work began at the chevet. It was to take a long time because the community's financial resources were limited. At his death, the body of Don García had been buried at the Cluniac monastery at Sahagún, as he had requested in his will of 1157. But it is possible that at the death of Doña Teresa in 1187, the remains of the two spouses were united at Gradefes and they are the contents of the 13th century tomb with the two recumbent figures kept in the abbey church. This is only a hypothesis because, according to the abbey's chronicles written in the 16th century, Doña Teresa was buried in the chapter house and, furthermore, the characteristics of the two figures do not correspond to the picture that one might have of the couple. When the Congregation of Las Huelgas Reales was instituted in 1187, both Gradefes and Perales, daughters of Tulebras, were rather reticent. But the comprehensive attitude of the abbess of the Navarrese establishment helped, and the first General Chapter of the Congregation desired by King Alfonso VIII was held on April 27, 1189, under the authority of Doña Misol, the abbess of Las Huelgas.

In 1245, on the basis of a donation to Gradefes made in 1240 by the Countess of Villalba de la Loma, the abbey diffused to Otero de la Dueñas, in the valley of the Luna River, north-west of Leon. Since the noble lady was a nun at Carrizo, the situation created some conflict between the two houses which were close neighbours and members of the same congregation. It was probably reduced at the end of the 13th century when the abbesses of Gradefes and Carrizo were two sisters from the same great family of Leon, the González. In 1591, several nuns from Gradefes were at the origin of the reform movement of the Recoletas. In 1629, for reasons of security, the Gradefes community was transferred to Medina de Rioseco, a bigger and less isolated town to the north-west of Valladolid. In 1632, the abbess of Carrizo, Doña Isabel María de Quiñones y Acuña, came to the banks of the Sequillo River to run the Gradefes community and to organize its return almost immediately. In 1809, as Napoleon's armies approached Gradefes, with the exception of the abbess and one lay sister, the nuns left the abbey, which was spared when it was protected by the town's inhabitants. After the *Desamortización*, only two nuns remained. The abbey was

Our Lady of Gradefes

Abbey church capital

repopulated in 1880 by nuns from Avilés and, in 1882, by nuns coming from Otero de las Dueñas. The community of Gradefes has been incorporated into the Cistercian Congregation of Saint Bernard.

The abbey church appears disproportionate between, on the one hand, the 12th century apse, and what may have been the transept from the 13th and 14th centuries, and on the other hand, the later nave, barely deeper and very narrow. The choir is surrounded by an ambulatory with five apsidal chapels, of which the two closest to the nave hardly protrude. The capitals are sculpted with geometrical and plant motifs, as well as human and animal figures. In the cloister's east wing, the chapter house, dating from the end of the 12th and beginning of the 13th centuries, opens through a door framed on either side by three openings. The semicircular arches of these windows are decorated on the outside with a star motif, which is reproduced on the abbey church's doorway. Their springs are supported on sets of six, three or two columns, topped with capitals. The chevet's structure reflects the interior plan. The roofing of the choir and the apsidal chapels rest on modillions carved with plant and animal themes and with human figures. But on three of them, more original subjects have been presented: the struggle of Leon, a noble and a man cutting a tree. The central apsidal chapel is flanked by two columns topped with historiated capitals. The one on the left shows the weighing of souls with the devil on the left of the scale and Christ on the right.

Entrance to the chapter house

SAN MIGUEL DE LA ESCALADA

Under the reign of Mohamed 1st (852-886), the Christians of al Andalus were persecuted. They had no alternative but to convert or to flee northward in the Iberian peninsula. This was why, under the reign of Alfonso III (866-910), a community of monks from Cordoba, probably placed under the Rule of Saint Isidore of Sevilla, founded the monastery of San Miguel de la Escalada near Leon, on lands granted to them by the King of Asturias. Under the authority of their abbot, Alfonso, a church was immediately built on the ruins of a Visigothic church and named for the Archangel Michael. This original shrine turned out to be too small when the number of monks at the monastery increased and a new church was consecrated on November 20, 913, by the Bishop of Astorga. In the middle of the 11th century, when the community adopted the Rule of Saint Benedict, the church underwent new transformations. San Miguel de la Escalada was part of the *Infantando* or *Infantazgo* of Doña Elvira, the daughter of Alfonso VI, King of Castile (1072-1109) and sister of the future Queen Urraca (1109-1126). In the kingdoms of Leon and Castile of the 11th and 12th centuries, the *Infantando* was a seigniory given as a dowry for an Infante who chose not to marry. This seigniory was usually organized around a monastery and its possessions. In her will dated 1095, Doña Elvira bequeathed San Miguel de la Escalada to Doña Sancha, her niece, daughter of Urraca and sister of the future king Alfonso VII (1126-1157). San Miguel de la Escalada thus entered the *Infantando* of Doña Sancha which also comprised, after the death of Urraca, the monastery of San Isidoro in Leon, where she was buried. In 1124, Doña Sancha considered granting San Miguel de la Escalada to Cluny, but the transaction was not concluded. In 1127, she offered the Leon monastery to the cathedral of Santiago de Compostela but the act of donation was not written up. The final assignees were the canons of Saint Ruf, near Avignon, in an act dated December 16, 1155. It is surprising that Doña Sancha thought of Saint Ruf, which she perhaps knew through the wife of Alfonso VII, Berengaria, the daughter of Ramon Berenguer III, the Count of Barcelona (1096-1131), also Count of Provence. Extremely generous with religious orders, in 1147 Doña Sancha had donated lands at La Espina, near Valladolid, to Clairvaux so that a Cistercian abbey be established there. Halfway between Gradefes and Mansilla de las Mulas, the church of San Miguel de la Escalada has a basilica plan with three naves and six bays. In the widest bay, on the side with the chevet which takes the place of the transept, three apses open. Their floor plan is that of a very closed horseshoe, a stylistic effect characteristic of Mozarab art, and a figure that reappears in the Moorish arches inside the church, the portico and the window of the outside gallery. The very squat steeple, dating from the 11th century, is Romanesque.

San Miguel de la Escalada

The belltower and cloister of the abbey

Entrances to the abbey church and the chapter house

Cañas

Since its foundation in 1170, the abbey of Santa María de Cañas has continuously contained a community of Cistercian nuns, and is today part of the Cistercian Congregation of Saint Bernard. It was in 1169 that Count Lope Díaz de Haro, *alférez* of the king of Castile Alfonso VIII, and his wife Doña Aldonza Ruiz de Castro donated the abbey of Benedictine nuns of Hayuela to the Order of Citeaux. But this village in la Rioja, attached to Santo Domingo de la Calzada, which was a stopping point for pilgrims on their way to Santiago de Compostela, did not provide the nuns with the tranquility and silence they wanted, especially when the armies of the kings of Castile and Navarre were fighting over the region's rich lands. In 1170, the donors granted the nuns lands at Cañas and Canillas so they could transfer their monastery. It was barely two leagues south of Hayuela, in the valley of the Tuerto, a tributary of the Najerilla, at Cañas, the village where Saint Dominic of Silos was born in 1000, that the nuns settled, dedicating their new abbey to Santa María. In the 17th century, their house was dedicated to Santa María de San Salvador, or the Holy Saviour, perhaps to avoid confusion with Santa María Hermitage, also in Cañas, which had been restored by St Dominic. Count Lope Díaz de Haro died on May 6, 1170 at Redecilla del Camino. He was buried in the Cluniac monastery of Santa María la Real in Nájera, the city where he had exercised his power. Barely a month after the death of her husband, with whom she had eleven children, Doña Aldonza entered Cañas monastery, with four of her youngest daughters, including Apolonia, aged seven, and María Urraca, barely one year old. In 1181, Apolonia married Ferdinand II of Leon. In 1188, after her husband's death, she and her children returned to Cañas to escape the persecution of Alfonso IX of Leon, her husband's son by a first marriage. In 1222, she retired to the Cistercian abbey of Vileña, near Burgos, of which her daughter Isabel was to become the abbess. As for María Urraca, in 1225 she became the fourth abbess of Cañas. In 1171, Doña Aldonza bequeathed her goods to the abbey where she was to die in 1225. Doña Anderquina (1169-1199) was the first abbess of Cañas. In 1189, the year of the election of Doña Toda (1199-1212), who succeeded her, Cañas joined the congregation that had formed in 1187 around Las Huelgas Reales of Burgos. Two years later, while Alfonso VIII was fighting the Moors, Sancho VI, King of Navarre, invaded the Rioja. Conscious of the danger, Doña Toda, Doña Aldonza, and the community took refuge at the monastery of San Millán de la Cogolla, one league south of Cañas on the lowest foothills of the Sierra de la Demanda. This insecure situation obviously lasted because in 1199 Pope Innocent III threatened to excommunicate anyone who took violent action against Cañas. In 1213, during the abbacy of Doña Emerenzana (1212-1225), Francis of Assisi stopped at Cañas during his pilgrimage to Santiago de Compostela. The *Poverello* impressed the nuns, and particularly the future abbess Doña Urraca who later had a

Columns in the chapter house

To Well-Born Souls

Don Diego Díaz de Haro, the son of the founder of Cañas, had, like his father, the charge of *alférez* of the kingdom to King Alfonso VIII of Castile. On July 16, 1212, he was present at Las Navas de Tolosa. He was accompanied by two of his brothers, his son Lope, two nephews including the son of his sister Apolonia, and the King of Leon Ferdinand II. Don Diego commanded the Castilian vanguard and, because of his bravery, played an important part in this Christian victory over the Moors. During the battle, the Almohad chief, Miramamolin al Nasir, read verses from the Koran in his tent, surrounded by thousands of chained slaves armed with lances. At the announcement of his troops' rout, he fled to Sevilla. The captured loot was considerable. Alfonso VIII charged his *alférez* with distributing it among the Christian chiefs and Don Diego Díaz de Haro carried out his mission. Among the booty was a *pendón*, part of the defeated man's tent, that is now at Las Huelgas Reales de Burgos. But Don Diego wanted nothing for himself. Faced with his king's insistence, Doña Urraca's brother requested that the port of Santoña be returned to Santa María la Real de Nájera, where his remains were transferred after his death in 1214.

The Devotion Reredos (detail)

statue, no longer in existence, made of St Francis, who was canonized in 1228.

Hardly had she been elected, Doña Urraca López de Haro (1225-1262), considered the second founder of Cañas, and who also had the title of Countess, donated her inheritance to the abbey. Half of it was used to build a hospital for the poor in the village; the other half on work at the abbey. The apses and transept of the abbey church, as well as the chapter house, date from this construction period. An inscription on a cloister wall mentioned 1236 as the year the monastery was built, the year Cordoba was captured by Christian troops. It should be understood that Cañas was under construction. There is also no doubt that Canas took advantage of the many privileges granted by King Alfonso X the Wise (1252-1284) who went there several times. About ten years after her death in 1262, the body of Doña Urraca, who was proclaimed blessed, was placed in a tomb whose stone was carved by Ruy Martinez de Bureba. In the chapter house, it stands on three consoles, sculpted at each end with wolves' heads. The tomb was opened in 1898, 1899, 1933 and 1938. Each time the body, which gave off a fragrance, appeared intact. The chapter house in Gothic style also contains the tombstones of four other abbesses. It opens onto the cloister's east wing through a door with ogival voussoirs, framed with openings of the same kind. It is covered with four ribbed vaults that rest on a single central column. The abbey has been beautified over the centuries. The Gothic section of the abbey church built during the abbacy of Doña Urraca consisted of a deep central apse, flanked by two shorter lateral apses, opening onto a transept. These apses were supposed to be extended beyond the transept by a central nave with two aisles. But only the central nave had been built by the beginning of the 16th century. In 1531, Abbess Doña Leonor de Osorio (1523-1570) entrusted the creation of a reredos of The Devotion to the sculptor Guillen of Holland and the painter Andrés of Melgar. Today, the work is placed on the back of the western façade of the abbey church. On five levels divided by pilasters and columns, it presents twenty-eight painted or sculpted scenes from the life of the Virgin, and the lives of saints, including Bernard and Benedict. The painting on the right on the second level from the bottom, shows the commisioner of the work and St Bernard praying facing the Virgin. The cloister was entirely rebuilt during the 17th and 18th centuries. In the west gallery, a doorway dating from the 13th century is that of the cellar and the abbey's storeroom, from the same period. This large room, called a *cilla*, divided into two parts that communicate through five Gothic arcades supported on solid pillars, contains the museum's collections, composed of reredos, paintings, tabernacles and statues which arrived to enrich Cañas's furnishings starting in the 16th century, but also Romanesque and Gothic statues: one of Saint John from the 12th century; one of Saint Peter from the 13th. In the Relic Room, which is adjacent but entered from the south gallery, relics and reliquaries are gathered. There is also a carved group of the Virgin, Saint Anne and the child Jesus from the 13th century.

Reliquary of St Bernard

Head of Doña Urraca's recumbent figure

Three abbots and three bishops officiating at Doña Urraca's funeral

Three noble ladies and six monks, Doña Urraca's tomb

On Earth as in Heaven

The tomb of Doña Urraca, the fourth abbess of Cañas, is a masterpiece of Gothic funerary art. The recumbent figure represents the blessed nun, her head covered with a veil and resting on two cushions, dressed in a finely draped robe which emphasizes her height. Doña Urraca was one metre seventy tall. At her feet sit three praying nuns. On the right side of the tomb, the deceased woman's funeral is taking place: three abbots, three bishops, four officiants, six weeping men and women around the tomb, four noble ladies with tall headdresses, six monks including two Franciscans recognizable by the rope around their waists. On the left side, an abbot receives a theory from eleven nuns to whom he presents his condolences. Some of them hold the book with the Order's Rule, others say the rosary or hide their faces, the last one turns towards the abbot at the end of the procession. On the small end behind the recumbent figure's head, a nun takes a novice's hand, while another holds a book and a third kneels before St Peter, the keys to paradise in his left hand, blessing with his right. On the other end, Doña Urraca arrives in Heaven, her joined hands emerging from a shroud held by two angels.

Doña Urraca's tomb (detail)

The steeple and the cloister

Vallbona

On the lands in the south of the County of Barcelona which, in 1150, had just been freed from the Saracen yoke, hermits chose solitude. Some of them had retired to the north slope of the Tallat Sierra. In 1154, a woman called Agnes gave them a domain in this *good valley*, the place called Vallbona, where they settled and where she asked to be buried in the original chapel dedicated to the Virgin, Santa María, built by anchorites directed by a certain Ramón. On July 20, 1157, the community of Vallbona received a freehold from Ramón of Cervera. Two months earlier, on May 26, 1157, in Tortosa, the Count of Barcelona Ramon Berenguer IV (1131-1162) had ceded to Ramón of Vallbona properties at Sórboles, in the valley of the Montsant, near the current locality of Pobla de Cérvoles, to found a Benedictine abbey there. On July 18, 1164, Ramón of Cervera gave the castle of Colobrers, near Vallbona, to Ramón who managed an eremitic community spread over three locations: Vallbona, Colobrers, and half a league from Vallbona, Holy Spirit. However, despite efforts by Ramón of Vallbona, and despite the king of Aragon, Alfonso II (1162-1196) on September 12, 1164 making a new donation of the domain of Poboleda, near Sórboles, along with the right to set up a mill on the Montsant River, the Benedictine monastery was not founded. It must be said that Poblet Abbey was less than two leagues away to the east and that it already ran a grange in the Montsant valley. But

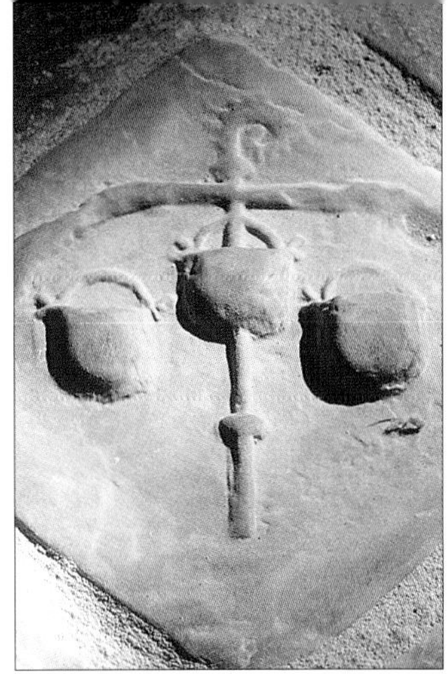

Tile on chapter house floor

Two Towers

Vallbona abbey church is topped with two towers. The lantern-tower topping the dome at the transept crossing dates from the 13th century; the steeple/bell-tower rising above the nave's second bay, from the 14th.

Santa María Abbey

Recumbent figures of the lords of Guimerà

West gallery in cloister

Ramón established hermits at Poboleda. On April 1, 1171, he ceded Sórboles to Poblet, joined this Cistercian community and, with the support of Berengaria of Cervera, negotiated the incorporation of Vallbona into the Order of Citeaux. It was to be an establishment of nuns. In Octobre 1172, Oria and some nuns from the Navarrese abbey of Tulebras settled at Colobrers. The male hermits left Vallbona for Poboleda, and the women remained. Ramón, who had continued directing Vallbona, died on April 8, 1176. He was buried in the "old" church of Santa María, one hundred metres north-west of the place where the new abbey was shortly to be established. He had organized his succession by placing Vallbona under the authority of Colobrers. But on October 17, 1176, Oria logically decided to transfer the community from Colobrers to Vallbona, where construction of the abbey church was undertaken. In 1177, Alfonso II (1162-1196) and his wife Sancha granted lands and privileges to the monastery. When they stayed there the following year, they agreed to pay it an income. They also granted it a domain close to Lerida to set up an abbey for Cistercian nuns. Saint Hilarius opened in 1204. Berengaria of Cervera was an important personality for Vallbona. Having become the widow of Guillem of Cervera in 1172, she dedicated her life to the abbey. It was thanks to her that the Aragonese monarchs came there in 1178. She did not take the veil, but acted at the side of the abbess, attracting many heiresses of the Catalonian nobility to Vallbona. They studied at the abbey school, which could rely on the considerable production of its *scriptorium.*

Berengaria died in 1225. As for Oria, she directed Vallbona for over ten years and, during her abbacy, construction continued and the abbey's possessions increased. To work the land, since there were no men within the community, the abbess was able to call on the men from the Holy Spirit Hermitage. But most of all, she began the system of *familiaritas*, in which laypersons of both sexes, the *familiares*, in return for the contribution they made to the abbey benefited at their death from the same offices and prayers as those said for the community's members. The richest paid an annuity, gave some goods or left something to the abbey in their wills. The others, by contributing their physical strength, earned a living in this world and worked for the salvation of their souls in the next world. The abbey also used servile labour, as attested in a donation to the abbey in1298 by Bernat Gilabert de Vilafranca of a black Saracen named Joseph. In 1275, the remains of the second wife of James 1st the Conqueror (1213-1276), Yolanda of Hungary, and their daughter, Sancha, were transferred to the abbey. A century later, in 1380, Vallbona was raised to the rank of a barony when Peter III the Ceremonious (1336-1387) ceded to it his powers of civil and criminal jurisdiction on his territory, in return for the sum of 22,000 sols, destined to finance the monarch's campaign in Sardinia. At the beginning of the 16th century, the nuns of Vallbona were no longer constrained by enclosure, but it was re-established by the Council of Trent. At its sessions of December 3-4, 1563, the same council imposed on the regular nuns to move their houses near inhabited areas for reasons of security. The abbess Estefanía de Piquer (1563-1576) invited the inhabitants of Montesquiu to settle within the walls of the monastery, previously isolated, providing them with a roof and lands. This led to the creation of the village of Vallbona de los Monges. Although the *Desamortización* of 1835 deprived the nuns of their temporal abbey, they remained in Vallbona where their presence has thus been continuous since 1176. Today, Santa María de Vallbona is a member of the Cistercian Congregation of the Crown of Aragon.

Access to the monastery, which is completely enclosed by the village, is through a Baroque door. The cloister forms an irregular quadrilateral. The south gallery, dating from the 11th century, is Romanesque, as is the east gallery from the early 13th century. The Gothic north gallery dates from the 14th century, and the west gallery from the 15th and 16th. Abbess's tombstones, including that of Estefanía de Piquer, are set in the floor of the chapter house, with its Gothic doorway. Construction of the church essentially dates from the 13th and 14th centuries. Its plan, that of a Latin cross, has an oblong nave and a transept whose crossing is topped by a dome on squinches. During the 15th century, the 14th c. tomb with recumbent figures of the lords of Guimerà was placed in the southern arm. They were benefactors of Vallsanta, a daughter of Vallbona. Beyond the transept prolonging the nave, the presbyterium with a flat chevet, like the two chapels flanking it, contains the tombs of Yolanda of Hungary and her daughter Sancha. In another chapel, built in the north-west corner of the cloister at the end of the 19th century, stands the venerated statue of Our Lady of the Cloister from the 12th and 13th centuries.

Entrance to the chapter house

Statue of Our Lady of the Cloister

Square tower of the abbey church

Las Huelgas Reales

The King of Castile, Alfonso VIII (1158-1214) and his wife Alienor Plantagenet founded the abbey of Santa María la Real in 1187, near Burgos, on the location of a residence used until then for royal pleasures. It became better known as Las Huelgas Reales from *holganza,* leisure. William II, Abbot of Citeaux (1186-1189) gave his agreement in a letter dated September that specified that the nuns themselves would choose one or two abbots from the area's Cistercian monasteries to do the visits. Alienor played an important role in this decision. She was the daughter of Eleanor of Aquitaine, who had retired to Fontevrault Abbey, and of Henry II of England, and hence the sister of Richard the Lionheart and John Landless. Nuns from Tulebras Abbey in Navarre, founded in 1157, arrived to make up the core of the community, of which Doña Misol was the first abbess. Alfonso VIII wished that his foundation would be at the head of a congregation consisting of other Castilian houses of Cistercian nuns. With that in mind, he addressed the Order's General Chapter through the intermediary of Martín de Finojosa, Bishop of Sigüenza and the former abbot of Huerta. Despite the reticence of several abbeys, the first General Chapter of the Congregation was held on April 27, 1189 at Las Huelgas under the authority of Doña Misol. Abbesses from Gradefes, Carrizo, San Andrés de Arroyo, Fuencaliente, Torquemada, Perales and Cañas all attended. Las Huelgas Monastery was richly endowed by its founders who donated to it forty-nine properties, including Hospital del Rey, several hundred metres away. Many young ladies of the Castilian nobility pronounced their vows in this abbey which, in a decision by Alfonso VIII in 1199, became the pantheon of the royal family. Las Huelgas soon came to command a real seigniory, enjoying temporal and spiritual jurisdiction and encroaching on that of the bishoprics, to such an extent that, in 1210, Innocent III (1195-1216) intervened through the bishops of Burgos and Palencia and the abbot of Morimond to restore order. Powerful and wealthy, over the course of time the abbey amassed a large library. Among other treasures, it possessed a lectionary made in the *scriptorium* of the neighbouring Cistercian abbey of San Pedro de Cardeña, a Bible copied in 1181, a *Commentary on the Apocalypse* by Beatus of Liebana from 1220, and a *Rule of Saint Benedict* from 1246. Strong because of support from the kings of Castile, then of Spain, it always showed great independence, particularly towards the Order's General Chapter. In 1260, the abbess even opposed a visit from the abbot of Citeaux. She was excommunicated and the measure was repeated in 1263. In 1332, Alfonso XI (1312-1350) had himself armed as a knight by the articulated arm of the abbey's statue of Saint James. On August 30, 1334, Queen Maria of Portugal gave birth to the future King Peter 1st (1350-1369) in the square tower that rises to the east of the church. Some chronicles claimed that the queen had given birth to a still-born daughter and that a servant had immediately substituted the newborn

Christ on the cross

A Disputed Succession

Among the royal tombs in Las Huelgas are those of Ferdinand de la Cerda, eldest son of Alfonso X (1252-1284), who died in 1275, and his son, Alfonso. In 1281, the king of Castile wished to entrust the kingdom of Jaén to the children of la Cerda, but his second son, Sancho, opposed it. Sancho succeeded him in 1284. In vain Alfonso de la Cerda proclaimed himself King of Castile in Jaca in 1288, then in Sahagún in 1296. In 1331, he recognized Alfonso XI (1312-1350).

Tomb of Alfonso de la Cerda (detail)

Chevets of the abbey church and St John's Chapel

son of a Jewish couple from Burgos. In 1379, John 1st (1379-1390) was crowned king at Las Huelgas and, for the occasion, dubbed about a hundred knights. In 1429, the abbess was once again punished for refusing to receive visitors and failing to keep the Rule. During the 16th century, relations between Las Huelgas and the Citeaux General Chapter improved when the latter certainly appreciated that the royal abbey did not join the Congregation of Castile. And in September 1533, during his Spanish journey, Edmund de Saulieu, Abbot of Clairvaux, visited the abbey without meeting any obstacles and presented it as the most important Cistercian abbey in Spain. In 1573, the Order's General Chapter approved the written request to "expand" its jurisdiction from Abbess Doña Francesca Manrique, its "obedient daughter". At that time, Las Huelgas controlled twelve houses of nuns within its congregation. And in 1591, with its approval, the Congregation of Recoletas was instituted at the initiative of nuns from Gradefes. At the beginning of the 19th century, fourteen abbeys depended on Las Huelgas. In 1809, Napoleon's army rabble sacked the abbey and desecrated the royal tombs. The *Desamortización* of 1836 interrupted the history of this abbey of nuns, which is today the mother-abbey of the Cistercian Congregation of Saint Bernard of Spain.

The exterior architecture of the abbey is rather severe, in the Cistercian spirit, and is dominated by the square tower dating from the 14th century. The abbey church is in Gothic style. Work began in 1187 and was completed in the second half of the 13th

San Fernando cloister gallery

Detail of turning pulpit

century. The sanctuary is divided into two parts by the enclosure. In the central chapel, behind the high altar, stands a Baroque reredos made in 1665, on which the Assumption of the Virgin is framed by statues of Saint Benedict and Saint Bernard as well as the founders praying. Above the door communicating with the central nave, a painting illustrating the battle of Las Navas de Tolosa, in which Alfonso VIII participated, is a work from 1594 by Jerónimo and Pedro Ruiz de Camargo. Because of its articulated support, a pulpit made in 1560 of gilded, embossed iron allowed the preacher to be heard on either side of the enclosure, by the faithful on the side of the transept and choir, and by the nuns sitting in their stalls in the nave. The central nave, flanked by two side naves – St Catherine's in the north, and St John's in the south – contains the double tomb of Alfonso VIII and Alienor, who both died in 1214. On the nave side, the enclosure is surmounted by a 13th century *Deposition from the Cross*. In the central nave, as in the two aisles, many other tombs have been placed. St Catherine's nave contains the 1275 tomb of the Infant Don Ferdinand de la Cerda, the son of Alfonso X the Wise. This tomb was not plundered by Napoleon's soldiers in 1809 and the Infant's clothing – a *pellote*, a kind of tunic, a cape and a *birrete*, a silk cap decorated with pearls and precious stones – are presented at the remarkable museum of Ricas Telas, which is located in a room opening onto the cloister. Two doors in St John's nave, where the tomb of Mary of Aragon, a nun at Las Huelgas and

Double sarcophagus of the founders of Las Huelgas, Alfonso VIII and Alienor Plantagenet

Stucco décor in gallery of San Fernando cloister

daughter of Ferdinand the Catholic (1474-1516), stands, provide access in the south to the Gothic San Fernando cloister from the 13th century. A few decorative elements in stucco, made in Mudejar style between 1230 and 1260, are still visible on the galleries' vaults. In the chapter house, opening onto the east gallery, the *pendón* from Las Navas de Tolosa comes from the tent of Miramamolin al Nasir, the vanquished Almohad chief. The Romanesque cloister, south-east of the preceding one, dates from 1180-1190, as does the Mudejar-style Chapel of the Assumption in its north-east corner. And some distance away, to the east of the monastery, Saint James's Chapel from the end of the 13th century contains a Gothic statue of the apostle, with articulated arms used for dubbing princes of royal blood as knights.

MUDEJAR ART

The Muslims who remained on lands recaptured from al Andalus by the Christian kingdoms during the *Reconquista* were called *mudejars*, giving the name to their architectural or artistic productions, greatly influenced by their origins.

Pendón from Las Navas de Tolosa

"Las Claustrillas", the Romanesque cloister

Bridge over the Arga at Puenta la Reina

Saint Martin's Church in Frómista

Tomb of St James, Santiago de Compostela cathedral

The *Camino francés*

During the decade 820-830, a hermit called Pelagius discovered the tomb of James the Greater in Galicia. Pilgrims converged on this site that was to become Santiago de Compostela. The first to come from beyond the Pyrenees was Godescalc, Bishop of Le Puy, in 950. In the course of the centuries, Santiago de Compostela became one of the most important pilgrimage sites of Christianity, along with Rome and Jerusalem. Little information is available about the itineraries taken by the Jamesian pilgrims from all over Europe before the 11th century. But it is likely that after crossing the passes at Roncesvalles or Somport, they went through Pamplona and reached Burgos via Salvatierra, Vitoria and Briviesca. According to the *Chronicle of Silos* from 1110, it was Sancho III Garcés el Mayor, King of Navarre (1000-1035) who encouraged pilgrims to go from Pamplona to Burgos by Puente la Reina, Estella, Logroño and Nájera. On this *Camino francés* leading from Puenta la Reina to Compostela, the Hospital del Rey de Burgos, a possession of Las Huelgas Reales, was an appreciated stop-over for the walkers for God who, afterwards, continued their travels by Carrión, Frómista, Sahagún, Leon, Villafranca del Bierzo and the Cebreiro Pass, the gate to Galicia.

Entrances to chapter house and parlour

Fontaine Guérard

A priory for women was founded between 1184 and 1190 east of Rouen with the agreement of the city's archbishop, Gautier of Coutances, and thanks to the generosity of Robert with White Hands, Count of Leicester. Set in a wooded location in the valley of the Andelle where there was a spring with healing virtues, the priory took the name Fontaine Guérard, or the curing (*guérir*) fountain. Joined to Citeaux in 1207, it was raised to the rank of an abbey in 1253. Ida, the first abbess, received the abbey benediction on July 20 from the archbishop of Rouen. Favoured by local lords and the kings of France, such as Saint Louis, the monastery flourished. But a drama happened there in 1399: pursued by the hatred of her former husband, the lord of Hacqueville, Marie de Ferrière was murdered inside the abbey where she had taken refuge. During the 17th century, Abbess Élisabeth de Bigars de La Londe (1619-1661) worked to restore the spiritual and material well-being of Fontaine Guérard. Closed at the French Revolution, the abbey was sold as state property. It was used as a quarry and many of its stones were used to build a nearby textile mill. The Marquis of Radepont used others to decorate the park around his castle. Listed by the Historical Monuments in 1937, it has since been restored by its architects.

Consecrated in 1218, the abbey church consists of a single nave ending with a flat chevet pierced by three lancet windows. The sexpartite ribbed vaulting of the nave has disappeared and a good part of the furnishings – stalls, statues, altar – are kept in the church at Pont Saint Pierre. South of the abbey church, only the east wing of the convent buildings from the beginning of the 13th century has been preserved. The ground floor contains the chapter house, which opens onto the cloister through three arcades with pointed arches, their piers decorated with thin columns set edgewise. Inside, four columns with worked capitals support the springs of the ogival vaults, whose keystones are finely sculpted. A stone bench runs around three sides of the room. After the parlour and the passage leading to the garden, the nuns' workroom forms the southern end of the east wing. Divided into two naves by three central columns, it has ribbed vaulting. Beside the chapter house, a stairway leads upstairs where a dormitory takes up the entire length. Lit in the east and the west by narrow windows, it used to be divided into cells set along either side of a central corridor. The ceiling has disappeared, leaving beautiful beams exposed. A private room with a fireplace was perhaps the abbess's room. Nothing remains of the building's south wing which contained the warming room and the refectory, nor of the west wing where the lay sisters probably lived. To the north, and away from the convent buildings, stands Saint Michael's Chapel, built at the beginning of the 15th century by the Lord of Hacqueville in repentance for the murder of his ex-wife. The chapel is built over a storeroom from the end of the 12th century, composed of a large rectangular crypt giving access to a cellar that extends about thirty metres underground.

Saint Michael's Chapel

Conjugal Tragedy

The choir of the church at Fontaine Guérard contains the mutilated statue of a recumbent figure in a place covered by a dome which used to be the nuns' sacristy. The statue was named Marie de Ferrière, although it is probable that the statue predates the murder. This shows how deeply her story is linked to Fontaine Guérard. Marie was the daughter of the chamberlain of King Charles VI. Married to William of Leon, Lord of Hacqueveille, and then repudiated by him, she took refuge at her brother's, Lord of Radepont, before being taken in by the nuns at the abbey. But her ex-husband, with his implacable hatred, decided to kill her. One night in 1399, his henchmen entered the abbey. They pushed away the nuns and killed the chaplain who had come to help the victim, then cut Marie's throat. Arrested shortly afterwards, two of them denounced William of Leon. Imprisoned at the Châtelet in Paris, he did not die in his cell. Released, he carried out pilgrimages to atone for his crime and built Saint Michael's Chapel at Fontaine Guérard, by paying an annuity so that daily masses be said in memory of the tragic Marie. He died at Azincourt in 1415.

The nuns' room

The abbey

Maubuisson

Blanche of Castile, who often stayed in Pontoise during her regency (1226-1235), decided in 1236 to found an abbey of Cistercian nuns close to the town but on the other bank of the Oise River. Raised on the domain of Maubuisson, from which it was to take its name, Notre Dame la Royale was completed in 1242. Cistercian nuns from Saint Anthony in the Fields near Paris came to settle there. In 1244, the year the abbey church was consecrated by the archbishop of Paris, the abbey was attached directly to the mother-abbey of Citeaux. Beside the regular buildings, a manor house was built and it was there that in 1244 Saint Louis vowed to leave for the Seventh Crusade (1248-1254). Blanche, who died in Paris in 1252 after taking the Cistercian habit, was buried in the choir of the abbey church. Lavishly endowed, Notre Dame la Royale developed rapidly and contained as many as 120 nuns and lay sisters by 1268. Philip the Fair was in Maubuisson in 1307 when he signed the order to arrest the Templars. He was there once again when, in 1314, the affair of the "king's daughters-in-law" broke out. To take advantage of the nuns' prayers, King Charles IV (1322-1328) and his wife, Jeanne of Evreux, as well as Charles V (1336-1380) chose to have their entrails buried at the abbey, where Countess Mahaut of Artois was buried in 1329. Damaged during the Hundred Years War and the Wars of Religion, Maubuisson, whose nuns were recruited from the aristocracy, was quickly restored. Starting in 1596, its abbess was Angélique d'Estrée, the sister of Gabrielle, mistress of King Henry IV.

Vaulting in nuns' room

The King's Daughters-in-Law

In 1314, King Philip the Fair was staying at Maubuisson when he learned that his daughters-in-law, Marguerite, the wife of Louis le Hutin, and Blanche, the wife of Charles de la Marche, had allegedly committed adultery with Philippe and Gautier of Aunai, knights of the royal house, conniving with their sister-in-law Jeanne, the wife of Philippe le Long, who had not revealed anything. The doubts that could hereafter stain the legitimacy of the royal succession – Philip the Fair's three sons reigned successively from 1314 to 1328 – explain the cruelty with which the king punished the accused. The knights of Aunai were skinned alive in Pontoise and castrated, their genitals thrown to the dogs. As for the three young women, they were put in prison – Blanche and Marguerite in Château Gaillard, Jeanne in the castle at Dourdan. Marguerite, who had confessed to her sins, was shaved and imprisoned in a room open to the elements, where she rapidly froze to death. After spending seven years in prison, Blanche was repudiated by her husband in 1322 and took the veil in Maubuisson. As for Jeanne, supported by her mother, Countess Mahaut of Artois, she reconciled with Philippe le Long, with whom she was to have five children.

Main channel and latrines

Angélique turned her new abbey palace into a place of worldly gatherings, but her indiscretions led to her being deposed in 1618. The abbot of Citeaux then called Mother Angélique of Port Royal to Maubuisson. Her restoration work was pursued by abbesses such as Marie Suireau (†1648) or Louise-Hollandine of Bavaria (†1709). But after 1730, recruitment declined regularly. In 1786, Louis XVI sent the last abbess into exile and forbade the community from accepting new novices or professed nuns. After the Revolution, the abbey became a military hospital in 1794. Sold in 1797, it was used as a quarry and its buildings were partially demolished. Purchased by the Rothschild Foundation in 1926, it was listed as a historical monument in 1947. Restoration of the domain, acquired by the general council of Val d'Oise in 1979, has been carried out by the chief architect of historical monuments.

The east wing of the cloister subsists of the convent buildings located north of the church, and nowadays it contains exhibitions of visual, fine and digital arts. It contains the sacristy, vaulted with Romanesque arches, the chapter house and the parlour with their Gothic vaulting, and the nuns' workroom which is separated into two naves by three columns holding the springs of the vaults' ribs. Upstairs, the dormitory used to communicate with the church in the north and in the south, with the latrines, built over a canal. Further west within the monastic enclosure stand the former guest house, enlarged during the 19th and 20th centuries, and the large tithe grange from the 13th century.

The tithe grange

Blanche of Castile

The daughter of King Alfonso VIII of Castile and Alienor Plantagenet, Blanche was born in 1188 in Palencia. In 1201, at the instigation of her grandmother Eleanor of Aquitaine, she married the future king Louis VII with whom she had twelve children. Queen in 1223, she became a widow in 1226 and carried out the regency during the minority of Louis IX, aged twelve at the death of his father. She skilfully overcame the revolt of the barons, encouraged particularly by Count Thibaud of Champagne, who were hostile to being governed by a queen of foreign origin, supported by another foreigner and especially by a cleric, the Cardinal of Saint Angelo Romano Frangipani. In 1229, with the treaty of Meaux-Paris, Blanche imposed her authority in the south by marrying her son Alphonse of Poitiers to the sole heiress of Raymond VII of Toulouse. She continued to use her influence in the royal government after Louis IX's coming of age, although he gradually became independent from her. It was nonetheless to his mother that Saint Louis entrusted the kingdom on his first departure for the Crusades in 1248. A year later, at the death of Raymond VII, Blanche took possession of the County of Toulouse in the name of her son Alphonse, who had gone crusading with the king. In 1251, she had to suppress the excesses of the crusaders called the Pastoureaux, aroused by the capture of Saint Louis at al Mansurah in Egypt. After her death in November 1252, she was buried at the Cistercian abbey of Notre Dame la Royale which she had founded. This abbey of Maubuisson was not the only Cistercian abbey due to Blanche of Castile. She had been a very devout queen who wished to provide her children with a strict upbringing, with an obsessive fear of sin. As a benefactress of Citeaux, Blanche continued a family tradition. Her parents, Alfonso VIII of Castile and Alienor Plantagenet, had founded the abbey of Las Huelgas Reales near Burgos in 1187, and populated it with Cistercian nuns. Alfonso and Alienor wished to make Las Huelgas the principal abbey of the female branch of the Cistercian Order in Castile by allowing its abbess to annually convoke a General Chapter which all the kingdom's abbesses had to attend. As for their daughter Blanche, in 1236 she founded two Cistercian abbeys for nuns: that of Notre Dame la Royale in Maubuisson; and Notre Dame du Lys near Melun where, in 1253, her heart was solemnly transferred. Also in 1236, she had also supported the creation of Cistercian abbeys for nuns at Biaches, near Péronne, as she had supported the creation of La Joie at Saint Pierre lès Nemours in 1231, and La Joie in Berneuil, near Soissons, in 1234. In 1244, she personally attended the Order's General Chapter in Citeaux at the side of the king of France, along with two other sons, the Counts of Artois and Poitiers, and her daughter Isabelle. By a decision of the General Chapter, Blanche was registered, along with Saint Louis, in the *memento* of all the Cistercian monasteries in France. In the same year of 1244, she obtained the direct connection of Notre Dame la Royale Abbey with Citeaux.

Vestiges of Notre Dame du Lys abbey church

Reference Points

54°
Edinburgh
SCOTLAND
Melrose
Sweetheart
BELFAST
St Patrick's tomb
Boyle
Clonmacnois
Mellifont (142)
Bective
Corcomroe
IRLAND
DUBLIN
Glendalough
Nenay
Hore
Jerpoint
Dunbrody
Tintern Minor
Furness
Rievaulx (114)
Fountains (122)
Leeds
Manchester
NORTH SEA
51°
Valle Crucis (188)
Buildwas
Birmingham
WALES
ENGLAND
Tintern
Tamise
NETHERLANDS
AMSTERDAM
LONDON
Canterbury
Buckland
Meuse
BELGIUM
BRUSSELS
Villers (158)
48°
ATLANTIC
OCEAN
Vaucelles
Bonnefontaine
Ourscamp (106)
Seine
Orval (112)
Fontaine-Guérard (304)
Royaumont (266)
Longpont (110)
Le Val
Chaalis
Maubuisson (306)
PARIS
Le Relecq
Boquen
La Trappe
Port-Royal (280)
Marne
Trois-Fontaines
Rennes
Perseigne
Les Vaux-de-Cernay (164)
Preuilly
L'Épau (262)
CLAIRVAUX (96)
PONTIGNY (198)
MORIMOND
Loire
Saint-Benoît-sur-Loire
Molesme
Auxerre
Fontenay (98)
45°
Fontevraud
Lorroy
Vézelay
La Prée
Tart
L'Étoile
La Bussière
Acey
Poitiers
Noirlac (132)
LA FERTÉ
CITEAUX
Sept-Fons
Le Miroir
FRANCE
Bellaigue
Allier
Cluny
Saône
Limoges
Cressac
Boschaud
La Bénisson-Dieu
Lyons
Aulps
Hautecombe
Obazine (226)
BONNEVAUX
Dordogne
Sarlat
Bordeaux
La Chaise-Dieu
Mazan
Léoncel (216)
Cadouin (202)
Conques
Valcroissant
Santiago de Compostela
Sobrado
Loc-Dieu (258)
N.-D. des Neiges
Rhône
Valdedios
Moissac
Aiguebelle (210)
42°
Flaran (244)
Beaulieu (148)
Saint-Guilhem-le-Désert
Sénanque (234)
Carracedo
Gradefes (286)
Viaceli
Gimont
Sylvanès (204)
Oseira (138)
Avignon
Ganagobie
Carrizo
Sandoval
Les Feuillants
Toulouse
Silvacane
Las Huelgas Reales (298)
L'Escale-Dieu (212)
Valmagne (254)
Garonne
Montmajour
Iranzu
Ebre
Vignogoul
Moreruela (146)
Cañas (290)
Leyre (272)
Fontfroide (150)
Marseilles
Le Thoronet (206)
Duero
La Espina (162)
Palazuelos
La Oliva (240)
Saint-Michel de Cuxa
Fitero
Tulebras
Tarouca
Valparaiso
Valbuena (252)
Veruela (222)
Arles-sur-Tech
PORTUGAL
Huerta (248)
Piedra (184)
Rueda (260)
Vallbona (294)
Poblet (172)
Montserrat
Alcobaça (178)
MADRID
Santes Creus (168)
Barcelona
39°
LISBON
Montesión
Tage
Toledo
SPAIN
Guadiana
Majorca
Zaidía
Valencia
Júcar
Calatrava
Palma
Alzira
Valldigna
Las Navas de Tolosa
Cordoba
Sevilla
Guadalquivir
Murcia
MEDITERRANEAN
36°
0
300 km
6°
3°
0°
3°
6°

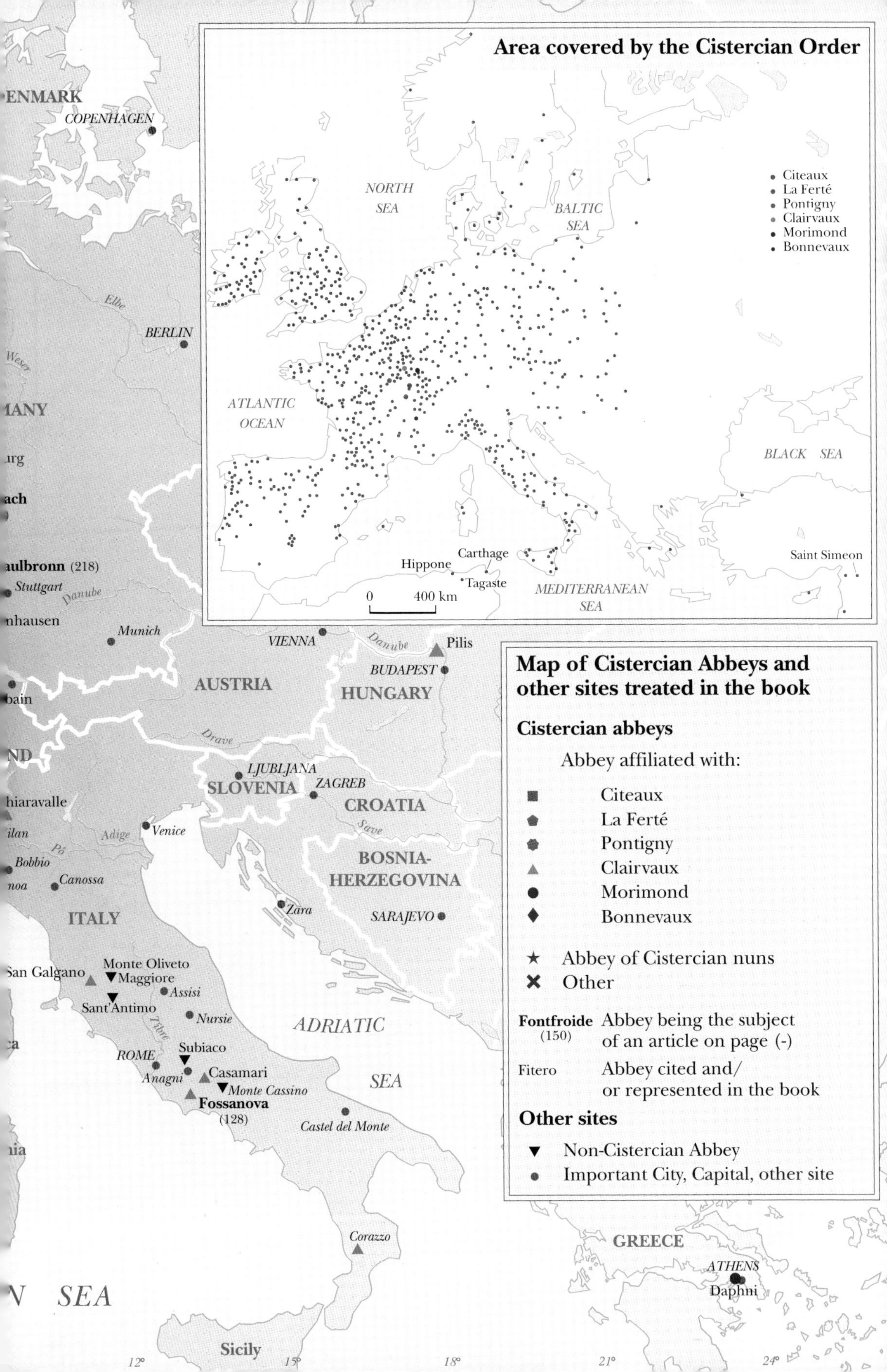

Area covered by the Cistercian Order
NORTH SEA
BALTIC SEA
ATLANTIC OCEAN
BLACK SEA
MEDITERRANEAN SEA
Citeaux
La Ferté
Pontigny
Clairvaux
Morimond
Bonnevaux
Carthage
Hippone
Tagaste
Saint Simeon
0 400 km
Map of Cistercian Abbeys and other sites treated in the book
Cistercian abbeys
Abbey affiliated with:
Citeaux
La Ferté
Pontigny
Clairvaux
Morimond
Bonnevaux
Abbey of Cistercian nuns
Other
Fontfroide (150) Abbey being the subject of an article on page (-)
Fitero Abbey cited and/ or represented in the book
Other sites
Non-Cistercian Abbey
Important City, Capital, other site
ENMARK
COPENHAGEN
Elbe
BERLIN
Weser
MANY
ach
aulbronn (218)
Stuttgart
Danube
nhausen
Munich
VIENNA
Danube
Pilis
BUDAPEST
AUSTRIA
HUNGARY
Drave
LJUBLJANA
SLOVENIA
ZAGREB
CROATIA
Save
BOSNIA-HERZEGOVINA
SARAJEVO
hiaravalle
Milan
Adige
Venice
Pô
Bobbio
Canossa
Zara
ITALY
San Galgano
Monte Oliveto Maggiore
Assisi
Sant'Antimo
Nursie
Tibre
ADRIATIC SEA
ROME
Subiaco
Anagni
Casamari
Monte Cassino
Fossanova (128)
Castel del Monte
Corazzo
GREECE
ATHENS
Daphni
SEA
Sicily
12°
15°
18°
21°
24°

INDEX

D/E/F

G/H

I/J/K

L

INDEX

M/N/O

P/Q/R

S

T/U/V/W

Y/Z

BIBLIOGRAPHY

HISTORY:

BARNAY (S.), "Lactations et apparitions de la Vierge: une relecture de la règle, une lecture de la vie de saint Bernard" in *Unanimité et diversité cisterciennes,* Acts of the 4th International C.E.R.C.O.R. Colloquium, Publications of Saint-Étienne University, 2000.
BARRAL AND ALTET (X.), *L'Art Médiéval,* coll. "Que Sais-Je ?", PUF, Paris, 1991
BAUD (P.), *La ruche de Cîteaux,* Les Éditions du Cerf, Paris, 1997
BERLIOZ (J.), *Saint Bernard en Bourgogne - Lieux et mémoire,* Les Éditions du Bien Public, 1990
BERNARD DE CLAIRVAUX, *Lettres* (vol.I.), Les Éditions du Cerf, Paris, 1997
BERNARD DE CLAIRVAUX, *De la Considération,* translated by Pierre Dalloz, followed by an essay on St. Bernard's architecture], Les Éditions du Cerf, Paris, 1986
BERNARD DE CLAIRVAUX, *Œuvres mystiques,* Le Seuil, 1953
BRUNEL (G.) AND LALOU (E.) (under the direction of), *Sources d'Histoire Médiévale - XIe siècle-milieu du XIVe siècle,* Larousse, Paris, 1992
CAILLET (J.-P.) (under the direction of), *L'Art au Moyen Âge,* Éditions de la Réunion des musées nationaux/ Éditions Gallimard, 1995
CASTICAU (T.), *L'Art Roman,* Flammarion, Paris, 1982
CONRAD D'EBERBACH, *Le grand exorde de Cîteaux ou Récit des débuts de l'Ordre cistercien,* [translated from Latin by Anthelmette Piébourg, introduction by Brian P. McGuire], Brepols/Cîteaux - Commentarii cistercienses, 1998
CROIX BOUTON (J. DE LA) (under the direction of), *Les Moniales Cisterciennes* (vols.I. and II.), Commission for the History of the Order of Citeaux, N.D. of Aiguebelle Abbey, Grignan, 1986-1987
DESMONS (G.), *Mystères et beauté des abbayes cisterciennes,* Privat, 1996
DIMIER (A.), *L'Art Cistercien* (vols.I. and II.), Zodiaque
DUBOIS (J.), *Les Ordres Monastiques,* PUF, 1985
DUBY (G.), *Saint Bernard - L'art cistercien,* Flammarion, Paris, 1979
DUCHET-SUCHAUX (G. AND M.), *Les Ordres religieux,* coll. "Guide Historique", Flammarion, Paris, 1993-2000
DURLIAT (M.), *L'Art Roman,* Mazenod, 1982;
Espagne romane, coll. "Les formes de la nuit", Zodiaque, Ateliers de la Pierre-qui-Vire, 1993
FONTAINE (J.), *L'art Mozarabe - L'art préroman hispanique,* coll. "La nuit des temps", Zodiaque, Sainte-Marie de la Pierre-qui-Vire
GAUVARD (C.), LIBERA (A. DE) AND ZINCK(M.) (under the direction of), *Dictionnaire du Moyen Âge,* Quadrige/PUF, 2002
GERBET (M.-C.), *L'Espagne au Moyen Âge (VIIIe-XVe siècle)* Armand Colin, Paris, 1992
GOBRY (I.), *Les moines en Occident* (vol.V.), Cîteaux François- Xavier de Guibert, 1997
GOBRY (I.), *Saint Bernard,* Éditions de La Table Ronde, Paris, 1990
GRENTE (G.) (under the direction of), *Dictionnaire des lettres françaises - Le Moyen Âge,* Fayard, 1964-1994, and for the article by P.M. Bagaert: "la Bible française au Moyen Âge"
HAMMEL (J. P.) AND LADRIÈRE (M.), *La culture occidentale dans ses racines religieuses,* Hatier, 1991
JEAN-NESMY (DOM CLAUDE), *Saint Benoît et la vie monastique,* Maîtres Spirituels, Le Seuil, 1959
KINDER (T. N.), *L'Europe cistercienne,* coll. "Les formes de la nuit", Zodiaque, 1997
LACARRIÈRE (J.), *Les hommes ivres de Dieu,* Fayard, 1975
LEBEAU (M.), *Chronologie de l'Histoire de Cîteaux,* Dijon, 1997
LECLERCQ (J.), *Bernard de Clairvaux,* Desclée de Brouwer, Paris, 1989
LEKAI (L.), *Los Cistercienses Ideales y realidad,* Editorial Herder, Barcelona, 1987
LUTTRELL (A.) AND PRESSOUYRE (L.) (under the direction of), *La Commanderie - Institution des ordres militaires dans l'Occident médiéval,* CTHS, Paris, 2001
MENJOT (D.), *Les Espagnes médiévales 409-1474,* Hachette, 1996
MESTRE I CAMPI (J.) AND Hurtado (V.) (under the direction of), *Atlas d'Història de Catalunya,* Edicions 62, Barcelona, 1995
MOURRE (M.), *Dictionnaire encyclopédique d'Histoire* (8 vol.), Bordas, 1978
OURY (G. M.), *Les moines,* Desclée de Brouwer, Paris, 1987
PACAUT (M.), *Les moines blancs,* Fayard, 1993;
L'Ordre de Cluny, Fayard, 1986;
Les ordres monastiques et religieux au Moyen Âge, Nathan, 1993
PENCO (G., O.S.B.), *Els cistercencs, Historia, espiritualitat,* [traducció de Just M. Llorens, monjo], Publicaciones de l'Abadia de Montserrat, 2002
PETZOLD (A.), *Le monde roman,* Flammarion, Paris, 1995
PRESSOUYRE (L.) (under the direction of), *L'espace Cistercien,* CTHS, Paris, 1994
REGNAULT (L.), *Les chemins de Dieu au Désert,* Solesme, 1992
RICHÉ (P.), *Petite vie de Saint Bernard,* Desclée de Brouwer, Paris, 1989
RICHÉ (P.), *Petite vie de Saint Grégoire le Grand,* Desclée de Brouwer, Paris, 1995
RUCQUOI (A.), *Histoire médiévale de la Péninsule ibérique,* Le Seuil, 1993
SAINT-THIERRY (G. DE), *Vie de saint Bernard,* [translation, introduction and notes by Ivan Gobry], François-Xavier de Guibert, Paris, 1997
SBALCHIERO (P.) (under the direction of), *Dictionnaire des miracles et de l'extraordinaire chrétiens,* [preface by René Laurentin], Librairie Arthème Fayard, 2002
STIERLIN (H.), *L'art du Haut Moyen Âge en Espagne,* coll. "Que Sais-Je ?", PUF, Paris, 1994
VAUCHEZ (A.), *La spiritualité du Moyen Âge occidental (VIIIe-XIIIe siècle),* Le Seuil, 1994
VEYSSIÈRE (L.), "Les différences de vues et de réalisation entre Étienne Harding et Bernard de Clairvaux à propos des premières moniales cisterciennes" in *Unanimité et diversité cisterciennes,* Actes du IVe colloque international du C.E.R.C.O.R., Publications de l'université de Saint-Étienne, 2000
VOET (T.), *La colonie phalanstérienne de Cîteaux, 1841-1846,* Eud, 2001

COLLECTIVES:

Les Cathares, coll. "In Situ", MSM, Vic-en-Bigorre, 2003
Les Chemins de Saint-Jacques-de-Compostelle, coll. "In Situ", MSM, Vic-en-Bigorre, 2001
Cîteaux et les Femmes, Texts from a colloquium held in Royaumont under the direction of B. Barrière and M-E Hennau, éditions Creaphis, 2001
Crónica de España, Plaza & Janés Editores, 1998
Dictionnaire encyclopédique du Moyen Âge, Les Éditions du Cerf, Paris, 1997
L'Encyclopédie des Religions, Bayard, 1997
L'hydraulique monastique, Créaphys, 1996
Liens cisterciens, Association pour le rayonnement de la culture cistercienne, n° 1, 2001
La Introducción del Cister en España y Portugal, Fundación Santa María de Bujedo, Editorial La Olmeda, 1991
Moines d'Occident - De Martin de Tour à Bernard de Clairvaux, Bayard Centurion, 1996
Moines et religieux au Moyen Âge, Le Seuil, 1994
Origines Cisterciennes, [presentation, translation and notes by a group of Cistercian monks], Les Éditions du Cerf, Paris, 1998
Réformes et continuité dans l'Ordre de Cîteaux. De l'Étroite Observance à la Stricte Observance, Acts of a colloquium on monastic history by Saint Mihiel, 2-3 octobre 1992
La Règle de saint Benoît, texte Latin text according to the S. Gall manuscript [French version by Henri Rochais], Desclée de Brouwer, Paris, 1980-1997
Saint Bernard Homme d'Église, Les cahiers de la Pierre-qui-Vire, Desclée de Brouwer, Paris, 1953
Secrètes clartés sur le chemin de Dieu: Cisterciens - Trappistes, coll. "La tradition vivante", Édition CIF, Épinay-sur-Seine, 1981
Le temps des Cathares, coll.

"Regards sur", MSM, Vic-en-Bigorre, 1996
Theo, l'Encyclopédie catholique pour tous, Droguet-Ardant/Fayard, 1993

ABBEYS:

Alonso Bermejo (P.), *Oseira - Donde se posa el Fénix*, Murcia, 2001
Altarriba (E.) and Baluja (J.), *Poblet*, La bola de vidre, 1994 ;
Santes Creus, La bola de vidre, 1992 ;
Vallbona, La bola de vidre, 1991
Andoque (N. d') and Mècle (A.), Abbaye de Fonfroide, Éditions Gaud, Moisenay, 1996
Armengaud (R.), *Boulbonne, Le Saint-Denis des comtes de Foix*, Mazères, 1993
Aussibal (R.) and Gouzes (A.), *Sylvanes*, Éditions du Beffroi, 1991
Bonis (A.) and Wabont (M.), *L'abbaye de Maubuisson*, éditions Ouest-France, Rennes, 1997
Cabestany i Fort (J.-F.), *L'abbaye royale de Santes Creus - Guide historique et architectural*, Generalitat de Catalunya, Departament de Cultura, Barcelona, 2001
Canellas López (A.) and San Vicente (A.), *Aragon roman*, coll. "La nuit des temps", Zodiaque, 1971
Casado (C.) and Cea (A.), *El monasterio de Santa María de Gradefes*, Ediciones Lancia, León, 1996;
Los monasterios de Santa María de Carrizo, Santa María de Sandoval, Ediciones Lancia, León, 2000
Cortés Borroy (F. J.), *El monasterio de Rueda*, Diputación General de Aragón, 2000
Cruz (V. de la), *El monasterio de las Huelgas de Burgos*, Everest, León, 1990
Dailliez (L.), *Veruela*, 1984
Étienne (C.) and Verdier (F.), *Abbayes cisterciennes, Eure*, Connaissance du Patrimoine de Haute-Normandie, 1996
Evans (D. H.), *Valle Crucis Abbey*, Cadw : Welsh Historic Monuments, 1995
Felipe Abad Leon, *Real Monasterio de Cañas, nueve siglos de fidelidad*, Talleres Gráficos de Editorial Ochoa, Logroño, 1984
Godeau (J.), Mégevand (M.-C.), Brégeat (R.), *Musée des Granges de Port-Royal - Le jansénisme au XVIIe siècle*, Dossier pour les enseignants n° 13, Centre des publications de l'action culturelle, Direction des musées de France, 1992
González García (M. Á) and Yáñez Neira (D.), *Santa María la Real de Oseira*, Guía del monasterio, Elidesa
Guía turística de San Juan de La Peña, Santa Cruz de la Serós y Botaya, Prames, Zaragoza, 1997
Heinen (E.), *L'ancienne église abbatiale d'Altenberg*, Altenberger Dom-Laden, 1984
Hernández Basurko (J. M.) and Pérez Lerendegui (J. M.), *El monasterio de La Oliva - Un estilo de arte para un estilo de vida*, Edilesa, León, 2000
Herrero Carretero (C.), *Museo de Telas Medievales - Monasterio de Santa María la Real de Huelgas*, Editorial Patrimonio Nacional, Madrid, 1988
Herrero Sanz (M. J.), *Monasterio de Santa María la Real de Huelgas. Burgos*, Editorial Patrimonio Nacional, Madrid, 1999
Iglesias Arias (J. A.), *El monasterio de Carracedo*, ediciones Lancia, León, 1991
Jusué (C.), *Monasterios*, Gobierno de Navarra, Departamento de Industria, Comercio, Turismo y Trabajo, 1994
Lacarra Ducay (M. del C.), *Monasterio de Leyre*, Editur, 2000
Lancelot (M. F.), *Boquen - 1936-1965, réponse à une question*, Société du Vieux Lamballe et du Penthièvre
Lapostolle (C.), *L'abbaye de Royaumont*, Éditions Ouest-France, Rennes, 1995
Lojendio (L. M. de), *Navarre romane*, coll. "La nuit des temps », Zodiaque, 1967
Lojendo (L. M. de) and Rodríguez (A.), *Castile romane* (2 vol.), coll. "La nuit des temps », Zodiaque, Sainte-Marie de la Pierre-qui-Vire, 1966
Masson (R.), *Abbaye de Villers - Guide général*, Syndicat d'Initiative et de Tourisme de Villers-la-Ville, 1995
Meyer (A.), *Das ehemalige Zisterzienserkloster St. Urban*, Gesellschaft für Schweizerische Kunstgeschichte, Bern, 1994
Montesquiou (A.-P. de), *Abbaye de Longpont*, Éditions Gaud, Moisenay, 2001
Oliver (J. M.), *Abadia de Poblet*, Fisa, Barcelona, 1991
Pablo Trindade Ferreira (M. A.), *Monasterio de Santa Maria de Alcobaça*, Elo, Lisbonne, 1993
Pedrosa dos Santos Graça (L. M.), *El Castillo de los templarios de Tomar*, Elo, Lisbonne, 1994
Peugniez (B.), *Routier des abbayes cisterciennes de France*, Éditions du signe, Strasbourg, 1994
Phaure (J.), *L'abbaye Notre-Dame du Lys*, Imp. S.D.T.
Piquer i Jover (J. J.), *Abaciologi de Vallbona (1153-1977)*, Fundació d'Història i Art Roger de Belfort, 1978 ;
Vallbona, Guía Espiritual i Artística, Editorial Claret, 1993
Puente Lopez (R.), *La iglesia mozárabe de San Miguel de Escalada*, Editorial Albanega, León, 1997 ;
El monasterio cisterciense de La Espina, Editorial Albanega, León, 2002 ;
El monasterio cisterciense de Santa María de Gradefes, León, 1991
Ritt (A.), *Les Cisterciens en Alsace*, Imp. Reproset, 1999
Roucy (T.), *L'abbaye Notre-Dame d'Ourscamp*, S.A.E.P. Édition, Ingersheim, 1995
Sans i Travé (J. M.), *Precedents i orígens del monastir de Santa Maria de Vallbona (1154-1185)*, Pagès editors, Lleida, 2002
Schweitzer (M.), *Espagne*, Les Guides Bleus, Hachette, 1967
Tobin (S.), *Les Cisterciens, Moines et monastères d'Europe*, [traduit de l'anglais par Sr. Emmanuel Billoteau], Les Éditions du Cerf, Paris, 1995
Trepat (C.-A.), *L'hora del Cister (Santes Creus, Poblet, Vallbona)*, Barcanova, Barcelona, 1991
Vaubourgoin (J. R.), *El Real Monasterio de Nuestra Señora de Rueda*, Institución Fernando el Católico, 1990
Viñayo González (A.), *L'ancien royaume de Léon roman*, coll. "La nuit des temps », Zodiaque, Sainte-Marie de la Pierre-qui-Vire, 1972

COLLECTIVES:
L'Abbaye Blanche, Communauté catholique des Béatitudes
L'abbaye de Clairvaux, Revue n° 14 de "La Vie en Champagne », avril-juin 1998
Abbaye de Sénanque, Éditions Gaud, Moisenay, 1993
Abbaye de Valmagne, S.A.E.P. Édition, Ingersheim, 1989
Abbaye des Vaulx de Cernay, Éditions Gaud, Moisenay
Abbaye des Vaulx de Cernay - Historique, Les "Hôtels Particuliers"
Abbaye Notre-Dame d'Acey, Éditions Protete, Dole, 1989
Abbaye Notre-Dame de la Grâce-Dieu, S.A.E.P. Édition, Ingersheim, 1985
Abbaye Notre-Dame des Neiges, Imprimerie Lescuyer, Lyon
L'abbaye Notre-Dame du Pin - Une abbaye cistercienne dans la vallée de la Boivre, Imp. Orcades, 1995
La Beata Doña María Urraca y su Sepulcro en Cañas, Monasterio Cisterciense de Cañas, La Rioja, 1994
Bourgogne, Les Guides Bleus, Hachette, Paris, 1994
Barcelone et la Catalogne, Le Guide Vert, Michelin, 2002
Champagne Ardenne, Le Guide Vert, Michelin, 2002
Château du Clos de Vougeot, SER, 1995
Cîteaux, Éditions du Signe, Strasbourg
Espagne, Le Guide Vert, Michelin, 2000-2002
Guía - Abadía Cisterciense de Cañas, Fundación Caja Rioja, 2001
Île-de-France, Les Guides Bleus, Hachette, Paris, 1988
Monasterio de Piedra, Fisa, Barcelona, 1997
Monasterio de Veruela, Guía Histórica, Diputación de Zaragoza, 1993
Els monestirs cistercencs de la Vall del Corb, Grup de Recerques Terres de Ponent, 1989
Port-Royal des Champs, notice historique à l'usage des visiteurs, Imprimerie J. Semichon et Cie, Paris, 1893
La ruta del Cister, Cossetània Edicions, 2001
Santa María de Huerta, un monasterio cisterciense, Monasterio Cisterciense de Santa María de Huerta, 1995

ILLUSTRATIONS

This table provides more information on some illustrations and their origin where space in the figure caption was not sufficient.

Front cover (from left to right and top to bottom): The choir in Noirlac abbey church; Benedict teaching his doctrine to peasants, detail of a fresco in Monte Olivet Maggiore Abbey (Italy); detail of Saint Stephen's tomb in Obazine; capitals in Orval Abbey (Belgium); the abbey of Sénanque; monk harvesting, *Moralia in Job*, Saint Gregory, Municipal Library of Dijon; the cloister in Fontfroide Abbey; the abbey of Poblet (Spain); the grange of Maubuisson; a gallery in the cloister of Fontenay Abbey; Saint Bernard, reredos in the Museum of Palma de Majorca; the cloister in the abbey of Alcobaça (Portugal).
Back cover (from left to right and from top to bottom): Saint Thibault's Fountain at Les Vaux de Cernay Abbey; a keystone in the abbey of Hauterive (Switzerland); rose window in Flaran Abbey; a capital in the abbey of Boschaud; Fountains Abbey (England); the south aisle in Silvacane Abbey; the fountain in Relecq Abbey; painting showing Saint Bernard, abbey of Saint Urbain (Switzerland); the blazon of the abbey of L'Étoile; Bellaigue abbey church; tiles in the apsidal chapel in Aiguebelle Abbey.
Summary: Reredos of Saint Anthony and reredos of Saint Bernard, Museum of Palma de Majorca.
Pages 4-5: Gallery in the cloister in Fontenay Abbey
Page 6: Fresco of the life of Saint Benedict, Monte Oliveto Maggiore (Italy)
Page 7: Gallery in the abbey of Serrabone
Page 8: Reredos of Issenheim; Unterlinden Museum, Colmar
Page 10: Reredos of Issenheim; Unterlinden Museum, Colmar
Page 11: Saint Onufre; Museum of Palma de Majorca
Page 13. Capital in abbey church of Fleury, Saint-Benoît-sur-Loire
Pages 14-15: Frescoes of the life of Saint Benedict; Monte Oliveto Maggiore (Italy)
Page 19: Tombstone of Saint Patrick, Downpatrick (Ireland)
Page 24: Judas's Kiss, detail from the façade of Saint Gilles abbey church; statue-reliquary of Saint Foy; treasure of Conques abbey church
Page 31: *Saint Augustine teaching the hermits* by Defendente Ferrari, Dijon Museum of Fine Arts
Page 32: Reredos of Clairvaux, anonymous from Burgundy, Dijon Museum of Fine Arts
Page 33: The nave in the abbey of Bonnefontaine
Page 34: Stained glass window in Miroir Abbey
Page 35: Crosier of Saint Robert; Dijon Museum of Fine Arts; Reredos of Saint Anthony and reredos of Saint Bernard, Museum of Palma de Majorca
Page 40: Painting on wood from the 15th century showing the monastery's foundation, Maulbronn (Germany)
Page 41: Stephen Harding and Saint Vaast offering the model of their abbey to the Virgin, *Commentary on Jeremy by Saint Jerome*, Dijon Municipal Library
Page 43: Woodcutting monks, *Moralia in Job*, Saint Gregory, Dijon Municipal Library
Page 45: Stephen Harding receives Bernard and his companions, *Miroir Historial* by Vincent of Beauvais, Condé Museum, Chantilly
Page 52: *Saint Bernard preaching the Second Crusade in Vézelay* Museum of the History of France, Versailles
Page 54: *The Virgin Protector of the Cistercians* by Jean Bellegambe, Museum of the Chartreuse, Douai
Page 55: Lactation of Saint Bernard, reredos, Museum of Palma de Majorca
Page 60: Decorated letter of Stephen Harding's Bible, Dijon Municipal Library
Page 63: Detail of the life of Pope Alexander III, Bailli Room, Public Palace, Siena (Italy)
Page 65: Fragment of the monochromatic Great Bible of Citeaux, Dijon Municipal Library
Page 67: Tomb of John XXII, Palace of the Popes, Avignon
Page 68: Saint Dominic, Santa Maria Novella Chapel, Florence (Italy); Saint Francis by Cimabue, San Francesco Basilica, Assisi (Italy)
Page 69: Studium of Benedict XII, Palace of the Popes, Avignon
Page 73: *Katharina von Bora* by Lucas Cranach the Ancient (1472-1553), Uffizi Museum, Florence (Italy)
Page 74: *Cardinal Richelieu* by Philippe de Champaigne, Louvre Museum, Paris; the last meal of Benedict and Saint Scholastica, fresco in the transept of the upper church in Saint Benedict's Monastery, Subiaco (Italy)
Page 77: *Armand Jean Le Bouthillier de Rancé*, painting on metal, Condé Museum, Chantilly; the family tree of the male monasteries of the Order of Citeaux in France, Dijon Municipal Library
Page 79: The Christ of Carrizo, San Marcos Museum, Leon (Spain)
Page 80: *The Virgin Protector of the Cistercians* (detail) by Jean Bellegambe, Museum of the Chartreuse, Douai
Page 81: Hombeline enters Jully, *Miroir Historial* by Vincent of Beauvais, Condé Museum, Chantilly
Page 82: Detail from the tomb of Doña Urraca, Abbey of Cañas (Spain)
Page 85: *Portrait of Jacqueline Arnauld* (detail) adapted from Philippe de Champaigne, Museum of the Granges of Port Royal, Magny-le-Hameaux
Page 90: *Charles de Foucauld*, Notre Dame des Neiges Abbey
Pages 92-93: The cloister in Fontfroide Abbey
Page 94: The nave in the Abbey of Alcobaça (Portugal)
Page 95: Columns and capitals in Orval Abbey (Belgium)
Page 97: Saint Bernard (known as *Vera effigies*), treasure of Troyes Cathedral
Page 153: *Jacques de Molay*, Museum of the History of France, Versailles
Page 190: The Abbey of Sénanque
Page 191: Gallery in the cloister at Thoronet
Page 193: Decorated letter, *Moralia in Job*, Saint Gregory, Dijon Municipal Library
Page 194: Gothic Virgin and Child from the Abbey of Citeaux, Louvre Museum, Paris
Page 257: Recumbent figure of Eleanor d'Aquitaine, Fontevrault Abbey
Page 274: Detail of the reliquary-chest of Nunilo and Alodia from the Abbey of Leyre, Museum of Navarre, Pamplona (Spain)
Page 278: *The holy nuns of the Order of Citeaux*, Boucher de Perthus Museum, Abbeville
Page 279: The Abbey of Fontaine Guérard
Page 280: *General view of Port Royal des Champs in the 18th century before its destruction*, Museum of the Granges of Port Royal, Magny-les-Hameaux
Page 281: *Jacqueline Arnauld* by Philippe de Champaigne, Museum of the Château de Versailles
Page 282: *Antoine Arnauld* by Philippe de Champaigne, Museum of the Château de Versailles
Page 283: *The ex-voto of 1662* by Philippe de Champaigne, showing the healing of his daughter Catherine, Louvre Museum, Paris
Page 284: *D'Argenson notifying the nuns of Port Royal of the order to disperse*, Museum of the Granges of Port Royal, Magny-les-Hameaux; Blaise Pascal, Museum of the Granges of Port Royal, Magny-les-Hameaux
Page 310: The lavatorium of Maulbronn Abbey (Germany)
Page 311: The dormitory in Sénanque Abbey